MARKETING YO

For a complete list of Management Books 2000 titles,
visit our web-site on http://www.mb2000.com

MARKETING YOUR BUSINESS

A theoretical and practical guide
to cost-effective promotion

Second Edition

Martin Bailey

2000

All trademarks acknowledged. Original cover design by Emma Balk & Martin Bailey.

Visit **www.marketingyour.biz** for up-to-date information, tips and advice.

First published in 2005 by Management Books 2000 Ltd
Forge House, Limes Road
Kemble, Cirencester
Gloucestershire, GL7 6AD, UK
Tel: 0044 (0) 1285 771441
Fax: 0044 (0) 1285 771055
E-mail: info@mb2000.com
Web: www.mb2000.com

Printed and bound in Great Britain by 4edge Ltd of Hockley, Essex

British Library Cataloguing in Publication Data is available
ISBN 1-85252-489-8

Contents

Acknowledgements

We are the sum of our experiences and there are a number of people I would like to thank for their influences, support and assistance with this book.

Thanks to Dr Andrzej Kotas BSc PhD MBA, Devi Roy BA (Hons), Emma Balk BA (Hons), Lezlee Burke MInstSMM, Robert Abercrombie and Sara Waddington for their advice, support, input and fastidious attention to detail. A special thanks to Emma for her assistance with the cover design.

I would also like to thank the companies and individuals that provided additional content, for the book and CD-ROM, including Actinic, Adobe, Alison Jackson, Cunning Stunts, Executive Protocol Group, Macromedia, .net magazine, Nimlok, Sage, Sue Knight, Sugar CRM Inc, Saatchi & Saatchi, The Marckis Group, Virgin Group and Weber Shandwick.

Acknowledgement must also go to my friends and colleagues at JETCAM, Camtek and Rent-I.T., whose positive attitudes and team spirit act as encouragement that makes day-to-day life so much more enjoyable.

This book is dedicated to the three ladies in my life: To my mother, whose sacrifices during my early years are appreciated more every day. To my wife, for whom my love, admiration, trust and respect continue only to grow. And finally, to my daughter, who can make a day complete with a single smile. At the end of the day these are the things that matter.

About the Author

I have several friends who run their own businesses, and over the years I have helped them with various issues and ideas, from databases to demo CDs to advert design. Most small businesses start with one or two people that have extensive skill in their chosen field, but not necessarily the marketing skills to adequately promote themselves. As their businesses developed I noticed the one problem common to all of them – obtaining quality staff with the right skills and knowledge, an example being a friend that kept coming back to me to help write and maintain his customer database. There was nobody within their organisation that understood the full  capabilities of a database or the requirement to structure information correctly in order to retrieve relevant information at a later date. When they did finally hire someone he left them in a worse state than they were in before, prompting a quick phone call to me again. Fortunately they did find the right person in the end – she had good communication and computer skills and has subsequently brought the company and its methods of working forward.

You don't have to be an academic genius with letters after your name to come up with good ideas, or to be able to put them into action. I was a 'Sinclair baby' – growing up as a teenager with one of the first home computers available in the UK in the early 80s – the Sinclair ZX81, boasting an unprecedented 1KB of RAM, block black and white graphics and a membrane keyboard. This got me hooked on computers and technology in general – an interest I still have today and one that has stood me in good stead.

I left school at the age of sixteen to start as an Office Junior in a printing company, but quickly migrated into telesales, becoming Manager of a sales desk within three years. At the age of 22 I was first introduced to real marketing techniques while in a sales role for a technology company, and got involved in the designing of trade magazine adverts and generating PR.

We went from two people working in the back of a house to a recognised industry brand turning over £2m ($3.3m) within two years. I'll not bore you with the rest of my résumé but my point is that you don't have to get a degree in marketing to be able to market your company successfully, although I'm sure it helps!

Since 1992 I have attained increasing success in building small business brands, streamlining internal and customer information flows and generally improving the reputation of the companies that I have worked with to their specific customer and prospect bases. For example, I negotiated prime-time TV coverage by giving away a relatively low-cost PC, also providing us with a free database of all the people that called in to win. I cannot take all the credit for these successes – the people I've worked with believed in what I was trying to achieve and delivered these ideas to market quickly and accurately. Regular press coverage, adverts designed in-house (either for us or dealers), impressive booths at trade shows and seminars are just a few of the ongoing successes that keep the company name in the eyes of its prospects and it is exactly this ongoing campaign methodology that I want to lay out in the following chapters.

I have stayed in or near the computer hardware and software industry ever since, mainly because it is a subject that holds a personal interest for me; that interest and excitement hopefully comes across in what I do. I take great satisfaction in being able to help others see what they are capable of achieving armed with only a PC, Internet connection, a word processing/DTP package and a few ideas.

The response received from the first edition of this book was very encouraging, especially from the companies that co-branded the cover. While many readers were aware of what they should be doing most of them rarely put it into practice, and several had commented that they used this book as a guide to prompt themselves to perform certain promotion activities at regular intervals. It gave me great encouragement to work on this edition; to enhance the existing content, add new areas of interest and focus on emerging technologies and trends.

I have never professed to be a genius – just fortunate that I was born in an age where computers were starting to take a hold of the world and at time in my life where I was able to understand and take advantage of it. Couple that with the sales and communication skills picked up over the years, and then throw in the odd good idea and that pretty much sums up how I do what I do and what I'm trying to put across to you.

Martin Bailey
August 2005

Introduction

Although the dictionary may use a single sentence to describe it, marketing is a very hard subject to define – it covers a multitude of areas for any business and no one can be an expert in all of them. I make no guarantees that you'll make your first million within days, weeks or months of reading this book – I'm still waiting to make my own – but I am confident that you'll have a better idea of how to market your company and products more effectively, at lower cost and faster.

The common thread with most of my previous employers is that they have either never had the resources or the desire to invest heavily in advertising, forcing me to promote the company within a very tight budget. As several of these companies were very small, I concentrated on increasing customers' perception of the size of the company, ensuring that they felt safe dealing with us. This is relatively easy to do, and at low cost – even more so now with the Internet.

Who should read this book?
I have aimed much of the content at the small to medium sized business. Maybe you're a small business of 15 people or less and you're the MD, or maybe you're the Marketing Manager in a company of 200 – either way there will be many relevant ideas and solutions that you can make use of here.

What geographical areas does this book cover?
While written in English (as opposed to American English), this book focuses on marketing methods common to virtually all markets, with examples taken from around the world. Many US and European companies have also contributed to the content in this book.

What skills will you need to understand this book?
If you're already in marketing, chances are that you have many of the skills you will need, so the rest will follow as you put the pieces into place. If this area is new to you, then the first skill you'll need to brush up on is communication. The ability to convey your ideas orally and with the written word is quintessential, and the basis of everything you will do. Basic to intermediate computer skills are also essential if you are to take full advantage of this book. In several chapters I have gone into relatively in-depth technical detail, but to a level where users with general 'Office'

software skills should be able to pick up and follow. In any case, where you need to hone up on any particular skills there is certainly a wide array of books to choose from in the computer field. This book can help you identify the areas of marketing in your business that you wish to bring in-house and the skill-sets required to achieve this.

Aside from the above, the only limit is your own creativity, and you'll be surprised how creative you can actually be! How many times have you seen a commercial and thought how it could have been made better? Have you ever thought of a really good billboard or magazine ad?

What does this book cover?

Primarily this book is about showing you what you could actually take on yourself rather than outsourcing it to a third party at great expense, such as:

- **press releases and case studies** – do you need to use a PR company?
- **adverts/brochures** – do you need to use a design house?
- **website design and promotion** – do you need to use a web design company?
- **mailshots** – do you need to use a mailing house?

If you're outsourcing any of the above, ask yourself if you need to, then read on. If you're not even doing any of the above then get ready to increase your business! In addition to showing you what you can take control of yourself, I also wanted to demonstrate how tasks that you may already be doing in-house could be done better, quicker and perhaps more cost-effectively, and to give guidance on what works and what doesn't – this is exceptionally useful if, for example you're branching out into new areas such as trade shows and don't know where to start. There are also other practices, such as viral marketing, which cost next to nothing to set up but can yield untold benefits.

Much of the content in this book relates to the Internet and its usefulness within your business. Even if you believe your business is not right for online promotion do not dismiss it altogether – you may find that you are already losing out to your competitors.

I hope this book will give you guidance either through some of the business practices I suggest or the real-world examples I have used myself or admired of others. If just one of them works for you then I've justified your outlay for this book. If nothing else, remember to have fun – this will come across in everything you do...

Part 1

The Theory

1.1

Marketing Overview – Your Company Image

On the CD

- Skoda adverts
- Web links

According to the *American Heritage Dictionary*, Marketing is defined as:

1. The act or process of buying and selling in a market.
2. The commercial functions involved in transferring goods from producer to consumer.

This could be clarified further by saying that marketing is working out the best way to package and promote your products/services and/or company to your target audience. The target audience is also a key area, as it is actually audiences – marketing starts from within your company to your own employees – if they don't understand your products or services how will they communicate this effectively to your prospects? We'll cover this in more detail later on with the Internal Communications chapter.

Business to Business (B2B) or Business to Consumer (B2C)?

The type of customers you sell to will reflect the approach you take when carrying out your marketing activities. If you work within a B2B environment, then you will generally have a smaller number of customers, many requiring personalised marketing aspects such as products and prices. B2B also demands deeper relationships with partners in the supply chain with focus being placed on your key accounts. B2C usually consists of a much larger number of small, shorter cycle transactions across a large customer base, with the focus on brand management. We'll cover this in more detail later.

Let's focus on the packaging elements for starters. Whatever a company sells, it is your company that is selling them. People will not buy from a company they do not trust, unless the circumstances are exceptional, such as very low price or lack of choice. Therefore you need to ensure that the customer's perception of your company is right. Every company needs an angle – be it price, service, brand name etc.

Reputation: Would you buy a car from this company?

Depending on your line of business, marketing your company will take many different forms, each being unique to your company. As a B2C orientated business a dentist still needs to market his services to achieve the same result as a B2B software company selling its products through a network of dealers – more sales – but obviously in very different ways. If the company is not trusted then sales will be negatively affected, however well your products may be perceived and regardless of your supply channel.

A good case in point is the Eastern European car manufacturer Skoda. They sold a range of very low cost vehicles and were the butt of many an excellent joke, such as:

Q. What do you call a convertible Skoda?
A. A skip.

Q. Why do Skodas have rear-heated windscreens?
A. To keep your hands warm when pushing them.

Q. What do you call a Skoda with a long radio aerial?
A. A dodgem car.

Q. How do you double the value of a Skoda?
A. Fill it with fuel.

The market perceived that their products were of poor quality. Their reliability was not as good as their competitors and because of their low cost were seen as sub-standard. Volkswagen acquired Skoda in 1991 and has since sought to use their reputation for 'cheap and nasty' to their advantage, firstly concentrating on quality issues using Volkswagen's superior skills and resources and then turning their attention to public perception of the brand. They made sure that the first new range of models released not only looked better but also performed better. They then proceeded to do what many thought might have been commercial suicide – running ad campaigns joking about their own cars, the slogan being 'It's a Skoda – Honest!' Although still seen as a low-cost alternative to mainstream models, Skoda sales have rocketed and their cars now receive excellent reviews for quality and value for money, with the cars even performing well in motor rally events around the world. Customer perception was changed because they felt they could trust a brand now in the hands of a group with a proven track record.

Fig 1.1.1 Skoda's 'It's a Skoda, Honest' campaign helped turn brand perception around.

Similarly a company can be ruined by reputation just as quickly. The UK-based Ratner high street jewellery chain was thriving in the 1980s selling low cost jewellery until owner Gerald Ratner made a throwaway comment during a speech to the Institute of Directors relating to a cheap necklace that 'everyone knows is crap'. He continued by famously boasting that a pair of earrings his company also sold were 'cheaper than a prawn sandwich'. These comments wiped an estimated £500m ($835m) from Ratner's value within months and signified the downfall of the company; not because people believed that the jewellery was not as valuable but because they felt insulted. Even sixteen years after the event people still use the phrase 'doing a Ratner' when describing similar situations.

At this point you may be asking 'Didn't Ratners just do the same as Skoda?' Yes and no. Both companies were ridiculing their own products but Skoda did it in a very different way. They knew that they had an image problem that they had to remove from their new model range. Their TV adverts, which showed various people being impressed by the car, then refusing to believe it to be a Skoda, invited viewers to review their own opinion of them.

Gerard Ratner appeared to show arrogance and almost contempt for his customers, although in 2004 he launched an online jewellery store (**www.geraldonline.com**). With no advertising budget and only press coverage to fuel interest, the site had taken £3m within the first three weeks of trading, proving that past mistakes can be forgiven. The site partnered with Goldsmiths Jewellers retail outlets, offering a 30-day no quibble returns policy and alterations either online or in-store.

Everybody hates me – what do I do about it?

If your company is currently suffering from a bad reputation, what can you do about it? Firstly you need to understand why you have this reputation. There are normally four main answers to this: service, quality, reliability or price. As Microsoft founder Bill Gates once said, "Your most unhappy customers are your greatest source of learning". Conducting a survey with your existing customer base can be a good way to identify this. This book obviously cannot help you solve the underlying problems within your organisation, but once you have identified and rectified them it can help you with ways to win back customer trust. This is covered in detail in the Customer/Prospects communication and Press chapters, but in short once you've resolved the problems that the world hated you for, you now have to get out and tell the world about it.

The invisible company

Assuming that your company has a respectable reputation, reasonable products, competitive pricing and reliable service, why are you not number one in your field? Simple – not enough people know about you.

Selling is a numbers game – the more prospects you have in the funnel the more sales you will close (unless of course you're still suffering from some of the issues mentioned earlier). This is where the promotion comes in! You don't have to spend megabucks on advertising to reach a wider audience and this is essentially what we'll be concentrating on. From mailshotting your existing customers and prospects to gaining regular press coverage, there are many low-cost methods of putting your name in front of people and getting it remembered – the rest of the theory chapters in this book take you through the various methods and resources you can make available, while the practical chapters give you hands-on advice on how to put your plans into action.

Compare your company to your competitors. Where do they advertise? What size of business are they in comparison to you? Why do they win business? What is the general perception of their company? Seeing what others are doing right (and more importantly, wrong) can help you take your own marketing efforts forward.

Keep a healthy product range

In the 1970s, The Boston Consulting Group (**www.bcg.com**) developed a business approach known as the *Growth Share Matrix*. It was developed to help managers determine when they should consider using profits from "cash cow" businesses to fund growth in other businesses. This theory also translates well for product pricing. So great was the initial success of BCG's matrix that for the greater part of two decades it became the standard approach to capital allocation in multisector, multisegment companies. "Stars," "dogs," "cash-cows," and "question marks" have become firmly embedded in the language of business. These break down as follows:

Stars: Defined by BCG as a market leader in a high growth market. This may not be a highly profitable product, but it is your bestseller and is likely to become a cash-cow in the future.

Cash-cows: These are the products that produce the most profit for your company.

Dogs: Typically they are products with weak market share, generating low profits or losses and are slow moving.

Question marks: Products in high-growth markets that have relatively low market share. They could move on to become stars and then cash cows, or conversely could turn into dogs if the product's market takes a downturn.

A company needs to balance the mix of these categories within its product range to ensure that it has an adequate number of products bringing in sustainable revenue.

Pricing your products correctly

Many brands are built on the strength of price – Walmart being a prime example. Their reputation is that of a company with formidable purchasing power, which passes savings onto its customers with low priced products, regardless of brand. This factor is important as they demonstrate they still sell the perceived higher quality brands priced lower than their competitors.
The price of a product is defined by two main factors:

- the functional value of the product – will it do what it is required to do – **Need**
- the brand value of the product – **Want**

Therefore the price is defined by its value to the customer in respect to the next best alternative, depending on their functional requirements or brand desire. Let's compare two very different products: a 15-piece screwdriver set vs. a relatively expensive brand of make-up. The screwdriver set serves a need. Brand will play a smaller, but not insignificant role in the consumer's purchasing decision. However, if faced with two similar products at very different prices, it is likely the consumer will buy the cheaper. In the case of make-up this role is reversed. The need is there of course, but the 'want-factor' justifies the price tag.

What motivates customers?

This can be broken down further by Maslow's theory of motivation. In 1943 Abraham Maslow published an article that attempted to formulate a needs based framework of human motivation based upon his clinical experiences of humans, rather than the psychological theories of the time (many of which were either largely theoretical or based on animal behaviour).

Maslow's theory suggests that human needs are arranged in a hierarchy, from the most pressing to the least pressing. His 'needs pyramid' demonstrates the theory that when a need is satisfied it no longer motivates and the next higher need takes its place.

Figure 1.1.2 - Maslow's Hierarchy of Needs

An extreme example would be that of a man dying of thirst in the desert. He would not be interested in the latest showbiz gossip (esteem needs), how he is viewed and thought of by others (social needs) or even where he would be sleeping that night (safety need). If he finds water, then the next most important need would become his priority.

To put this in a more general context, someone buying a new computer would no doubt automatically fulfil the first three needs. It may increase their self-esteem but would also meet their need for wisdom (self-actualisation).

It should be reasonably obvious where your products or services fall, but it is well worth spending the time to fully understand what motivates every type of customer you serve. Knowing why they buy allows you to target more precisely your marketing material to meet their needs.

Where to find industry pricing levels?

Trade associations can be a very good source of pricing information, as are your competitors! Before setting your pricing strategy, carefully examine your market. Visit websites selling similar products. Are you pitching your products/services towards quality or purely 'cheap and cheerful'? If you are targeting the higher end, then do not undersell yourself as this will be more damaging that over-pricing – you can always discount but it is very difficult to raise a low price.

Retail stores such as Walmart and Costco are fighting the 'name' brands with own-branded products. In the US in 2003, one in five items sold were stores' own-branded products, and in Europe this has soared to two in five. Costco's 'Kirkland' label covers everything from barbecues to baby wipes. According to market information suppliers A.C. Nielson, unit sales of store-brand goods grew 8.6% between 2001 and 2003. National brands grew only 1.5% during the same period. A 2001 Gallup poll found 45% of shoppers more likely to switch to a store brand, while only 31% said so in 1996. In 2005, Proctor & Gamble and Gillette announced a $57 billion merger, with analysts citing the strengths of store brands as a possible factor for the merger. The products that both companies manufacture, such as washing powder, shaving products and toothpaste, generally sell for higher margins than food products and are more difficult for store brands to compete against – in terms of both product development and marketing aspects.

Summary

❑ If you've got a good company or product image this will inevitably help your sales. Research regularly shows that expensive cosmetics and anti-ageing products may do little more than their low cost equivalent but they still sell by the truckload because of people's trust in the brand. The brand is the company, even if the names are not the same.

❑ Why did you buy the car that you drive, the mobile in your jacket or handbag or the perfume or aftershave you're wearing? Because you trusted, liked, respected and/or wanted them. The product met one or several motivational needs, and this is the critical thought process we all make many times every day.

❑ Price plays an important role in defining both product placement and company perception. Set your prices too low and this may be perceived to be at the expense of quality – too high and you run the risk of pricing yourself out of the market unless you have the brand to support it.

Pearls of Wisdom

'If you have an important point to make, don't try to be subtle or clever. Use the pile driver. Hit the point once. Then come back and hit it again. Then hit it a third time; a tremendous whack.'

Winston Churchill

1.2

Personal Presentation and Communication

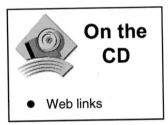

On the CD

● Web links

In the Marketing Overview chapter we discussed the topic of image – this is where you put that image into practice. Everything that you communicate, be it by voice, print or electronic means speaks volumes about you and your company – both consciously and subconsciously. If you already have your portfolio of marketing material that has a common brand you're halfway there.

Before we leap into discussing various methods of communicating with customers let's start with a basic issue that is often overlooked. In any first-time meeting or discussion, regardless of whether you are in a sales role the first 'sale' you close in the eyes of the client is yourself – you are someone they can trust and do business with. The way you look, speak and act can make all the difference in any situation.

Mind your Ps and Qs

According to 'Mr Manners' – Paul Siddle of US business etiquette company, The Executive Protocol Group (pictured), we form our impression of people within 4-7 seconds of meeting them. Therefore whenever you are in any environment where you may make contact with business contacts, act the part. He continues to say, 'Having proper manners is just acting with thoughtful consideration for the other person. Everything with manners is based on the Golden Rule – treating someone the way you would want to be treated.'

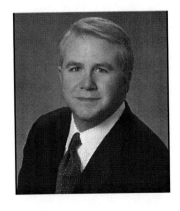

Siddle offers 13 key tips on business etiquette.

- Unlike social etiquette, business etiquette is genderless or gender-neutral. Therefore, both men and women should always stand when introduced and offer a firm handshake.
- The first person to the door opens it, regardless of gender.
- Always make introductions; if you forget someone's name, apologise and ask for the name again.
- Introduce people in business based on rank, not gender (introduce the person of lower rank to the person of higher rank). The client or customer is always the most important person. Begin the introduction by identifying the most important person – the client – first.
- Always refer to someone as Mr or Ms until he or she asks you to use a first name.
- First impressions are formed in four to seven seconds. Make sure your handshake is firm!
- Hugs and kisses are inappropriate in the business environment (unless you're in Hollywood). The handshake is the only acceptable physical contact between men and women in a business setting.
- When attending business functions that require wearing a nametag, pin or stick the nametag on your right shoulder (or lapel) because the natural line of eyesight follows the right hand and arm as you shake hands and it will be easier for people to read.
- When entering an office or conference room for a meeting, do not sit down until you have asked the person who called the meeting where he or she wants you to sit.
- Do not put your briefcase, handbag, papers or keys on the table during a meal or meeting; place them on the floor beside you or under your seat.
- Never let your mobile phone ring during a meal or meeting; set the phone on the vibrate mode.
- A handwritten thank-you note to your customer will distinguish you from your competition.
- Return voice-mail, e-mail and phone calls within 24 hours. If you don't have an appropriate reply, call and set up another time to communicate.

Standard etiquette rules can be applied to any situation – whether you are having a staff meeting, talking with suppliers or meeting with editors, but of course your sales staff should be adhering to the above when in contact with clients! Manners cost nothing but a lack of them can cost you a great deal.

Look the part – dress correctly

Now that you're acting the part, you should also dress the part, and there are plenty of good books on this subject that can point you in the right direction, such as the Chic Simple books (Men's Wardrobe, Women's Wardrobe). There's no need to go overboard – a three-piece suit at an informal staff meeting would be overkill, however jeans and trainers do not set the right tone either. Your aim is to be listened to – to be seen as someone who commands respect and attention.

It can in fact be intimidating to others if you overdress for an occasion. People treat you differently when you are dressed to impress, so make sure that in any business environment your attire matches your position (or the position that you aspire to) and fits in with those around you.

The Marckis Group (**www.marckisgroup.com**), a leading recruitment firm based in Ontario, Canada suggests you 'k.i.s.s.' – keep it simple and sophisticated, and recommends several key tips to make that first impression last:

- A great haircut is worth as much as, if not more than, a new outfit.
- Buy the best quality business suit you can afford.
- Appropriate colours for business suits are grey, black, taupe, olive green, and navy.
- Socks and shoes should be dark and not too casual. Leather lace-up shoes or slip-ons are best for men.
- Never ever chew gum! It's probably the biggest turn-off of all.
- Business dress for women may be dependent on the culture of the country you are in, so dress appropriately:
  1. Always wear stockings or tights; offices are often air-conditioned
  2. Consider wearing more formal shoes rather than open-toed shoes
  3. Consider wearing more formal skirts/tops or trouser-suits rather than sleeveless tops or dresses
- Women's earrings should be small and business-like.
- Men's jewellery should be limited to a classic watch, and one ring on each hand.
- Be sure your clothing is always clean and pressed, and shoes are polished.

Personal presentation travel tips

While these tips have no relation to marketing they may ensure that you are remembered for all the right reasons rather than the wrong ones!

- When travelling by plane, always wrap your toiletries in a plastic carrier bag – after the baggage handlers have finished playing football with your luggage you can be safe in the knowledge that the single suit and shirt will not be complimented by the various fragrances normally reserved for the shower.

- If you're drinking gallons of coffee at a show or meeting, take the breath antidote with you at all times – mints. You don't want to gas your prospects with death breath. Also, if you grab a snack, dash to the restroom before you return to make sure you don't have something sticking to your teeth or you will be remembered as 'the guy who had an egg and cress sandwich' rather than for your products.
- Wear the most comfortable shoes for trade shows. There is nothing worse than finding out two hours into a five-day trade show that your most expensive pair of shoes is also your most ill-fitting.
- Keep essential toiletries and a brush/comb in your car. It may also be handy to keep a spare shirt/tie if you travel frequently – buy a non-iron one and keep it shrink-wrapped and neat for emergencies.

Think smarter, not harder

So you're minding your manners and dressed to kill, but are you putting your foot in it as soon as you open your mouth? In marketing, you're the one in the company that's supposed to have the silver tongue, but while you should be relatively articulate you may not be the best orator in the world. This is not a problem if you're not hosting massive press events where you have to deliver an inspiring speech. You should, however try to improve your communication skills in general, as it's not just about what you say, but also about what you hear, understand and interpret. Again, there are plenty of good books that go into this subject, with many focussing on NLP – *Neuro Linguistic Programming*. This is the study of the way you filter and process your world through your senses, interpreting it through language and process the resulting information – in other words, people skills. It covers such subjects as body language, perceptual positioning (being able to empathise with others by 'putting yourself in their shoes') and building rapport. While this may sound like a 'touchy-feely' new age fad it is tried, tested and respected by businesses and professionals around the world.

NLP initially focuses on your own frame of mind – **Neuro** – allowing you to manage your thoughts effectively. By doing so you can change the way you feel, and subsequently react to situations, influence the reaction of others and build better relationships. People think in different ways. For some, a picture is worth a thousand words whereas others think in terms of audio or emotional responses. For example, when you think of toast what springs to mind? Do you think of a plate with hot toast and butter? Or perhaps it may be the sound of the toaster popping up? Alternatively it may be the feeling of tasting or smelling it. Everyone is different, and the chances are you might be able to pinpoint your own thinking pattern from the above example. If everyone thinks so differently it's no wonder that communication is one of the most common problems in business. Recognising that everyone thinks differently is the first step to understanding how you can effectively communicate across each individual barrier.

Your **linguistic** skills are the tools with which you bridge the communication divide. The language type you use will depend on your thought patterns as described above. Visual people are prone to using expressions and words that draw a picture (e.g. clear, colour, view) whereas others use auditory responses (tell, say, hear). Others focus on feelings (impact, taste, feel, smell). A good communication can identify the preferred thinking pattern of others and tailor their communication accordingly. You will also learn to enrich your language to appeal to each type of person within your audience.

Once you understand the way that you and others think, and can modify the language you use to best suit your audience, you can set about the process of **programming**, or modelling excellence. This is a skill that everyone possesses from birth – learning from others. Self-belief is also a large part of the NLP code of practice. Many of the beliefs we have (good and bad) stem from those taught to us by parents and teachers or any other major role models. If someone tells you enough times that you cannot do something you will start to believe it. NLP gives you the skills to build your own set of positive beliefs that support the way you want to be.

Sue Knight (pictured), a leading trainer and speaker on NLP and author of *'NLP at Work – the difference that makes a difference in business'*, has several statements and key questions you can ask yourself to help see the bigger picture:

- The meaning of the communication is the effect – *in what way is the response that I am getting feedback on what I am doing?*
- There is no failure, only feedback – *how can I learn from what is happening?*
- The map is not the territory – *how is each person's perception true for him or her?*
- The person with the most flexibility is the person with potentially the most influence – *if what I am doing isn't working, how can I do something else?*
- Behind every behaviour is a positive intention – *how am I meant to benefit from what is happening?*

- Mind and body are one system – *what is my body telling me?*
- Everyone makes the best choice available to them at the time – *how can I understand why someone has done something rather than condemn them?*

With a clearer understanding of the conscious and unconscious processes you use to understand the world around you, this can only help you to build better, stronger relationships and achieve win-win situations.

Summary

❏ If you want to leave a positive lasting impression, be remembered for what you did right. Be attentive and listen – you have two eyes, two ears and one mouth – use them in that order. A wise person said it is better to keep your mouth closed and look stupid than to open it and confirm the fact, so don't talk just because you feel you need to. Talk because you need to ask questions or give answers. Dress to fit in with your surroundings and colleagues, and treat others in a way that you would wish to be treated – do all of this at least half right and you won't go too far wrong.

Pearls of Wisdom

'Develop yourself, your interests and your talents. Learn to love what you do and you will without doubt attract others who want to share in that passion. I had this belief reinforced recently by Penny Tompkins who said to someone asking a similar question – tend to your own knitting before attempting to help anyone else with theirs.'

Sue Knight, Author of *NLP at Work*

1.3

Defining your Marketing Activities for a Marketing Plan

On the CD

- Sample marketing plan
- Web links

If you run a local shop, there's not much point in embarking on a country-wide advertising campaign backed by a full e-commerce website. Conversely, if you were running a business which sells nationally you'd probably not consider a small ad in the local paper. You need to define your customer type to ascertain which standard marketing methods are most suitable. Once you have clearly identified your target audience, you can then set about structuring a marketing plan, which will help you focus on your overall market, your competition, sales forecast, budget requirements and implementation – then put in place methods to measure your plan's effectiveness over time.

Customers normally fall into one or two of the following categories.

Local

Your business mainly sells to individuals/companies within a very local region, such as local stores and services (builders, plumbers etc). Potential customers might perhaps need to see products or discuss detailed services before making a purchase, or perhaps you provide services on-site making face-to-face meetings a requirement.

Telesales

Most of your customers trade with you over the phone. Your products generally have a shorter sales cycle and may require limited technical pre-sales support, such as consumer electrical goods. Goods/services can be supplied by mail order or services given over the phone.

Field Sales

Your customers span a wider geographical area, requiring you to have regional sales staff to visit them. Your products may have a longer sales cycle or require face-to-face discussions/demonstrations, such as technical hardware/software.

Global (Internet)

Your products and/or services are already suited to online sale and perhaps even delivery. Customers can obtain enough information about your products through online literature/demonstrations without generally calling your sales staff.

It may be that you operate two or even three of the above methods of attracting business – there are activities that you can pursue that are relevant to each particular business type and some that span all of them. The table below gives an overview of some of the general activities that you can/should be doing that fit with each customer type:

Activity	Local	Telesales	Field Sales	Internet
Mailshots to customers/prospects	Yes	Yes	Yes	Yes (via email)
Press releases to either local, general or trade press	Yes	Yes	Yes	Yes
Telesales campaign	Possibly	Yes	Yes	Possibly
Local advertising campaign	Yes	Maybe	Maybe	Probably not
National advertising campaign (in general or trade press)	No	Possibly	Yes	Possibly
Web advertising/marketing	Yes	Yes	Yes	Yes
Case Studies	Yes	Yes	Yes	Yes
Trade Shows	Local	Possibly	Yes	Possibly

Example 1: Local Building Contractor

A local firm of builders is looking to expand their customer base. All of their customers are normally within a 30-minute drive from their offices. Customers normally require a face-to-face consultation, followed by written quotes and further discussions over the phone. They currently only advertise in the Yellow Pages telephone directory.

Recommendations:

- An advertising campaign in the local newspapers, possibly backed up

with negotiated 'advertorial' (which could be a case study of an existing satisfied customer) would be a very cost-effective way of getting good coverage.
- Leaflet distribution to local residents.
- Building up a case study dossier would be useful when visiting prospects. Ideally, ask customers if you can place a billboard outside the property while you are working.
- A basic website containing the above-mentioned case studies would help to build credibility and the image of the company in the customer's mind.
- It is important to maintain a good database of prospects, and allocate someone to follow up all enquiries. This is a role that many local services tend to forget as customers are local and there's the belief that 'they'll call us when they want our services'.

Example 2: Waste Management Company

A firm that sells waste management equipment (compaction machines, skips, bins, crushers etc) to hotels, hospitals and general business is looking to raise the quality of their image with customers. They have a team of sales reps on the road across the country, backed by sales and support staff in their office. Customers prefer to have a sales rep visit them, with most deals being closed face-to-face after 2-3 meetings. Products are quite technical and specific to each customer, with off-the-shelf products sometimes requiring customisation.

Recommendations:
- As they are in a niche market (e.g. B2B selling a product that is of interest to a relatively small market sector), adverts in the trade press are the only mainstream media advertising opportunities they should really consider.
- It may be more cost-effective to see if they could address more of the customer requirements through telesales – if the number of meetings required to close a sale can be reduced, this frees up the sales reps to make more visits, and reduces the overall cost of sale.
- Regular press releases to the trade press on products and customer case studies will keep the general exposure high at very low cost (time and mail costs only).
- A basic website with full product information, case studies and customer information request forms would be of use. E-commerce could be added for consumable items, however this should be weighed up against likely numbers of customers using this.

31

Example 3: Mail Order Software Company

This company writes and distributes its own range of office applications and is looking to sell these products internationally as well as increasing national business. The applications are easy to install and learn. The main driver is price, with their products being substantially cheaper than the brand leader. Software is currently sent out on CD-ROM. Customers place all orders by phone/mail and are happy to purchase after either discussing over the phone or seeing a brochure.

Recommendations:

- A good website is a must! Full product specification sheets should be included, along with 'FAQs' (frequently asked questions) and support areas. There should also be full technical support areas, perhaps even customer discussion forums to reduce the number of technical enquiries received at the office – help users to help themselves.
- Online ordering via credit card would reduce the number of telesales calls received. If credit card processing is also performed online this would again reduce back office overheads and may even give a better credit card surcharge rate with the payment providers. A discount structure could also be put into place if the customer is happy to receive the software and documentation electronically instead of receiving a disc and manuals, further reducing production costs and allowing for immediate delivery.
- Depending on whether the software is protected and the size (in Megabytes) of the software, there should be downloadable trial versions available.
- Press releases to the trade (computer) press would also be of major benefit – also, submit programs for review in the magazines. A review costs nothing and, if good yields many times over the number of orders you'd receive from the same size coverage of an advert.
- Telesales effort would only be of use to chase up existing enquiries – there would be little point in cold-calling unless you had a very accurately targeted database of prospects, and your time and money would probably be better spent doing more of the above instead.

Example 4: Mobile Phone Ring Tone Company

Purely an Internet-only company, they don't even publish a telephone number, except an automated order processing system. Each sales value tends to be low. There is no major cost of sale and the customer does the decision-making process with no input from the company other than advertising from its website.

Recommendations:

- As this particular product attracts a younger audience, any advertising should be confined to magazines that attract this type of clientele.
- A web marketing campaign may be a more cost-effective way of reaching new customers as they are more likely to be online – again target sites that attract younger visitors.
- Start up a mailing list online to maintain customer loyalty and keep your company in their minds.
- Organising joint marketing ventures with relevant magazines, such as competitions, prize giveaways etc – can be much cheaper than standard advertising and generates a database of prospects for you to contact as well!

Low-cost press-related activities such as case studies and press releases should be performed at least once a month – surprisingly this is generally the area that most companies overlook.

Of course, some of the above ideas may not be entirely relevant to your business, especially if you are in a niche market. They are the general mainstream activities that most companies use to attract business – we'll cover some of the more bizarre methods later on (in Chapter 1.6 – Customer/Prospect Communications). In all of the examples above, the main emphasis is in providing customers with information from as many sources as possible (news stories, case studies, online material) and also increasing the trust factor of your company in the eyes of the customer.

Writing a marketing plan

Now that you have a rough idea of the methods you want to employ you need to put this into a structured format, either to gain financial approval from directors or to confirm in your own mind that you have realistic expectations of your sales and expenditure. A good marketing plan will help you to correctly structure and optimise your resources.

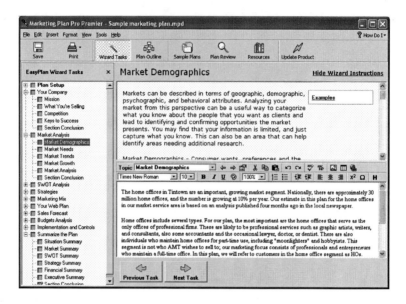

*Fig 1.3.1. Marketing Plan software can help you structure
your plan properly*

There are plenty of books, websites and programs dedicated to producing a well-structured marketing plan, and it is well worth acquainting yourself with one or several of these before you write your own. By using a pre-defined template you ensure that you don't miss important elements or costs out of your plan. One of the leading software products is PaloAlto Software's Marketing Plan Pro/Premier; from around £60 ($110), it will lead you through a step-by-step process of building your plan. A sample marketing plan generated from their software has been included on the CD-ROM.

Your marketing plan needs to cover every element of your business strategy, including the following topics.

Market Analysis: This section needs to clearly categorise the types of customers you intend to serve, taking into consideration (where relevant) factors such as age, gender, nationality, education, location, income etc. The market needs must be identified with the benefits that your product/service will provide (e.g. time/money saved, enriched skills, better self-esteem etc). Defining market trends and growth is also important – if a pattern of movement is appearing, how are your products placed to evolve to keep pace with the changes?

Competitors: By outlining your competitors, you can pinpoint where your product is likely to sit in the eyes of your prospect. Include information such as their target market and share, company size, product quality, growth, available capital and market image. Some of this information may be difficult to obtain, however most companies will have a 'Company information' page on their website that may provide much of this.

Suppliers: If you rely heavily on one or a limited number of vendors, how can this affect your business? For example, if your sole source for your main product ceases trading, can your business survive on the remaining sales?

Your product range: By providing a breakdown of your products, along with projected sales, you can clearly see the split of sales revenue and where each product is positioned within your marketplace.

SWOT Analysis (strengths, weaknesses, opportunities, threats): A conceptually simple method of analysing your company's current market position. Write down relevant factors under each heading. For example, Strengths may have 'Price, industry knowledge'; Weaknesses may have 'Brand awareness'; Opportunities might list where markets are going and why you are better placed to react to these changes, and Threats may cover the same but from the potentially more negative angle.

Strategies: Take elements from the SWOT analysis to create marketing and financial objectives, target marketing and your position in the marketplace. The strategies section effectively suggests 'where I want to be within X months/years time'. Financial objectives are generally easier to pinpoint than marketing as this will generally focus on tangible figures. They should be S.M.A.R.T. – Specific, Measurable, Attainable, Realistic and Timed. You should also document target marketing; where and why your company might be placing specific focus to a target customer group.

Budget analysis: A complete and realistic breakdown of where you will spend money to promote the company and products. By now you should already have a clearer view of where the majority of your marketing costs will lie. Identify each cost and explain in detail how and why the budget will change over a period of time. Larger marketing expenses will need to be justified in more detail.

Implementation and goals: Milestones, break-even analysis and result tracking. Every marketing plan needs to have targets and methods of demonstrating success or failure. By assigning milestones against each marketing activity, showing costs against projected income to visualise the break-even point, then putting controls in place to track and monitor whether your plan is on track, you are more likely to be successful and will be able to react quicker for those activities that are not.

Sales forecast, summarising key expenses and sales figures: The sales forecast allows you to easily visualise your actual/projected sales against the cost of sale. You will already have created most of the figures that you need to start with in the above sections. When explaining your figures you need to discuss the level of sales you are projecting and why. Obviously any projection is based on several assumptions, so ensure that these are adequately explained.

Overall summaries: This should be broken down into relevant sections (market, SWOT, Strategy, Financial, Executive). Effectively you are bringing all of the above into a single section to summarise the key objectives and findings of the plan. Although you will probably write this section last it will generally appear near or at the front of the plan. The summaries are the reader's entry into the plan and therefore have to succinctly bring the purpose of the plan to the fore.

Once you have compiled the above information, you are ready to structure your plan. Tim Berry, President of PaloAlto Software indicates that intuitive software can take the complexity and time out of developing a well defined plan. *"We developed a product that offers resources and links to assist in the research process. It also presents questions and issues that may be invaluable to address prior to implementation of your marketing strategy. With the help Marketing Plan Pro offers in developing your marketing strategy through the actual milestone steps for implementation, it prompts you to acquire the information you need for a plan that can make a difference."*

Summary

☐ Once you understand who your target audience is you can spend time and money on the activities that are most likely to work. Write a marketing plan to provide you with a structured way forward with targets to check that your plan is working. Concentrate on elements that will be effective for the greatest number of prospects as a priority. Ensure that momentum is continued on items such as case studies and press releases, as it is easy to become complacent. Remember: the marketing that you do today is creating the customers of tomorrow.

Pearls of Wisdom

'Define your marketing strategy, create an action plan around it and find a way to measure and assess the results. The tighter the link between these steps the higher your chances are of finding what works and what needs to be changed.'

Tim Berry, President of PaloAlto Software

1.4

Resources

On the CD

- Various freeware and trial software
- Web links

Before you start to create and disseminate your material, you need to ensure that you have the necessary tools to do the job in the first place. Let's assume that you're starting a company from scratch – you've got a killer product that you know will sell, it's priced right and you have no problems with manufacture/delivery. How do you start promoting it? By defining what you can do in-house you can reduce costly outsourcing, especially important if you're running on a tight budget. What you need will depend on how you intend to market your products and this again will depend on your industry – our dentist is not going to need movie-editing skills or equipment but will still need to manage information on customers and prospects like any other type of business.

This chapter covers the various different resources that you may, or perhaps should have in your business. Much of this chapter is dedicated to the hardware and software sections, as this is where you will consistently see savings in time and money.

Staff

The hardest thing to get right in any business is obtaining and retaining quality staff – if you have a committed team, this will come across in your company's overall quality and ability to deliver. Also, if your sales team conduct themselves in a professional and friendly manner, customers will want to do business with them. Hiring the right person to promote your company is probably one of the most difficult positions you'll have to fill. Firstly you need to decide whether marketing within your company is a full-time occupation or not. Maybe it's not to start with but could expand into a full-time position, so let's assume you're doing it yourself for the time being.

If you do decide to hire someone, or even to do the job yourself, what magical qualities must a person possess to warrant placing your company's reputation in their hands and hold the esteemed title of 'Marketing Manager'? This will depend on the breadth of the role, but in general there are three main skill sets that will be required.

Communication skills

As covered in the Personal Presentation and Communication chapter, your Marketing Manager has to shine both over the phone and face to face, and also be able to string a decent sentence together on paper. They don't, however have to be highly knowledgeable about your products – that's the salesman's job. I have worked for a company where I had only a general understanding about their main products but I never felt that it hindered me – more importantly neither did my boss. Obviously the more you know the better, as you will be able to talk more competently about your product range. You will also be more respected, both from staff internally and customer/prospects/editors that you talk to.

Design skills

You don't need to be Van Gogh, Picasso or Pollock – just have an eye for what looks good and what doesn't. If you intend to design material in-house, then the right person will need the ability to take a set of bullet point features and benefits and flesh them out into a fully descriptive set of words, mixed with a healthy balance of imagery.

IT skills

If your marketing role requires brochures, press releases, websites, adverts, video etc, and you want to keep as much in-house as possible then good IT skills are essential. As I mentioned in the beginning of this book, I have always had a passion for technology, so when the Internet came along, I was in my element, which also stood me in good stead career-wise. If your marketing person has either good IT knowledge or can delegate this work to someone within your company, you'll reduce a massive overhead and bottleneck.

The main benefit of having all of the above skills is speed of turnaround. Let's say you've just been handed a new product – *'I want to launch this at the show next month,'* the MD says as your brain goes into overdrive. You'll need the communication skills to be able to pen the press release, the IT skills to create it electronically and design skills to back it up with product literature. The IT skills will come back into play again for the website, then back to the communication skills when you push your newly created material to the editors and consumers.

Don't mix and match sales and marketing roles!

One thing that is not recommended is to have a Sales/Marketing Manager. Invariably this person's role is to head up a sales team, obtain new business, keep existing customers happy and also perform marketing miracles. In this scenario marketing is always the poor cousin, especially when business is hard. You have a sales target to meet so you don't spend your time designing new literature, writing press releases or case studies because you're on the phone to prospects or out on the road. As a result it turns into a downward spiral – the following month will be harder than the last, as you have no ongoing marketing material/presence to back up your sales effort. Fewer prospects know about your company as there's no press, or out of date advertising and/or sales material so you have to work harder to find new leads...

Computer hardware and software

This is where you can really reduce your workload and overheads, either through cutting down on outsourcing or streamlining existing procedures. You will also require some of these items to undertake previously untried techniques.

Computer Hardware: The jury is still out between the Apple Mac and PC brigades. Apples are known for their ease of setup and use, whereas PCs tend to be more mainstream (especially in the office) with more software available. In the design industry, it's probably fair to say that Apple has the majority of market share, but that's not to say that if you buy a PC you won't be able to perform similar functions. I'm of the PC brigade so this section assumes that you will make the same choice.

By the time you read this book the standard computer may well be a Pentium 9 900GHz with 512GB Ram. If that is the norm then buy it! If you compare PC prices over the last decade they have dropped, although specifications have improved dramatically. Since the advent of Windows, it is customary for the newest version of the operating system to require a substantial leap in hardware to retain a similar performance, but you don't necessarily need the top-of-the-range system for the majority of tasks. The table below should give you a rough idea of the processing power required to perform certain tasks.

Entry Level	Mid Range	Top Range
Word processing Emails and emailshots Data management	Desktop publishing Graphics manipulation Web Design Audio editing	Video Editing
Special considerations: None	**Special considerations:** High-end graphics card	**Special considerations:** High-end graphics card Large Hard Disc Large memory Fast or Dual Processor

The desktop/laptop debate: Since notebooks became mainstream in the early 1990s, the debate has raged as to whether you should opt for the portability of a notebook against the power and expandability of a desktop. Today there is not as great a leap between the two on performance as there used to be, but there are still factors that may sway you either way. Desktop computers are generally much more upgradeable and expandable than notebooks – if something goes wrong or you need better performance only one component generally needs to be swapped. Notebooks are proprietary, and all of the main components are on a single board, except processor, RAM and hard drives which can be upgraded. Therefore if the graphics card is too slow in the notebook, there's little you can do, except prop it up with a faster CPU and more RAM. The table below gives a guide as to which is best for different requirements:

Desktop PC

- I rarely leave the office.
- I need the fastest system available.
- If it breaks down I want to be able repair it quickly and at low cost.
- I will need to keep the system upgraded to continually be the fastest available.

Notebook PC

- I need portability and wireless networking.
- I don't need top-of-the-range PC.
- If it breaks down, I'm happy to get it repaired under warranty, which may take a couple of days.
- The system's current speed will be adequate for as long as the machine lasts.

Connectivity: Historically, PCs have always been more flexible than laptops when it comes to plugging in accessories – not any more. The arrival of high-speed port technologies such as USB (Universal Serial Bus) and IEEE 1394 (Firewire), and the subsequent inclusion of these ports on most notebook computers means that they are as well equipped as their desk-mounted counterparts. Peripherals such as scanners, digital cameras and video cameras can be easily connected to either. If you still want to use a full-size keyboard, mouse and monitor when you're in the office, virtually all notebooks have the relevant ports at the rear. As many devices now have removable memory cards, PCs and notebooks now often have multi-card readers built in.

Networking: There are two types of networking – wired and wireless. The standard wired interface is known as 10/100 base T and operates at a speed of either 10 or 100Mbps. For users requiring higher speeds, or networking over long distances (over a mile) fibre optic cabling delivers a robust solution that is impervious to external radiation and providing break-neck speeds of several Gigabits. Wireless networking standards are constantly evolving, with the current standard (802.11g, also known as '54g') providing around half the speed of 100MBps over an area of up to 250 feet. All three types generally require a hub or router, which can also allow PCs to access the Internet if a suitable broadband connection is provided.

Input devices

If you are working with still or video images, then you will probably need additional hardware to get them into the computer. With still images you have two main options:

Scanners: A scanner is an absolute must, especially as the prices are now extremely low. Many come with OCR (optical character recognition) software, allowing you to scan a page and convert it to editable text, saving you time and finger strain. You'll use a scanner perhaps to pull in images for a brochure, or for scanning existing brochures to convert to a web page. Unless you need absolute colour matching or need to scan larger than a normal magazine page, any scanner should do. Opt for one with a resolution of 2400dpi (dots per inch) or greater. You have three ways to connect it to your PC – parallel port, USB or SCSI (Small Computer System Interface). USB or Parallel will be quite suitable unless you need high performance.

Digital Cameras: It is good that digital cameras have dropped dramatically in price over the last few years. These are much more flexible than standard cameras that take film, as pictures are stored on memory cards – download the pictures immediately to your PC and the card is empty again, ready for use, and the pictures are ready to load into your application. With many cameras capable of taking a 1GB card you'll be able to fit 100s or even 1000s of pictures on. Some allow you to record short movies, although the quality is generally only good enough for the web. Anything over 5 mega pixels should be more than suitable for general brochure pictures. If you need great detail or intend to enlarge photos to posters, then the greater the resolution, the better. There are several different standards of memory card, such as SD Cards, Compact Flash, Memory Stick and MMC, with varying prices for the same memory capacity.

Web Camera (webcam): If you intend to work remotely or travel frequently, then using a webcam in conjunction with video conferencing software (many of which are free) can give you a better method of communication that is cheaper than a telephone call. The advent of wireless networks at airports, cafés and hotels allows you to literally have a videoconference anywhere. Webcams are inexpensive, starting at around £20. Many notebooks have the option of an in-built webcam.

Output devices

Once you have created your material on-screen, you will need to output it, either on traditional printed media or via electronic means.

Printers: There are two main types of printer you should consider – maybe you should even buy both depending on your needs – you can pick up good inkjet and mono laser printers for well under £200 ($330) each. Inkjets are low cost colour printers that can produce photographic results when used with the right paper. The main drawbacks are speed and cost per page, although this is only a real issue if you are looking to do large print runs. Alternatively if much of your work is text only and you want a faster throughput, you should consider a laser printer, which runs on the same technology as a photocopier.

Colour laser printers have dropped substantially in price over the last few years, although they are still more expensive to buy than both mono lasers and inkjets, and would only be recommended if you have a regular use where speed and quality is of the essence. It is worth obtaining running cost comparisons, as colour lasers are now fiercely competitive so may be suitable for medium sized print runs – they may even work out cheaper in mono printing than their mono-only equivalents.

The table opposite shows a comparison between inkjet and laser printers.

You can do a great deal with a printer these days. In addition to printing out standard letters you can also consider:

- newsletters
- labels
- envelopes
- iron-on transfers for T-shirts, braiding etc
- CD Labels
- DVD case sleeves
- banners
- window stickers.

Inkjet printers		Mono laser printers	
For	**Against**	**For**	**Against**
• Low cost • Excellent quality • Colour • Can sometimes handle thicker media (e.g. card) than laser printers • Wider media range - window stickers, T-shirt printing etc • Large format printers (that handle larger size paper and even banner rolls are available at relatively low cost) • Some printers can print edge-to-edge	• Higher running cost, especially on large runs • Minimal paper handling - normally maximum 50 sheets • Slower than a laser on higher runs	• High speed, especially on long runs • Low running costs • Better paper handling - some lasers have multiple bins or duplex printing	• Expensive if you only do short runs • Limited handling for thicker or non-standard paper

Check out the different types of media that are available for any printer you consider purchasing. It is also worth investing in the 'official' consumables rather than cheap unbranded ink or toner. Companies such as Epson and

HP invest a great deal in the quality of both the consumables and the media they sell, and you will generally always produce substantially better results when using the right materials. After all, you wouldn't put vegetable oil in a sports car, would you?

CD/DVD Writers: Most users' computers will be fitted with a CD-ROM reader, so providing information to customers on a CD is an acceptable and cost-effective means of distribution. DVD writers have also come down to a very reasonable level, but be wary of the different formats available, such as DVD-R, DVD+R and DVD-RAM as well as the new Dual Layer (DL) standard that provides double the capacity. At present DVD+R is a standard that produces discs that are compatible with the majority of players. Dual-format writers are now available that read/write both +R and -R formats, so these are the best bets but you should be careful if you are burning discs for distribution. The safest option for mass DVD distribution is still a CD/DVD mastering company.

Software

Regardless of the hardware you have, the software you install is what really allows you to quickly create high quality material. With the right tools you can handle your accounts, send mail shots and press releases, design brochures, design and upload websites and produce demo CDs – all by yourself! Here are some recommendations:

Operating system: If you've opted for a PC, then there is only one real choice – Microsoft Windows. Linux is gaining popularity due to its stability and security, but is still mainly used for web servers, and unless you know what you are doing with it, then steer clear – your business depends on this, and if something goes wrong, you need to be able to get up and running quickly.

At the time of writing, Windows XP Home and Professional are the two main options – go for XP Professional. If you buy it with the PC then it's not much more than the Home version and will give additional security and network capabilities.

General office software: Again, the leading Office suite comes from Microsoft – Office XP. Whether you're deciding to use a standard contact management product or Microsoft Access will affect which version of Office you buy – the Standard version does not come with Access. If you're looking for a good alternative, why not try Open Office or E-press's Easy Office. Both offer compatibility with Microsoft's file formats (e.g. Word Documents,

Excel Spreadsheets), and best of all they are free! A good 'Office' suite will include:

- word processor
- spreadsheet
- presentation software
- database
- communications suite (email, calendar, task list etc).

Use Office software to:

- organise your diary
- store your emails
- write standard or custom letters
- 'crunch numbers', create graphs
- store customer information in databases (unless you use an alternative Customer Relationship Management (CRM) package – see below
- send emails to multiple recipients (you may also want to use a specialised e-mailshot package, as we've featured in the Customer/Prospect communications chapter)

Customer Relationship Management (CRM) Software: This is an application specifically designed to track prospects and customers, automatically providing you with a to-do list, calendar, relevant notes – all of which are interlinked. Sage Act! is one of the leading off-the-shelf products. Alternatively you could opt for a web-based product such as Sugar Suite CRM, which has the added benefit of being available in commercial and freeware versions.

Use CRM software to:

- provide a comprehensive storage and tracking solution for customer and prospect data
- allow you to quickly identify which leads require following up
- run reports on prospects and sales opportunities
- export data for mailshots.

Desk Top Publishing (DTP) Software: One of the best all-rounders is the CorelDraw Suite, although many people prefer products such as Adobe Illustrator or Microsoft Publisher. DTP software will allow you to design anything from mouse mats to brochures. Essentially a DTP package allows you to lay out content on a page with more flexibility than a Word processor, and can add many more powerful graphical features and effects. Many DTP suites such as Corel are also bundled with Graphics software (see Graphics Software section further on), offering a completely integrated solution with a common interface. A good, low-cost alternative is Typographicus.

Use DTP software when:

- you want to create an eye-catching brochure or poster
- you need more flexibility than your Word Processor can offer
- you want to create artwork for an advert – most publishing houses will accept electronic format files from known DTP packages, or alternatively you will be able to export it to a suitable format.

Electronic document creation software: Adobe's Portable Document Format (PDF) is widely recognised across the Internet, therefore it is worthwhile having the ability to easily create files in this format, either for direct emailing or for publication on your website. Adobe produces Acrobat Professional for creating and modifying PDFs, along with a free reader available from their website and virtually any CD-ROM that contains PDFs. Many products such as CorelDraw! have built in PDF export capabilities, but there are also dedicated products such as Jaws PDF Creator or the freeware program Cute PDF Writer that set themselves up as virtual printers, meaning you can produce PDF files from virtually any program. Alternatively PDFmoto can be configured to monitor a folder anywhere on your network, converting any files placed there automatically and uploading them, along with a navigation structure to your website. Adobe Acrobat Professional is still the better solution if you need more control over PDF creation, distribution and amendments.

Use PDF creation software when:

- you want to email documents or brochures to a customer
- you want to publish documents on your website.

Graphics Software: This would work hand-in-hand with your DTP software, together with many of the other applications you will use. The industry standard product is Adobe Photoshop, although Paint Shop Pro is an excellent shareware alternative. Corel's PhotoPaint!, shipped with the CorelDraw! Suite is also a viable product. For very basic file editing Picasa (owned by Google) not only offers brightness, contrast and cropping capabilities, but also red-eye removal and a slick way to browse the images on your hard disc.

A good graphics manipulation package will furnish you with a very powerful set of tools, from simply cropping a photo to creating amazing collages of graphics or effects that could never be produced with a camera.

Use Graphics software when:

- you want to resize/compress graphics for the web
- you want to create special effects on an image
- you want to clean up an image, make a background transparent etc.

Audio software: For mainstream marketing activities such as brochures and websites, this will probably not be an area you'll need to venture into, but if you're looking to create multimedia content for the web, CD or for presentations/shows then you will need to start looking at audio manipulation software. Mainstream packages such as Adobe Audition offer excellent features, but at a price. Goldwave and Audacity are good shareware/freeware alternatives that offer most of the features you'll ever need.

Use Audio software when:

- you are also working with Video editing
- you want to edit audio for inclusion on websites.

Video Capture/Editing Software: Many video capture cards are bundled with software that will be adequate for many users needs, but if you want to go for the best, then it has to be Adobe Premier. Most packages work by importing video from a variety of sources (including DV Camcorders), then creating a movie using a timeline of clips. You can then export your video either in a web format, for CD-ROM, DVD or output back onto DV tape. To take your video manipulation one stage further, also look at Adobe After Effects to add studio quality effects and sequences to your movies. Finally, if you want to create a fully functional DVD, then DVD authoring software such as Adobe Encore DVD provides the tools to create interactive menus, subtitling, multi-camera angles and all of the other media-rich features found on today's commercials DVDs.

Use Video Capture/Editing software when:

- creating movies for your website
- creating multi-media CD-ROMs
- creating DVDs/VHS tapes.

Website Development Software: If you are designing and possibly hosting your website in-house then there are several applications that will be essential.

Web Authoring Software: To create your web pages you will need a package such as Macromedia Dreamweaver, Adobe Go-Live or Microsoft

FrontPage, each of which offer an easy-to-use WYSIWYG (What You See Is What You Get) interface – making a relatively functional and aesthetically pleasing website can now be done knowing little or nothing about programming. You should also investigate programs such as Macromedia Flash, which allow you to produce media-rich content for websites. Low cost and freeware HTML authoring programs such as AceHTML may also be suitable if you're on a tight budget.

E-commerce software: If you want to sell your products online you will need a mechanism for taking orders and handling payments. The product you require will depend on the complexity and number of products you wish to sell. For more information on e-commerce solutions see Chapter 2.7 – How to sell online. One of the leading off-the-shelf products is Actinic Catalog and Actinic Business, which will allow over 10,000 products to be managed through a simple interface with little or no web design experience required (once configured). For online stores that have only a few products, PayPal's shopping cart facility may suffice, or even a simple fill-in-the-blanks order form that is processed offline – note however that credit card information should only be sent using secure methods such as PayPal and Actinic. If you have a little coding experience, the PHP/MySQL based Zen Cart (www.zen-cart.com) is a free alternative, but may take a little time to customise and be more restrictive than commercial products.

File Transfer Protocol (FTP) Software: Not as important as it used to be, but still useful, FTP software allows you to transfer files to and from your web space. Nowadays, Windows allows you to do this from Explorer, and all decent Web Authoring packages have FTP capabilities built in as standard. It's always useful to have a shareware/freeware program such as WS_FTP LE installed as a precaution – you never know when you may need it.

Web/Intranet/Extranet Server Software: You will only need this if you intend to host your website or intranet on your own server, and if you've decided to go this far then the chances are you know what you are doing! Windows NT and above is supplied with all the software you need to host multiple sites (IIS – Internet Information Server). If you intend to go one step further and have a database-drive site, then you will need another level of server technology that supports this, such as Macromedia's Cold Fusion, ASP (again supplied with IIS), Perl/CGI, PHP etc. Unless you have the resources in-house to install, support and develop a website or Intranet it is much better to pick one of the thousands of ISPs (Internet Service Providers) available. There are some very good Intranet services on the Internet. Sites such as **www.intranets.com** allow you to create your own intranet in seconds, charging a monthly fee thereafter. Most also offer a free trial so you can test their suitability. Yahoo offers a free calendar, 'briefcase' and address book service online that you can share with others – for small business this may be enough.

Security software: Although not strictly tools used for marketing purposes, they will ensure that your PC is available for use rather than a hacked 'zombie' PC, riddled with viruses and a stolen Internet connection that is spewing out junk emails by the million. There are two main tools that any PC should not be without before it is connected to the Internet – a firewall and antivirus software. A 'firewall' is a piece of software that only allows authorised programs to send and receive data through network connections. It also makes the computer invisible to incoming 'scans' from users looking for vulnerabilities. Antivirus software scans files and emails for known viruses and stops them from running. Antivirus companies generally release new virus databases every few days, with 'antidotes' to the latest threat, thus keeping your computer up-to-date.

Content Media – your company library of media resources

Once you've installed all the software you need, but before you have designed your brochures, website and other material, you need to build up a library of content. This means items such as your company logo, product pictures, staff pictures, video clips etc. Set up a directory on your server to contain the entire source and approved media elements so that you can quickly retrieve them. As you build your library keep the high resolution media in the one place – case study photos demonstrating real-world use of your products are always reusable for newsletters and the like. Separate them into relevant sub-folders so as not to mix content.

Obtaining new content

It may be that you do not have the time, skill or resources to get the images you need, so why not take advantage of pre-prepared stock? There are many sites on the Internet that will give you access to royalty-free images, sounds and movies. Alternatively you can purchase 'clipart' CD-ROMs, with thousands of images, fonts, backgrounds, sounds and movies without copyright restrictions. Sites such as Getty Images (**www.gettyimages.com**) allow you to search through a massive online database of stock and purchase single images or videos (priced either by usage or royalty free) as well as combination CDs. **Stockedimages.com** allows unlimited downloads for a fixed annual fee.

Marketing Material

This is defined as 'what you put in front of your customers', and will normally be in the shape of a brochure or booklet. Whenever you need to design material to promote a product, you should always think what medium you will be developing for. Will it only be a brochure or will you be making a web page as well? Will the content be used in other areas, such as a video? It is generally better to construct a set of words and pictures, and then tailor it to the media you are designing for.

If you're starting a project (or even a company brand) from scratch, you should create a common library of images and texts. For example, create a directory called \graphics and texts, then place items such as your company logo, standard company profile text, product text, product images etc in this folder. Separate each product into its own directory. Then, whenever you need to either design literature yourself or supply others you have a library of pre-vetted material ready to send. In larger companies this works very well as the approval process is reduced.

What printed marketing material will you need?

In addition to letterheads, compliments slips and business cards you will generally need the following items.

- **Details on each product.** The scale of this will depend on the sales cycle that surrounds it. For example, a pen probably requires only a picture and a few bullet points whereas a highly technical product may warrant a brochure spanning several pages

- **Company profile.** The first part of closing any sale is ensuring that the prospect has faith and trust in your company. Provide some background information on your company, its ethics and technical background of staff (if suitable). Rather than provide a separate leaflet you may wish to include this information as part of a folder into which product leaflets are inserted. This should only be two or three paragraphs unless you have a very long company history

- **Support/Service information** (if relevant). If your product requires after-sales service, then it is worthwhile providing information on this. This is an extremely important (and if done correctly, reliable) form of ongoing revenue

- **Case Studies.** This is also a part of making prospects feel comfortable with your company. In addition to this, they make great press releases! Either a single or double-sided sheet is sufficient for this

- **Company newsletter.** A low-cost, regular method of keeping your name in front of customers. This can be anything from a single sheet to several pages depending on how much you have to say

All of the above should also be prepared in electronic format. The best format for this will generally be Adobe Acrobat PDF files, which most people can read. Many applications, such as CorelDraw will export directly to PDF files, so you can create them in seconds as you're printing your material. Alternatively use a freeware program such as Cute PDF Writer, which sets itself up as a virtual printer on your system allowing you to produce a PDF from any application. PDFs can generally be small enough to email, which can really impress prospects when they receive an email from you with the information they requested, especially if they are still on the phone to you at the time!

Don't re-invent the wheel – templates save you time!
Attention to detail is important with your brand image. When you have a design you like, stick to it. Regardless of what format you are looking to output to, you can always design a template, or style to fit it to. Not only does this give you consistency across all of your material but it will make designing subsequent material much, much quicker! For example, product brochures will generally take a similar design.

- They will always have your company details in a certain place.
- They will always be based around the same corporate colour scheme.
- They will generally have a similar layout to each other.
- Pictures will generally be of a similar style and size.
- Text will always be the same font, size and colour.

A template can actually mean several things in software. The definition of a template used here are the boundaries that you set yourself once you have created something, so that you continue similar material with a similar look and feel. Many software applications, such as MS Word, Dreamweaver etc allow you to create templates which have certain settings pre-defined. For example, you can create web page templates that have your logo and navigation links on each page – when you create a new page you simply select 'Create from Template', thus creating a new page with the same style as every other page on your site – this is covered in detail in the 'How to build a website' chapter. If you have the skills to take advantage of templates within software, then you should do so. If not, it may be worth time and money investing in a good tutorial!

Many companies sell pre-defined layout templates with the creative flair

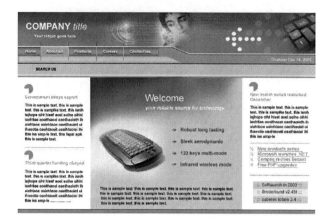

Fig 1.4.1. Pre-defined templates can take the pain out of designing a web site.

already impressed upon them, so allall you have to do is change the style to exactly fit your company's brand and modify the content to suit you. If you are starting from scratch it may be quicker to purchase a template (from the likes of **www.boxedart. com**, a sample of which is pictured here) and copy the design styles over to your brochures and news-letters. Very quickly you will havecreated a unique and professional image with very little work!

Check, check and re-check!

Before you release any material, check it thoroughly for mistakes. Ensure that you have permission to run text or image content if required. There is nothing worse than receiving several thousand brochures back from a printer to find glaring errors or omissions, or to find out that a person/company did not authorise use of material. If possible, get someone to proofread your work. A salesman once created a mail shot to several hundred customers inviting them to 'please hesitate to contact me for further assistance.' Fortunately it was spotted before leaving the office! Mistakes like this are very easy to make, and even easier to miss!

Summary

❑ Once you have a comprehensive library of material available in all of the formats that you need, creating new material is both quicker and easier. They say that a bad workman always blames his tools. How often have you cut your grass with a pair of scissors – you wouldn't. Therefore, make sure you have the right hardware and software to create the material you need. If you do not intend to do the designing yourself ensure that when you get material produced by an outside source they also supply it in an editable electronic format (such as the source application files), and not only just as a 'flat' image. Finally, make sure that you have a good method of storing and retrieving information on your prospects and customers.

Pearls of Wisdom

'Ensure that when positioning your company or product that you emphasise the benefits your company/product can bring to customers rather than what you consider to be the best selling points. You can do this by making sure you remain close to your customers' needs through ongoing contact, customer research and responding to any complaints they may have.'

David Pinches, Marketing Director, Sage CRM Solutions

1.5

Internal Communications

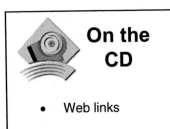

On the CD

- Web links

Before you even contemplate talking to your customers, make sure that the lines of communication are free flowing within your own organisation. Any new products or services must be fully introduced internally before being released publicly. If staff are not aware of your marketing strategies, they will not be best placed to support them.

Management must also take full advantage of all of the internal resources that may be available to support their external marketing and promotional effort. For example, all internal education, training and instruction with respect to the new product or service should be completed before the product is brought to market so that all the appropriate internal customer support personnel understand what the new service/product offering can provide to customers. How many times have you dealt with a large company (or a small one, for that matter), and on ringing their helpdesk for the third or fourth time, heard conflicting information from the first call? The larger your company, the more critical this is. Every member of staff that interfaces with your customers must be 'singing from the same song sheet'. Before we look at how this should be tackled on an ongoing basis, let's put the basics into place.

1. Ensure that there is a central repository of information. As covered in 'Resources', create a location on your network which hosts all source material.
2. Ensure that your staff can and do access this information. Confirm that everyone is using the most recent versions of material at every given opportunity.
3. Provide training for key sales and support staff on new products prior to release.
4. Send out regular internal news updates. People like to know how 'their' company is doing, and that the work they put in has a positive

effect. Monthly or bi-monthly intervals are generally adequate – more frequent and you run the risk of either running out of news or readers losing interest.

5. Set up an internal e-mailing list, so that important information can be immediately sent out to all staff.

Regular flow of information internally is the lifeblood of any business, so let's explore the various mechanisms you can put in place to maximise its effectiveness.

Centralise your information with an Intranet

If you have more staff than you can count on one hand, or if several staff work remotely, you may want to consider an Intranet. This is effectively a website that can only be viewed by your own staff, and can either simply be a collection of web pages and directories on your network, or a fully fledged database-driven site hosted on a real web server that users access with a password.

A good Intranet can offer many benefits.

- Users have a secure way of sharing information.
- The home page (or start page) can carry latest news updates.
- Diaries can be held in a single location, simplifying the organisation of group meetings.
- Customer information can be accessed by everyone.
- Projects can be set up, with specific tasks allocated to relevant members of staff – the precise status of a project can be viewed live at any time.
- Online discussions in private chat rooms can take place, regardless of where in the world the users may be.
- No-one has any excuses as the most up-to-date information is always available.

If you do not have the ability or resources to write an Intranet in-house, there are plenty of online services available at nominal costs. For more information on the resources required for an Intranet see the Internet and Resources Chapters.

The two-way street – listen to staff opinions

While there is a lot to be said for 'too many cooks spoil the broth' you should not dismiss the opinions of staff. Anyone who has contact with either your customers or your products/services will have valid input into how you can collectively improve the quality of service you offer. It is also very motivating for them to see their ideas acted upon. Just because you do the marketing it doesn't mean you have to be responsible for every good idea!

Not only should you accept the ideas of others, you should positively encourage it. It is said that everyone has at least one good advert inside them – it may be that someone provides you with the acorn of an idea that you can fully develop with the tools you have available. Make it easy for people to submit ideas – be 'accessible'. If your company holds sales meetings, ensure that a portion of this is dedicated to marketing. Discuss the activities you are working on to gauge others' perception – what you see as a flash of inspiration they might see as a flash in the pan and be able to justify with tangible reasons, possible supplying you with alternatives.

Tell the truth – good or bad

When keeping staff informed of current events, give them as much of the picture as you can, especially if it is bad news. There is nothing worse than staff finding out that you've lost your biggest customer directly from the horse's mouth, or worse still from a competitor when you could have told them a week earlier. By keeping a flow of information, you stop the rumour mill from starting. Most marketing experts agree that it is more important to communicate bad news internally than good news. Bad news heard through the grapevine is de-motivating and can have undesirable knock-on effects, but if this information is openly shared from within the company it can actually 'rally the troops'. If your company is going through a rocky patch and the grapevine gets up to full speed, you may find key staff jump ship because their perception of the problem is greater than the reality.

There is a limit, however as to how much information you should make public to staff. As a rule, never release more information than you would want your competitors to know. Chances are it may get back to them in some form or another, especially if they are perhaps already approaching your staff with alternative employment offers, which is common in any industry.

Staff newsletters

These are great ways to keep staff informed of current events but are often overlooked as unimportant and expensive exercises in internal PR, yet they need not be costly. In fact, if all your staff are on email then it will cost you nothing but the time to write them. If you do have to produce a printed newsletter, don't go overboard – although subconsciously most staff will appreciate being kept informed of the company's performance. If they receive a lavish full-colour newsletter that has obviously been put together at great time and expense, it will probably be seen as a luxury that the company could have done without. Keep it simple – if you're printing a couple of hundred single-sided (or double if you have the equipment) then laser/photo copies will be sufficient.

You can include a wide variety of topics in a staff newsletter, some of which need not even relate to your products or services at all! In addition to general business news subjects could also include:

- case studies on how employees (and not just sales people) have contributed to winning new/continued business
- 'Bright idea of the month' – the best money-saving idea, submitted by staff – you could also make this a prize-winning part of the newsletter
- highlighting some of the problem areas within the business, and showing how some staff are already trying to tackle them – by publicly airing such problems you make them less likely to re-occur
- long service awards (perhaps including several types marking different lengths of employment)
- new appointments and staff leaving (although you may not want to include dismissals!)
- staff hobbies/activities (e.g. strange pets, or charity work).

The format your newsletter will take will depend on the media you will use to deliver it. Emails could either be plain text or full graphical (HTML) based, if you have the skills and resources to design it. An alternative would be to deliver a text-only newsletter by email with hyperlinks into your company Intranet (if available), which could contain more detailed and/or graphical information. The printed design format of a newsletter is simple – just pick up any newspaper and copy that!

Think of a good, snappy title, rather than 'The XYZ company newsletter'. Keep the design simple and clean, and ensure that everything is approved 'from the top' before release. Include contact details at the bottom and invite readers to submit their own material for the next issue.

Shorter is sweeter!

Internet News reported that in 2002 US staff wasted 4.5 seconds deleting each unsolicited email (also known as SPAM), which Ferris Research claim accounted for up 20% of all emails. By the end of 2004 this had risen to an astronomical 85%, more than two thirds of which was generated in the UK or US (according to E-mail Systems, a spam filtering company). Meanwhile, in Italy, Europemedia reported that Italian employees were spending approximately 2 hours a day sending and receiving an average of 70 emails. People's attention spans have had to shrink to compensate for the barrage of unwanted, unnecessary and often unsavoury material that lands in their in-box. Therefore make sure that your emails are short, succinct and to the point – that way they'll get read!

Email mailing lists

Any email software worth its salt (such as Outlook Express, pictured) has the capability to not only store email addresses in an address book but also to create a group name that can send the same email to many recipients simultaneously. Therefore, creating a set of groups relating to internal staff (e.g. sales, accounts or just 'all staff') is a great way to ensure that no one gets left out. Once you've created a group you only have to type in thegroup name into an email to send it to all recipients specified within that group.

Fig 1.5.1 - Outlook Express can handle basic group emailing

Regular information such as memos or even news that may end up in the newsletter can be sent out by email rather than tying people up with meetings just to relay it. Don't write them in Word and attach them to the email – just write an email, the shorter the better.

Summary

❑ Every company relies on its staff, but employees also rely on their company. Most people work to live rather than live to work, but the more passionate they feel about the company they work for, the more this will come across in their work and to your customers. Miscommunication or a complete lack of communication can have a demoralising effect, and is inexcusable with the communication infrastructure available to most companies, and a company veiled in secrecy is no joy to work in and will command little respect and commitment from staff. A good Marketing Manager recognises that a regular flow of information between management and staff is just as important as any external PR exercise.

 Pearls of Wisdom

'None of our men are "experts". We have most unfortunately found it necessary to get rid of a man as soon as he thinks himself an expert because no one ever considers himself expert if he really knows his job. A man who knows a job sees so much more to be done than he has done, that he is always pressing forward and never gives up an instant of thought to how good and how efficient he is. Thinking always ahead, thinking always of trying to do more, brings a state of mind in which nothing is impossible. The moment one gets into the "expert" state of mind, a great number of things becomes impossible.'

Henry Ford, Sr.
The Ford Motor Co

1.6

Customer/Prospect Communications

On the CD

- Guerrilla marketing material
- Bulk email software
- Bulk fax mailing software
- Web links

Any salesman will tell you that sales is a numbers game – get more prospects in the funnel and sales will inevitably fall through. If you are doing things right and the market will support your product and pricing, then this is 100% true. To do this well you will need your portfolio of marketing material ready, be it in brochure, CD or web format to back up your approach.

The traditional methods of communication with prospects and customers (in addition to passive methods such as paid advertising and editorial) are:

- telemarketing, using either in-house or telemarketing companies
- direct mailing to existing or purchased databases
- newsletters, either included in press publications or direct mailed
- fax-shots and email-shots
- networking and joint seminars.

There are, however other methods by which you may make contact with customers. If you've already got a good flow of press hopefully the number of incoming calls, emails and mailed enquiries will be increasing. Viral and guerrilla marketing, covered later in this chapter are also extremely cost-effective ways to get your message to the masses – possibly reaching numbers you could not even anticipate.

Telemarketing
If done well, telemarketing can yield almost instantaneous results. There are two methods of telemarketing – inbound and outbound. Inbound involves sending material to a target list of prospects inviting them to call. When (or if) they do, your telemarketing staff will provide information on the product/ service with a view to closing the sale and taking the order there and then.

Outbound, or cold calling requires a proactive sales approach where your telemarketing staff call your target list of prospects. Telemarketing is not used just to call prospects and sell to them – you may be launching a new product and want to research the market, or invite a target audience to a seminar or show.

Whether you decide to do this in-house or through a telemarketing company will be defined by:

- **your internal resources** – do you have the numbers of staff required with the communication skills and discipline required to call out?
- **your product/service** – does it lend itself to this form of marketing?
- **your budget** – given that you may have adequate internal resources, is it still more cost-effective to use a telemarketing company instead so that internal resources can be better used?

If you decide to go the internal route, your costs will be limited to the number of staff who are dedicated to the task and the cost of the outgoing calls. A call-centre however will generally charge a basic fee plus a cost-per-call rate, or perhaps a cost per successful call rate, depending on what your requirements are. The drawback of using an external company is that their staff will only be able to act and react within given guidelines. If a prospect asks a question about the product or service they probably won't be able to answer it.

Making the call
Before you even pick up the phone, start by making a script. When making cold calls you only have around fifteen seconds to grab the person's attention. We've all done it – someone that we don't know calls us and launches into a sales pitch to which we reply 'No thanks', perhaps without really listening to what they were actually saying. After the initial greeting you'll need to be asking a key question to which you're looking for a 'Yes' answer. This then allows you to deliver your initial sales pitch to inform the person of who you are and why you are calling them.

When you do call, confirm that you are speaking to the right person – either the user or the decision-maker. If you are not, get as much information as you can (such as direct number, email address) before asking to be transferred. If they are not available, find out when a suitable time would be for you to call.

Once you're through to the right person you have your fifteen seconds to attract their interest with your initial pitch. If they immediately make it clear that they have absolutely no requirement for your product or service thank them for their time and move onto the next – there is no point in flogging a dead horse. Before you can go into greater detail with your pitch you need to qualify the person as a genuine target for your product/service. Ask key questions that will not only give you a better understanding of their needs, but will also keep their interest. For example, if you are trying to replace an existing product/service, you might want to ask what some of the problems the person might be experiencing with their current supplier (although don't be drawn into criticising competitors – sell on your strengths, not their weaknesses).

You will find that your script improves with experience as you learn the objections that you are likely to face and how to tackle them.

Direct mailing

More recently, direct mail has been overtaken by email as the chosen method for many companies, but in the main it is still the best method of targeting new business. A direct mail shot should consist of a specific covering letter that is customised to the recipient (e.g. Dear Mr Smith... and perhaps customised content if you have the relevant information).

Direct mailing is most effective when you have a well-structured database that allows you to pull out a specific range of records – perhaps all customers that previously purchased a product that has been updated recently. You could then send them a personalised letter mentioning that they had previously bought the said product, that a new version was out and list the advantages over their previous purchase. You might also include the new product brochure, any reviews or case studies and a current newsletter.

In-house mail merging is extremely easy nowadays, with Microsoft Word allowing you to create a document, attach it to an Access database or Excel spreadsheet and merge certain fields. In a matter of seconds you can merge a document with a database of hundreds or thousands of contacts, then press Print to start churning out the letters.

If you don't have a good database of prospects, or want to widen your customer base you might consider buying in a mailing list. Mailing houses, usually associated with trade magazines that use the same database for subscriptions, will sell you an address list for single or multiple uses. If they provide the names directly to you they may protect their interest by seeding the database with one or two false companies to ensure you don't abuse the terms by which you purchase the list. You can generally choose from a very select range of records, either by SIC code or other specific categories, then by the position of the person you want to contact, e.g. Managing Director, Buyer etc. If they are offering a complete mailing service, once you've produced your mailing material you can then send it to them for mail-merging – they will handle integrating names into the letter, adding any other material you supply, inserting it into envelopes and mailing it out. Purchasing a targeted list for a one-off mailing can be very cost-effective if you have a product that you feel is likely to attract a lot of attention.

Newsletters

80% of your revenue will probably come from 20% of your customers, and a newsletter is a great way to keep your name in front of them as well as providing current news in your packs to prospective clients. Its format can be flexible depending on budget and the amount of editorial content you can produce – from a single-sided inkjet or laser printed document to a full colour tabloid newspaper.

Once you start sending newsletters, keep producing them at regular intervals. Customers will start to look for your newsletter when it's due – its arrival will plant the subliminal seed that you are a reliable, consistent company. Make sure that the latest copy is included with invoices, goods shipments, placed in your reception and given out by sales staff. Send several copies to larger companies, marking each one for individuals that should receive a copy. Place it on your website as a downloadable PDF.

Designing a newsletter is covered in detail in Chapter 2.3.

Fax-shots and email-shots

In the late 1980s and early 90s, bulk fax mailing was a popular method of keeping customers informed of products and pricing, especially if you worked in a volatile market where pricing fluctuates regularly. This has now all but been replaced by bulk emailing, but should not be discounted altogether. The prevalence of viruses and the success of sending bulk email have actually worked in favour of the fax machine – buyers may receive dozens or even hundred of emails from suppliers but probably very few faxes, so you may stand a better chance of being noticed.

If you do choose to go the fax route, products such as Winfax or VentaFax make it very easy to set up an automated fax mailing system in-house. All you need is a PC with a fax/modem and one of the above or similar products. Most of these products set themselves up as a 'virtual printer'. Creating a fax to send to multiple recipients is as simple as printing from the application in which you designed your fax. You can then import the fax numbers from your customer database and the system will dutifully send out your faxes one after the other. Do not send out faxes overnight or at the weekend, as this can be annoying for users that work from home – nothing is worse than being woken at 3am by a fax machine, especially if it doubles as their phone line!

Although sending bulk emails is undoubtedly one of the most cost effective forms of informing people of your products, there is a fine line between providing useful information and 'spamming', the phrase given to unsolicited emails. Just because it's free to send an email it doesn't mean that you should do it daily. Email shots differ from newsletters in their structure. Where a newsletter contains a full story, an email can contain a brief headline with a link to the full story. People's attention spans are far less with emails, so the best way to grab and keep their attention is by using enticing hooklines, one or two sentences and a link to the full story on your website. According to US email marketing company DoubleClick, click-through rates from email marketing rose from 4.85 percent in the second quarter of 2002 to 6.13 percent in the third quarter, confirming that readers are more likely to follow a short, snappy hook line than read an entire email advert.

There are two types of email that you can send – plain text and HTML. The former consists of just text, generally in a standard font and with no pictures. HTML emails are effectively web pages that are sent as emails, giving you much more flexibility in design. The downside is that many people (myself included) will immediately aim for the Delete key on seeing any image loading in an email unless they recognise the sender. Even then they may regard it as spam as it is probably not a personally written email. And Windows XP (SP2) now includes HTML email filtering that blocks images from even loading unless the user confirms they wish to see them for each email. Therefore unless you know that your target audience is likely to be more receptive to a graphically pleasing email, stick to text only with hyperlinks – you'll probably get a better response rate.

Sending out bulk emails is extremely easy – the chances are you already have the software to do it, although you may want to use specific software for the job. Outlook Express, supplied with every Windows PC has the capability to build groups of email address, so you just type the group name in the email address field and it will duly send the email out to everyone in that group. This does mean that you have to have all of your customers and prospects listed in Outlook Express's address book, which can be cumbersome. Therefore, use a product such as Infacta's GroupMail, which is free. This will do the job just as well and offers a host of additional features.

Finally, at the bottom of your email or fax, include a contact number or email address where the person can request to be removed from future such mailings. Make sure you respect this wish. Not only will people be annoyed if you continue to bombard them with material they have specifically requested not to receive, but also you may find yourself at the wrong end of a lawsuit or find that your email domain name is blacklisted by organisations such as Spamcop – this will mean that any spam filtering software that links to Spamcop will see your emails automatically as spam and delete them before they are even read. Data protection laws differ from country to country, but legislation in some countries makes it an offence to send unsolicited mail or faxes where the user cannot request to be removed. In September 2004, Microsoft filed nine lawsuits at companies and individuals allegedly involved in the distribution of spam. In November of the same year, a spammer was jailed for 8 years.

For more information on how to send out bulk emails, read the Bulk Email section in Chapter 2.2 on distributing press releases.

Email harvesting – why you shouldn't do it!

Have you ever wondered how so many spammers manage to get hold of your email address? How do those Nigerian relatives of dead Princes know to contact you personally to assist with the transfer of $38 million? Or why is your life so poor that you will need to enhance various body parts, grow more hair, look more youthful or get a septic tank to die for. The answer is probably email harvesters – programs that scan websites, perhaps using specific keywords for relevance and extract every email address on every page. This includes news groups, chat rooms and email service directories. Internet News reports that spam cost corporate America close to $9 billion in 2002, with productivity losses accounting for 40% of the overall financial loss. In 2003 the US Federal Trade commission (FTC) seeded 175 Internet locations with 250 email addresses, monitoring them for 6 weeks. Altogether they attracted 3,349 instances of spam, with the first instance occurring just 9 minutes after a posting in a chat room. The problem has not got better over time, as new technologies make any email address vulnerable. In January 2005, Postini reported that of 18m emails that it monitored through its systems, 88% of it was SPAM, and also included directory harvest attacks (DHA). These occur when the spammer uses a company's email string (e.g. @yourdomain.com) and either runs through common names or every character and monitors the emails rejected by the company's server. Any that are not returned are assumed to be live and are heavily spammed. DHAs were up 30% on 2004.

Email harvesting programs are available for two-figure sums, but you would be ill advised to use one of these for several reasons. You have no way of knowing if your email will actually hit a large percentage of your target audience – all you will know is that every email address has been extracted from pages which may have some relevance to any keywords you specified. You could inadvertently be emailing all of your competitors – even if you don't recognise the email addresses they may be the private addresses to give your competitors anonymity in online forums. Also as mentioned previously you run the risk of being blacklisted, having your account terminated by your ISP, being hit by a lawsuit or even ending up in prison (although it must be said that this is an extreme scenario). In short, the drawbacks far outweigh any possible benefit.

User groups and workshops

If your product is regularly updated or users can benefit from ongoing training, organising a user group or workshop can help to secure ongoing loyalty with your existing customer base. Even those that don't take you up on it will at least be aware of its existence and will happier knowing that it is available should they need it. Situations change, staff leave and companies restructure, so ensuring that new staff are fully trained on your product reduces the risk of a competitor managing to unhook it due to the customer's lack of knowledge. It may not be unreasonable (depending on your industry) to charge for these events, meaning that it will even pay for itself as well as generating good publicity and customer retention.

If you do not have the premises to host such an event, or your customers are located too far to feasibly travel, find out what conferencing facilities are available. Choose a venue that is close to the main travel destinations your customers are likely to want to use, such as train stations or airports. A friendly customer may even be able to provide the venue at little or no cost. Provide customers with a full range of travel and accommodation options to make it as easy as possible for them to attend. And don't forget to list it on your website and send out a press release well in advance to your trade press announcing the event.

Networking and joint events

There is a lot to be said for partnering with businesses that service the same range of clients. For the price of a few phone calls, if you can build a good relationship with companies that sell non-competing products (or even if there is some overlap) to a similar clientele you can not only generate qualified sales leads but also gain excellent market information.

Once you have relationships like these in place, you can then organise joint events, sharing the cost. You can produce a leaflet that can be mailed to each company's prospect and customer list. Let's say that there are three companies involved, and each one mails 1,000 prospects. A hundred from each decide to attend – you therefore have access to up to 200 prospects that potentially you didn't know about in addition to the hundred of your own prospects/customers.

A tooling company held a joint seminar with a software company (which produces software driving the machines that the tools are used in) – an existing customer of the software company attended and initially wasn't interested in dealing with the tooling company due to a bad experience some twelve years previous. After leaving the seminar, he told the MD of the tooling company that he should have been dealing with them years ago, but did not because of the one bad experience with a salesman (who was fired three months later). This one customer alone paid for all of the costs with business placed in the months after the seminar.

Viral marketing

Word of mouth is normally the best recommendation, so if you can get people to spread the good word about you, your company and products then so much the better. This is what viral marketing is all about. One of the best of many great examples is Microsoft's Hotmail free web-based email service (**www.hotmail.com**). Anyone can set up an account for free and access it anywhere in the world using only a web browser. Every email that is sent by any Hotmail user has a tag line that invites the recipient to 'get your free Hotmail account', inciting new users to sign up. Microsoft can then get revenue from selling enhancements to your Hotmail account or selling targeted advertising, which is the price you pay for the free service. Nevertheless, millions of users are happy to put up with a Spam-filled In-box for a free service.

There are companies that will allow you to offer a Hotmail-style service to customers in return for split revenue from advertising and purchase of any service enhancements that may be offered with the package. Visit a site such as **www.bigmailbox.com** and you'll be able to create a web-based email service that users will want to come back to every day. Your brand will appear, you can get a percentage of shared banner revenue and you can also email all members using online tools. Every email that every user of your system sends will not only have your requested domain name (e.g. user@yourdomain.com) but will also have a hook line at the bottom of the email. Previously these services used to be free, but many companies will charge a small fee per user per month (normally only a few cents) because advertising revenue no longer yields adequate amounts.

Ambient and Guerrilla Marketing

You can, of course employ more unorthodox methods to get your message across. The phrase 'Guerrilla Marketing' was coined by Jay Conrad Levinson, author of several marketing books to describe getting maximum exposure using unusual, controversial and sometimes illegal methods at a fraction of the cost of traditional techniques. The term 'ambient' relates to advertising via out of home media such as taxi sides or telephone booths, with the idea being to fit into the target consumer's day-to-day environment getting as close to your prospective audience as possible.

Ambient advertising/marketing was until recently the preserve of low-budget advertisers who couldn't afford to pay for 'proper' media space, resorting to alternative low cost methods such as fly posting and sandwich bags. Over the past few years, the popularity of ambient media has taken off, with even blue-chip advertisers taking advantage of the host of new places, from 'viewrinals' to PR stunts where brands can be seen.

The format has increased by more than 500% since 1998 with revenues of just £17.4m ($29m) in 1996. Ambient media was the only form of advertising to see significant growth in 2002 with revenues up 12% to £100.8m ($169m), according to the outdoor advertising specialist, Concord. (See Chapter 1.9 for more information on ambient media advertising)

Fig 1.6.1. Gail Porter left quite an impression on the Houses of Parliament!

Companies have taken this approach to extraordinary lengths and created memorable stunts that, when you add up the equivalent tabloid advertising space, together with TV and radio coverage would have cost millions of dollars as opposed to the thousands they actually cost. One such company is the appropriately named Cunning Stunts, which operates in the US, Brazil and the UK. Since 1998 they have pulled a number of extremely high-profile stunts, including projecting model and TV star Gail Porter's naked rear onto the Houses of Parliament in London, England for men's magazine FHM (pictured left) to promote their '100 sexiest women' issue.

Cunning Stunts were also responsible for creating several waxwork heads of a new magazine's founder and, reminiscent of the film Se7en, packed them in boxes along with a copy of the magazine and sent them to key media figures. In February 2003 they created a media frenzy, obtaining worldwide TV, radio and press coverage with the 'invention' of foreheADS™ – renting the space on students foreheads for £88 per week (around $140) to include a corporate logo (as illustrated overleaf).

Anna Carloss, Managing Director of Cunning Stunts attributes the success of such drastic tactics to two factors; "The ad industry is constantly searching for new ways to communicate messages to consumers. It is now at a stage of development where the intro-duction of original forms of advertising and promotions are essential in order to satisfy the ever-increasing demands of the advertiser. Couple this with the fact that people are no longer spending their evenings in front of the TV and if they do, they may switch over or leave the room during the ad breaks. People travel more and more to and from work and enjoy more spare-time activities such as eating out, going to the gym, and socialising in bars and pubs. These two factors have combined to drive a demand for ambient marketing and the the sector has enjoyed tremendous growth and continues to grow as advertisers recognise its value, both in terms of creating direct sales and developing brand awareness."

Fig 1.6.2. foreheads™ was more about the 'PR about the PR' than real advertising, but it worked.

Another excellent case in point was the launch of the new MINI car in 2001. Cunning Stunts was appointed as the consumer PR and ambient agency for the launch, achieving more media coverage for MINI than any other car in the UK. This was achieved through a combined PR and ambient event strategy using the overall theme of 'MINI Adventure'. Prior to the launch no real cars were available so fifteen fibreglass replicas were made and 'parked' in surprising places, such as on top of buildings. 25,000 matchbooks were distributed by (unbranded) good-looking guys and girls to people in bars and clubs across ten target UK cities. Each book contained a provocative hand-written message and a phone number, creating the impression that the recipient had been chatted up. On calling the number a cheeky voice revealed the admirer to be 'MINI', with callers then invited to visit the website. Similar notes were

Fig 1.6.3. 'Fetish Mini' was just one of several custom cars build especially for the new car's launch.

also placed under windscreen wipers in car parks. This dual approach achieved a response rate of 11.2% when no other marketing activities were running.
The campaign continued after the car's launch in July 2001, with MINI appearing at several high-profile community events. A leather-clad 'fetish-MINI' (pictured) stole the show at the Mardi Gras festival, with other customised cars fitted with high-powered sound systems appearing across other UK events and even entertaining crowds on the dance capital of Ibiza. At the end of 2001, the fibreglass MINIs were rounded up and constructed into a Christmas tree, which was then floated down the River Thames in London, England, again receiving massive TV and tabloid coverage.

One potential drawback with guerrilla marketing is that there may be legal or moral issues relating to some tactics (such as fly-posting, projections onto buildings etc), but there is no doubt that off-the-wall ideas can grab attention and headlines and need not eat a large hole in your marketing budget. Anna Carver concluded; *'Where any activities are proposed that do fall foul of the law we make our client fully aware of the possible consequences in advance. Sometimes the potential fines are low enough to warrant the risk.'*

Below are some other examples of ingenious ways that have attracted consumer and media interest:

Body-painted logo
A company hired a model to have their logo painted on the top half of her body. She then proceeded to walk around a trade show that they were exhibiting at on a pair of stilts (ensuring no-one could smear the text). This technique is unlikely to work in many markets, such as the US, where public nudity is frowned upon.

Crop circles
A company 'rented' a field from a farmer for a month, and then used biodegradable paint to spray their web address across the field in extremely large letters. As the field was in the flight path of an international airport this was an innovative and cost-effective way of reaching people where they least expected it.

My name is Turok
Games developer Acclaim Entertainment set up a website and sent out a press release offering £500 (around $830), an XBOX games console plus the complete back-catalogue of the Turok game series for the first five people willing to change their name by deed poll for one year to 'Turok'. The closing date was set shortly before the game's release, so that the media

could cover the launch with the details of the five lucky (?) individuals. They spearheaded the campaign by heralding it as the launch of 'Identity MarketingTM – taking a brave step beyond the leading edge of marketing practice'. Within hours, this story was across every game-related website around the world and even reached several tabloid newspapers. Acclaim did back this campaign up with a comprehensive ad campaign, but the exposure they received through word of mouth and press was phenomenal.

Cheatingscum.com

Future Publishing's .net magazine in the UK wrote an article demonstrating how to generate web traffic with a marketing budget of zero. They wrote a fictitious site – **cheatingscum.com** – allowing people to submit pictures and accounts of love rats they knew to expose their cheating ways. (For legal reasons all of the 'rats' published were staff members with made-up names and stories). They set a time span of 10 days to see how much traffic they could generate. Day one saw them emailing out a press release that was immediately covered by London's leading radio station, and achieved a full page story in a UK tabloid newspaper, even finally gaining coverage in a Chinese newspaper! They then sent out an email with the story

Fig 1.6.4. .net magazine demonstrated a novel way to get promotion.

about a fictitious character that appeared on the web to a list made up of friends and family, asking them to forward it to all their friends. The final stroke of genius was to print placards and walk around key landmarks in London inviting passers-by to find out 'is your lover cheating on you – find out on cheating scum.com', again creating great awareness. The entire stunt netted them over 10,000 site visits in less than two weeks at virtually no cost.

Seeing Double

Artist and Photographer Alison Jackson caused several media storms by photographing look-alikes in unusual but easily believable situations. In May 2003 the story broke that the England footballer David Beckham was considering a transfer from Manchester United to Real Madrid. She

Fig 1.6.5. Alison Jackson created a media frenzy with this fake shoot.

immediately set up a photo shoot in the Spanish capital with doubles of David and his wife, ex Spice Girl, Victoria. The resulting media frenzy ensured that the photos made the headlines of almost every tabloid newspaper the following day. Not only did she increase her own exposure but also that of the 'Posh and Becks' look-alikes. When interviewed by the Evening Standard newspaper, Jackson said, "I like to be disruptive. Not for the sake of it, of course. But it's good to make people question their perceptions, otherwise they'll believe in anything."

Summary

❑ There are many methods over and above traditional and expensive advertising to attract new prospects. Keep your eyes and mind open, and see how other companies and individuals promote themselves – maybe you will be able to apply some of their techniques to your own business. Don't dismiss using a PR company unless your business cannot yet afford it or is in a market not suitably covered. Networking with crossover companies costs nothing and can yield significant results as well as giving you a finger on the pulse of your industry. Keeping a high visibility with customers and prospects through seminars and workgroups builds face-to-face relationships, trust and a feeling of reliability – people by their very nature stick with what and who they know.

 Pearls of Wisdom

'Word of mouth is one of the greatest marketing tools in the world. Good people create happy customers, who tell their friends and come back for more.'

Richard Branson
Chairman, Virgin Group of Companies

1.7

The Media

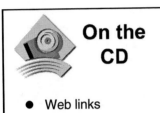

On the CD

- Web links

Many people confuse the media with advertising – publicity and advertising are two entirely different areas. Do not also make the mistake of picturing all journalists as hacks who will camp out in your back yard looking through your litter to get the dirt on your organisation! This chapter concentrates on what the media has to offer your business and how you can take full advantage of this. We'll go through establishing media contacts, how to talk to editors and the benefits of press events.

Firstly, let's establish the benefits of media publicity over general advertising:

Media Publicity:	Advertising:
• It's generally free	• You have control of content, but at a price
• Can often be seen as unbiased over an advert	• You choose when and where your material appears
• Gives your company more credibility	• You get 100% coverage (whereas an article may include competitors)
• Allows you to get a more technical message across in details that an advert could not convey	

Put simply, if your customers read an article about your company or product they are likely to view it more favourably than an advert.

In many industries advertising still has its place, and may indeed be necessary, however a continued press presence is a much more cost-effective way to get long-term results. You should place a high priority on trying to gain regular press coverage, be it in magazines, newspapers or even radio and television if your product is suitably mainstream. The trick is to make yourself and your company easier to deal with than your competitors, supplying the right information in the right format at the right time.

Most magazines will separate editorial and advertising, making it clear that placing adverts does not necessarily win you editorial. Ringing your ad sales rep and asking them to put a good word in for recently submitted editorial generally does not work, and in a worst case scenario could work against you. Publishing houses or titles catering for niche markets may buck this trend if they need to tie adverts to editorial because of low circulation or ad sales, but this will normally be made clear to you from the outset.

Public relations company vs. in-house

Publicity in the media may be free but getting your message to the media takes up a resource. The question is whether you have the resource and media knowledge available in-house to communicate this effectively, or whether you should pass this task to a company that specialises in this field. Weber Shandwick, the largest PR Company in the world, state that they offer much more than just a press release distribution service. Michelle McGlocklin, Managing Director of Weber Shandwick UK's Technology Practice states; *'The press release has a role to play in official communications but there are more effective ways of getting a company's message across. Increasingly, we recommend that our clients drive their message on the back of key issues and trends being reported in the media, and also look at what is happening at the EU level that their products or solutions could/do support. Additionally, visual communications such as eTeasers and online viral campaigns are used as a quick, impactful way to get clients' messages heard in a crowded marketplace.'*

Finding the dividing line as to when a company should move over to a PR company is blurred. McGlocklin gives further insight into why many companies have used Weber Shandwick's services. *'Essentially it's a business decision as opposed to a function of time or size. There are several reasons why companies use PR. The first may be because they have a negative perception in the market around their products or company and need to counter it. Alternatively they may be launching a new product into a sceptical market and so need to explain clearly to the key industry influencers why they are doing this, or to deposition a competitor and its products. Perhaps they are looking to reposition the company as part of a broader strategic initiative or it may be that they want to raise the profile of their company, products or brand amongst key decision makers. In most cases, it is to support sales by more clearly and credibly defining and explaining the benefits of their particular products or services to their target audiences. We have some clients that use us to handle their core press office functions but in most cases we work alongside an in-house team to combine their knowledge of their company and products with our insight into their industry, the relevant media, analysts and influencers as well as the depth and breadth of services we offer and geographies we cover.'*

PR companies will either generally charge a flat retainer fee or by way of a performance-based pricing plan. At the outset of the relationship a program of activity will be defined, with success milestones laid out along with associated costs. Weber Shandwick, for example, generally work on an overall campaign budget managed on a per-hour basis, with all work and time being openly tracked – this gives the client total visibility of the costs associated with a campaign.

So the question remains – do you use a PR company or handle it internally? Unless you have worked in the media within your given industry and know the various methods of public relations in detail, together with having the contacts to be able to pull it all together, you would be well advised to investigate a PR company. This is probably not an activity you (or indeed the PR company) will want to split – either they handle the PR or you do. Splitting your PR efforts will only result in a fragmented message being sent out to the respective media. Of course, budget will play a part in this, together with the industry you serve, but it costs nothing to investigate.

A good PR company will tell you if it is worthwhile for you to employ their services, and be able to clearly demonstrate the effect they are likely to have on your business. Also, if you intend to employ guerrilla tactics as mentioned in the previous chapter, you will need the advice of experts to carry your plans out and perform risk assessments. The bottom line is this: If your budget and industry allows, the cost of a PR company may be justifiable by the results. If the costs are just too high for you to consider at this time, the rest of this chapter is devoted to methods of gaining press coverage with minimal time, effort and cost.

Getting your foot in the door with editors
Many people are afraid to talk to editors, thinking that if they say anything slightly out of turn the editor will write a damning story on their company. While this may hold some remote truth with the mainstream press, if you work in a niche market the chances are that editors need you more than you need them. Most editors will be pleased if you contact them with a story of interest.

When you have an item of interest to discuss, just pick up the phone. You should not be calling editors for every release you send – only when you have a major news story or are inviting them to attend an event. Keep the call short unless they are interested and need more information. The call should generally be a precursor to providing them with more information in writing. For example, if you've just written a case study, you may want to find out whether it may be of interest to them as an exclusive story. If it is, then you've got your answer – tell them you'll forward it via email and wrap up the call. Check what format they'd like it in, e.g. Word, Adobe Acrobat, and whether they'd like some digital photos to go with it.

Don't be scared to ask them what they're looking for. Maybe they're writing a piece your product or service line and want some stats, or want to add another angle by way of including another company in the story. Ensure that they know that you are always on-hand to quickly provide them with the information they may need to get their job done. This makes you a valuable source in their eyes, while ensuring that you get a continual drip-feed of coverage, however small.

Product reviews

If your company manufacturers or sells a product, the chances are that there are magazines or TV shows that regularly run reviews, either singular or group test. It is imperative to ensure that you get included in these. A good review can be worth a dozen adverts. When working for a PC manufacturer in the early 1990's we placed a machine into a magazine for review and won 'Best Buy' – the phones rang off the wall! Entry is free – all you have to do is supply the product and the reviewer will do the rest! Most magazines will have a Reviews Editor who not only performs and writes the review, but will also manage the logistics of getting the right goods back to the right suppliers.

Give them what they want:

I receive regular exposure in a magazine that offers international coverage. The reason for this, the editor confided in me, was because although they were an international title, they were based in the UK and as such mainly received stories confined to that geographical region. I therefore ensured that I provided them with case studies and news articles in as many far-flung places as possible, giving them a regular supply of global material to choose from. While they didn't use everything they generally used most of it - the point is that I was providing them with as much of a service as they were providing me.

It is very rare (unless you have a very bad product) that reviewers will give a damning review – they may criticise certain elements of your product, but this is par for the course, and you will know where your weak points are anyway. If you are concerned about faring badly in a group review, stick to standalone reviews – they may still point out your flaws, but at least they won't be recommending an alternative. Amend the pricing provided with the review product to reflect how your product is likely to be priced when the review is printed – most magazines will run the review 6-10 weeks after seeing your product, and with volatile products such as computers the price may already be lower.

When preparing a product for review, ensure that you check it thoroughly. Include a covering letter that details exactly what you have provided, including pricing information. If your product is breakable, pay greater-than-normal attention to the packaging to make sure it gets there in one piece – computer magazines regularly have to refuse items for review after they arrive smashed or DOA (dead on arrival) because a piece of internal hardware has shifted. Check that all manuals and literature are included – in short make sure that it is the best representation of a product that your company can supply.

A reviewer should be able to give you a rough timescale for how long they'll need your equipment for. Once that time is up, give them a courtesy call to see if they need any assistance, perhaps even offering to arrange collection – this will be appreciated. Don't embarrass them by asking how your product performed, as they will not tell you.

Once the review is published, and assuming it is favourable, ask for permission to reprint copies, and to get it in electronic format (ideally a JPG or PDF) – you can then include it on your website and sales packs. Many magazines will charge for this, but if it's a good review it will be worth it. You effectively have a brochure that has taken no time to design, has been written by an external and respected source and gives an unbiased and positive opinion of your product.

Kill several birds with one stone – organise a press conference
If you have a product launch or major announcement that should be conveyed to many media contacts at once, then it makes sense to try to get them all together in the same place. A press conference is essentially a seminar, which is covered in detail in chapter 1.9. The success of such an event will depend on geography and the perceived importance of the event. An editor is unlikely to fly across three States for anything other than a major news story. Conversely, where there is a high congregation of press contacts in one city (an example being London, England) you are more likely

to get a higher attendance as the event will be relatively painless for them to get to. The other alternative is to host the press conference at a trade show. Most shows have either specific press days or set aside areas for presentations of this nature. This virtually guarantees that the people you want will be in attendance.

Make yourself a voice in your industry

In every industry, editors in every media type have their 'black book' of contacts to call when they need a quote. When a news event occurs they'll immediately get on the phone to get the opinion of the appropriate 'leading figure'. Take Sir Richard Branson (pictured), Chairman and founder of the Virgin group of companies. He has done a fantastic job of being instantly recognisable in a wide variety of markets, from condoms to soft drinks to airlines. Not a week goes by where his smiling face doesn't appear out of a glossy magazine or a news article on television. He has become synonymous with success and people will listen to what he has to say. Of course not everyone is suited to high exposure – Sir Richard is a particularly flamboyant individual – so although you may not wish to be the face of your company on TV there should be nothing stopping you from appearing in print.

Fig 1.7.1. Sir Richard Branson is the well-publicised face of the Virgin Group.

In your regular conversations with editors, bring the conversation around to general market conditions, then give your opinion, citing examples and statistics wherever possible. Watch what you say – stick to the facts, do not criticise competitors and do not make claims that you cannot substantiate. If you are giving an opinion then justify it with logical reasons rather than emotional statements. Make it clear to them that you will always be happy to provide them with 'inside information' on the industry.

Another good method of self-promotion is interviews; in print, on radio or TV. Let editors know that you are available for interview, mentioning topics that might be of interest to cover e.g. new product launch, recent successes etc. Not only does this give substantial credibility for your company as leader in its field, but it also looks good on your résumé! In general an editor would want to interview you face to face, however many will be happy to perform a telephone interview – you can supply them digital photos of yourself by mail or on CD. For ten minutes of your time you'll secure excellent media coverage.

Custom written articles are also an extremely good way to gain exposure, even if your company brand or products do not feature heavily in the article itself. For example a builder might write about the top home building problems (e.g. dry rot, leaky roof etc). Look for problems that are common amongst your customers, or perhaps even your competitors customers, and then discuss with editors whether they would like an article on the subject. Do not make it a blatant plug for your products – if your company name and contact details appear that is enough, but anything above that is a bonus.

Look for alternative opportunities

Being flexible and open-minded with promotion ideas can open very unexpected doors. Providing sample products or services gets you free publicity and can create great brand awareness and in some cases even gain cult status. Brian Clemens, best known for writing the UK hit detective shows The New Avengers and The Professionals (pictured) originally used

British Leyland vehicles when making The New Avengers, although suffered continual filming delays because of poor reliability and service. He then initially switched to Japanese manufacturers, and finally Ford. Of the decision to switch, Clemens said, *'When we needed a motorbike for Jo (Lumley), we went to a Japanese manufacturer and within hours they replied "How many bikes do you want? What colours?" If we gave them a little time they would be pleased to produce a special 'Purdey' bike for our use! In that one incident I realised why the Japanese industry was growing so rapidly – and the British one was*

doomed to oblivion. Later, on The Professionals, we involved Ford – a US company – and again received excellent and professional treatment.' (Quote courtesy of *'The Ultimate Avengers'* by Dave Rogers.) Ford's success was British Leyland's loss – by being inflexible, BL lost out on the opportunity to make their car an object of desire. Ford met the production company's needs, supplying vehicles as filming moved from location to location – The Professionals, which ran in the UK from 1977 to 1983 subsequently turned the Ford Capri and Escort RS2000 into the cars every would-be 'CI5' agent wanted to be seen in.

And the winner is ...

Another innovative way of gaining publicity is to host a contest or competition. If your product or service would make an attractive prize, why not talk to a major magazine in your industry to see if they are interested in running a competition – most magazines do. A deal can generally be brokered whereby you will receive details of all entrants, which immediately gives you an excellent database of prospects within your target audience. You will gain good exposure within the magazine, often also on the front cover – hard to do in any industry – and this can also elevate the status of your product as by association and by offering it as a prize they are stating that it is a prize worth having.

Keeping tabs on future editorial subjects – editorial calendars

Every publication will produce a schedule of what they intend to write about for at least a twelve-month period. This is normally included as part of the advertising media pack and is known as the Editorial Calendar. It will detail the subject matter of each issue and acts as a good reference for when you should be providing them with specific articles. If you know that in June they will be doing a group test of your product, then you need to ensure that you're in that issue (possibly also from an advertising standpoint). Note that many magazines' cover date is at least one month ahead, e.g. if it's January now, then it'll say February on the cover! Don't miss a deadline because you didn't leave enough time – as soon as you receive your editorial calendar, identify the items of interest and contact the magazine to find out when they will be starting to receive content for that topic.

Summary

☐ Remember that in any business conversation or transaction the other guy is thinking (consciously or sub-consciously) 'what's in it for me'? The same applies to editors. If you're thinking this on their behalf you can learn to push the right buttons sooner to attract and maintain their interest. Your aim is to get as much exposure as possible – their aim is to produce a magazine, radio or TV show that meets their target audience's requirements. By making their lives easier you ensure your success. If you provide them with what they want, when they want it and in a professional manner you will guarantee yourself continual exposure and build a positive and mutually beneficial relationship.

Pearls of Wisdom

'It sounds simple: be very clear from the outset what it is you are trying to communicate and to whom. Avoid hype and jargon and take time early on to clearly define what it is you need to communicate. Once set, stick to your goal and as much as possible measure performance along the way so you can clearly articulate and demonstrate the value you are adding to the business.'

Michelle McGlocklin
Managing Director – Technology Practice, Weber Shandwick UK

1.8

The Internet

In the last 10 years, the Internet has gone from geeks plaything to mainstream business tool. Most people in any commercial environment have some exposure to the Internet, be it for email or accessing the World Wide Web, but it offers far more than that. The Internet itself is a network structure (e.g. the Information superhighway), not just one type of program and as such there are many different types of application that can utilise it. A closer analogy is that the Internet is a road on which different types of vehicles can travel.

A brief history of the Internet

The Internet's history can be traced back as far as 1957 after the launch of the first USSR satellite, Sputnik. In response, the USA formed the Advanced Research Projects Agency (ARPA) to establish a US lead in science and technology for the military. In the 1960s, the RAND Corporation were commissioned by the US Air Force to do a study on how it could maintain its command and control over its missiles and bombers after a nuclear attack. This was to be a military research network that could survive a nuclear strike, decentralised so that if any locations (cities) in the US were attacked, the military could still have control of nuclear arms for a counter-attack. Their final proposal was a packet switched network, which became the basis of the first version of the Internet – ARPANET – a network connecting four university computers at the breakneck speed of 50Kbps.

The map overleaf shows what was to become the Internet in September 1971, with each point signifying a computer connected to the network.

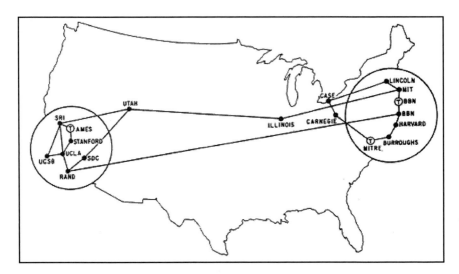

Fig 1.8.1 - The internet as it was back in September 1971

The early 1970s saw the development of TCP/IP – the protocol that allows different computers to communicate with each other, plus the invention of the Ethernet network and the first email program. 1979 saw the creation of the USENET decentralised newsgroup network, by which time APRANET now consisted of 110 host computers, or servers. In 1983 the Domain Name System (DNS) was created, allowing what we know today as www.domain.com to be attached to a computer's unique identifying 'IP address', although Hypertext Transfer Protocol was not created until 1990, the web itself following on two years later. The HTML language was created to allow documents to be linked together. By 1994, hundreds of thousands of new hosts were being added to the Internet bringing the number of host computers connected to almost 4 million. More importantly, the same year Pizza Hut started taking orders online!

In the early nineties, it was thought by many (including Microsoft) that the Internet was a passing fad. Now it touches almost every facet of daily life for many of us. We use the web for online banking, to download maps or to book flights. Checking email (and deleting the myriad unsolicited emails) is a daily occurrence. Many people also share files on peer-to-peer networks. But there are several other useful business applications that can put you one step ahead of your competitors and help you to reach new audiences. The Internet has now successfully broken away from being an application you must use in front of a PC. Digital TV now delivers email and online shopping access to those without PCs. Smart phones perform many more functions than just making and receiving calls or text messages, with video conferencing and remote access. Even the humble fridge can now be hooked up to the Internet to provide an inventory of products and provide you with a shopping list for either direct or online purchasing, as well as allowing you surf the Internet from your kitchen!

From a business perspective, there are eleven main areas that one should be aware of:

- email
- web browsing/search engines
- intranet/extranet
- instant messaging
- internet telephony
- FTP Sites
- peer to peer file sharing
- newsgroups
- website services
- web logs
- RSS news feeds

Let's take a look at each one in-depth, focusing on their uses in a business environment:

Email

This is the first application that many people became familiar with, before the Internet itself became commonplace. Many corporations set up internal networks with email capabilities, but this did not allow emails to be sent to other companies. The Internet solved that in the mid 1990s. Nowadays email is the most cost-effective way of communicating, with messages costing nothing to send and arriving in minutes, if not seconds. Do not make the mistake that this should be your main form of communication, as many people still find email an impersonal medium, preferring to speak to people over the phone or see them face-to-face.

All PCs are normally pre-loaded with an operating system that will have email software already installed. Microsoft Outlook, Outlook Express, Mozilla Thunderbird or Eudora are firm favourites, however there are many others out there that will perform the same tasks just as well. To send and receive email you will need an email account with an Internet Service Provider (ISP), of which there are hundreds to choose from.

When you sign up with an ISP they will normally assign you with an email address. However, it is much better to purchase a domain name relating to your company. The ISP's address will probably include their name e.g.

john@smith.ispname.co.uk, but if you purchase a domain name you can choose a name to suit your business. (See 'What's in a name' for more information on choosing a domain name).

Lastly, don't forget to add a signature to your outgoing emails. A signature should contain your name, company name and a link to your website. You may also want to include other information such as telephone, fax, mobile, address details and the now familiar disclaimer.

The World Wide Web

This is what many people consider 'The Internet' actually to be, but it is simply one of the many applications that run across the Internet infrastructure. The web started out as a collection of documents that were connected by threads, or hyperlinks. Nowadays websites, especially commercial sites, are no longer static pages – they can be linked to back-end computer systems providing live interaction. When you check your bank account balance, you are communicating live with the bank's computer systems in the same way as if you visit your local branch. This is a method of self-service that reduces the resources needed by the bank to run their business and also gives you 24-hour customer service.

There are three ways that you can use the web for your business – as a promotion tool, online store and as a research tool. The web is a cost-effective way to brand your company and provide your prospects and customers with a self-service shop for 24-hour information.

Sales of products online are growing extremely rapidly, with the E-commerce Times reporting retail sales in the US alone at $45 billion for 2002, and the IRMG reporting the UK as seeing almost $1.6 billion for January 2003 alone. Forrester Research reported that worldwide online sales hit $70 billion in 2004 and projects that they will hit $230 billion by 2008. According to Bruce Townsend, Marketing Manager for Actinic Software, anyone who can sell through traditional methods can also sell online; *'Compared with traditional retail, e-commerce is a relatively low cost, low risk way of opening a new channel to market, broadening coverage and increasing sales. If you can run a successful business offline, there is no reason why you cannot do the same online. The keys to success are not clever technology and big investment. One independent study, commissioned by Actinic and conducted by pfa Research, showed that many small retailers had established profitable online businesses for an investment as low as £1000 (around $1600), using boxed software. They succeeded by offering the right products at the right price, marketing them effectively, and offering good customer service.'*

The web also gives you an excellent way to find out what your competitors are up to and how they promote themselves. It's worth adding all of your competitors to your 'Favourites' list and revisiting their sites regularly.

Use the search engines such as Google or MSN Search to perform searches that your prospects are likely to perform to find your company to see what results you get. Armed with this information you can ensure that you remain competitive and keep abreast of goings on within your industry. Sign up to web-based forums (see Newsgroups below for more information) that cater for your industry and become an authority by helping users out while getting free promotion for your products.

Search engines are also moving towards the content stored on your local PC. Google's Desktop search is one of several PC-related search engines. Google works by constantly monitoring files and folders on your computer. Double-clicking on the icon placed in your taskbar will bring up the familiar Google web search, but the results will be limited to files on your PC. Not only is this much faster than performing a word search through the standard Windows method, but it scans Word documents, PDFs, emails etc! Also, when you go to Google's normal homepage and perform a search, it will detect that you have the Desktop Search installed and provide you with a summary of local results along with online results.

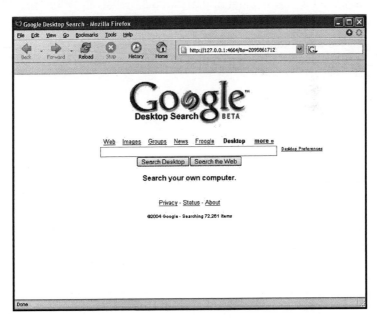

Fig 1.8.2. Google's Desktop search marries the web with your PC

There are so many innovative websites that offer useful services that it would be impossible to list them all here. As the Internet is such an effective tool for business promotion, make sure you keep up with latest developments by subscribing to one or more Internet magazines, or frequent technology news websites. They often list and review sites that offer invaluable tools for finding very particular information.

What's in a name – Choosing a domain name

A domain name is simply a mask for the 'real' address of your website. Every website in the world is accessible via an IP address – four groups of numbers, like 192.168.0.1. Imagine how difficult it would be to use the web if you had to remember up to 12 numbers for each website! Domain names were invented to make web addresses memorable, and are therefore no different to personalised telephone numbers or number plates.

Choosing the right domain name to represent your business is increasingly difficult. Not only do you have a wide array of domain suffixes to choose from (e.g. .com, .net, .info, .biz in addition to all of the country specific suffixes such as .co.uk, .fr, .cn etc) but virtually every word in the dictionary has already been registered.

There are several criteria you should consider when purchasing a domain name:

- It is very important to buy a domain that is easy to say so that people understand it correctly the first time they hear it over the phone
- Ensure that the domain has the main keyword or keywords that your customers are likely to search for, or buy several domains and point them at the same server. Use hyphens (-) but not underscores (_) as Google does not recognise them
- Always opt for a .com where possible, as this will be the suffix that people are most likely to try first

Go to one of the many companies selling domain names (such as **www.easyspace.com** or **www.verio.com**) – they will normally have a 'search for a domain name' box on the front page. You can now search to see if your chosen domain is available. Ideally you should purchase both the .com and your local country suffix. If the domain you want is not available, there are plenty of suffixes available where the main domain may still be free.

If you buy a .com domain, make sure that you buy the equivalent country code suffix as well and point it at the .com address. Price Waterhouse Cooper made a fateful mistake in June 2002 when they rebranded as Monday. They purchased introducingmonday.com but forgot to register the

.co.uk. Some bright spark registered the domain and posted a now famous taunt (written in Macromedia Flash) with a two fingered salute accompanied by a badly sung ditty of 'we've got your name, la la la...' On the other hand, beware of domain scammers. Many companies are falling foul of con-artists who call up and say that they have a customer wanting to buy a domain that is either similar to theirs or with a different suffix (for example, .tv, .org, .biz etc). They then offer the company first refusal as an apparent legitimate gesture. The bottom line is that if you own the trademark associated with the domain (e.g. your company or product brand name) then you should be able to win in a court of law if someone is misusing your trademark – Playboy has done this successfully on several occasions.

Intranets/Extranets
Both Intranets and Extranets are exactly the same as the Internet itself, however they each have a restricted range of access. An Intranet is effectively an internal LAN (local area network), although it normally relates to an internal website catering for staff. An Intranet might include online memos, calendar of staff holidays, company newsletters and access to company databases (e.g. customer records). An Extranet is the same but extended to customers, allowing them to access information directly from your system. Both can either be set up on servers within your organisation or purchased as online services offered by an increasing number of providers.

Providers such as **Intranets.com** offer a secure environment for staff and customers to access a variety of online services, including:

- document management – selected staff can upload files to a location only accessible by your staff or key customers
- online calendar
- online task lists
- discussion forums
- online databases.

All of the above is set up, administered and accessed purely by using a standard web browser from any location and is priced monthly based on the number of users. This is a cost-effective way to allow customers self-service access to information that a static website may not be able to provide. The main drawback is that you may have difficulty in migrating existing systems and data to fit with off-the-shelf solutions, and you will be limited to offering your users the functionality that the provider offers. In-house Intranet/Extranet solutions tend to be much more expensive as they will require technical staff to write a system that integrates with your existing software and data. Ultimately, however they offer a more comprehensive service – the larger your organisation the more likely you are to need an in-house solution.

There are several open source freeware applications which, if you have the time and technical ability, will allow you to offer a comprehensive range of online tools to staff and customers at little or no cost. PostNuke (also covered in chapter 2.8) is an open source content management system running on the popular MySQL database platform. It lends itself well to several Intranet/Extranet tasks, such as publishing of material, online calendar and discussion groups.

Instant messaging

Known as IM, Instant Messaging is similar in principle to Short Message Service (SMS) text messaging on mobile phones – some IM programs will even send and receive SMS messages. IM programs are an ideal way for keeping in touch with key work colleagues and customers, especially if you have a permanent Internet connection. They work by running in the background on your PC – anyone else who you authorise can see when you are online and send a message to you, which you can then reply to. Many companies are employing this technology to allow staff to work remotely. For the paranoid, there is the ability to set your current online 'status' so that other people don't know if you're connected to the Internet or not.

There are several IM programs available:

- MSN/Windows Messenger
- ICQ (I Seek You)
- AOL Instant Messenger (AIM)
- Yahoo Instant Messenger

IM is also spreading to other devices,such as smart phones. With the advent of the GPRS 'always on' Internet conn-ection for mobile phones, and phones becoming smarter themselves, applic- ations are starting to appear that allow users to connect to their Instant Messaging networks from anywhere. One example is Tipic, which allows users of several brands of phone (including Sony Ericsson P910, pictured) to connect to MSN, ICQ, Yahoo, AIM and any service using the XMPP/Jabber open standard.

Fig 1.8.3. IM programs can even be used on smart phones

In addition to the four main applications, several other companies have entered the arena. To make an impact in the market they have built in compatibility with some of the above IMs, allowing users to see when other users of other 'networks' are online. Two such examples are Trillian and Eyeball Chat. Both allow connection simultaneously to systems such as MSN, AOL and Yahoo, so you only need the one IM client installed on your PC.

Instant Messenger programs are not just for sending text messages – they offer a variety of other facilities as well. In addition to sending text messages, some programs allow you to send and receive files, have voice conversations or even full video conferencing – Eyeball is an excellent example of this, offering a free, sturdy application that works well across even the toughest of firewalls. Programs such as ivisit (**www.ivisit.com**) even allow for simultaneous multi-user videoconferencing, although strictly speaking this is not an IM program in the same vein as others mentioned here. The best part is that all of the above programs are free! Some, such as ICQ also offer the ability to 'log in' via a web browser with no need for the usual client end software – ideal if you don't have your computer with you and need to talk to someone online.

Internet Telephony

Also referred to as Voice Over IP (VOIP) this technology allows you to use a PC with a soundcard, microphone and speakers/headset to make telephone calls. Skype (**www.skype.com**) is one such product, which has the added benefit of working on Windows, Linux and Apple platforms. Depending on which product you choose, calls might be either to another PC or to a physical telephone. This can have major price advantages over standard call charges using your existing telephone network provider, so if you make a large number of international calls it may be worth investigating. Many traditional telcos are jumping on the VOIP bandwagon, but are pricing their products only marginally lower than their existing services. Some IM programs such as MSN Messenger will also allow you to integrate with VOIP/Telephony providers giving a single interface for both messaging and telephony.

FTP sites

FTP (File Transfer Protocol) software allows users to access, download and even upload data on other systems. For simple downloads it has been replaced in the main by web-based interfaces, but there are still many useful FTP sites. You will use FTP software in one form or another to upload web pages to your website, although this may be as transparent as pushing an

'Upload' button – the software itself is still utilising FTP to put your request into action. Alternatively you may use FTP technology to download information from sites of interest.

Using FTP software is simple. You need the 'host name', which is the unique identifying name of the server, plus a username and password. If it is a general site it may accept anonymous logins. Once logged in you are presented with two windows – one shows your hard drive and one shows the hard drive (or the part that you are allowed access to) of the server. You can then upload and download files accordingly.

There are many free-ware and shareware FTP software packages such as **Cute-FTP** or **WS_FTP** (pictured). They all perform the same basic task, so selecting a package will be down to cost and interface preference unless you require 'power user' features found only in prof-essional packages. You may not even need to obtain separate software, as most web browsers have basic FTP capabilities.

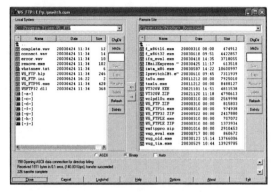

Fig 1.8.4. FTP software allows you to transfer files to and from your PC/Web server

You will only want to offer FTP capabilities to your customers if you have a large number of files that they may require access to, otherwise a web-based facility would offer a more user-friendly option. Intranet/Extranet service providers (mentioned earlier) can offer file-sharing capabilities that would remove the need for FTP.

Peer-to-peer file sharing

Similar to FTP, file sharing is the ability for computers across the Internet to share a directory of files on their computer, which is immediately searchable by all other users that are connected to the same file-sharing network. The most famous of these was the ill-fated, cat-logoed Napster that was originally put out of business by the recording industry due to the amount of illegal music file swapping that was taking place. It did resurface a couple of years later in a somewhat neutered form, selling legitimate music downloads.

P2P – peer to peer – can have viable benefits in business, especially in larger organisations that have thousands of documents that may need to be accessed from a wide variety of locations. Imagine, for example setting up a closed P2P, accessible only to staff that has all of your company invoices, sales orders and such like that can be searched and downloaded from anywhere. There are technical downsides to this, not least relating to security, but if remote access of a wide variety of files is of interest, you should investigate this option, although FTP is more likely to meet your needs.

Newsgroups and discussion forums

Newsgroups started way back in 1979 in an academic environment and until the early nineties were mainly used by students and those with software-related interests. Nowadays, there are some 60,000 newsgroups in addition to thousands of bulletin boards on any subject you care to think about, and there are probably several that are specific to key areas of your industry. News Groups and Bulletin Boards (also known as BBSs, discussion groups or forums) are two very different technologies using different infrastructures, but the appearance and usage is almost the same. Newsgroups use an infrastructure called Usenet, whereas bulletin boards appear on standard web pages.

A news group can be described as 'public, threaded email'. When entering a newsgroup, you will see a selection of messages 'posted' by other users. For example,

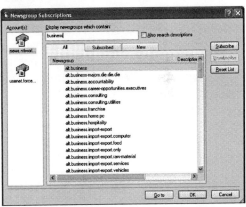

Fig 1.8.5. Outlook Express allows access to thousands of newsgroups.

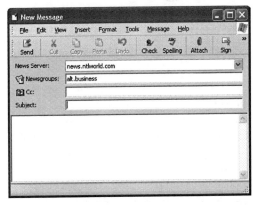

Fig 1.8.6. Posting a newsgroup message is as easy as sending an email.

someone may have placed a request for advice and opinions on buying a new product. Other users can then read and reply to this message, with resulting posts being attached to the first message as a thread. This gives you the ability to follow the conversation as it develops.

As with all of the other tasks you use the Internet for (such as email and web browsing), newsgroups are global, which is especially useful when working in a niche market, as geography no longer becomes the main obstacle. All you need to do is find one or several newsgroups that are relevant to your subject of interest. So what software do you need to harness this wealth of information? If you're using Outlook Express to read emails, you already have everything you need – you just need to know your Internet Service Provider's news server name. Alternatively there are many good freeware programs out there, such as Forte's Free Agent (**http://www.forteinc.com/agent/**) that will do the job just as well.

Posting messages on Usenet newsgroups is virtually the same as creating an email if you're using Outlook Express. Once you've configured your system to link to your service provider's newsgroup server, you can browse through a list of the thousands of newsgroups, or enter a keyword to shorten your search. Note that this search is searching on the newsgroup titles only, so limit this to a single relevant word. Double click on the newsgroup you wish to view and you'll see what appears to be a list of emails – these are the discussions. Where there is a reply to a discussion this will be marked with a + icon – this can be clicked on to expand the thread. If you want to add your own post to a thread click on New Post or reply.

Discussion forums/bulletin boards are very similar to Newsgroups, but are web-based. They work in exactly the same way, although you may need to register to use them – this is free on almost all sites. The main difference is the censorship of content that may appear on them, and this is dependent on the owners of the site on which the discussion group is hosted. For example a product manufacturer that hosts a newsgroup on their site will no doubt ensure that any posts that are irrelevant or perhaps show their product in a bad light are removed quickly.

There are two ways you will generally want to use newsgroups and forums – you'll either have a question that you want to ask or you may want to find out if someone has already answered the question for someone else. To ask a question on a newsgroup it's as simple as posting an email, and not much different for the web-based forums. If you want to look for previously answered questions, then you're best to start off with the web's most popular search engine – Google. In 2002 Google launched a new service (replacing Deja-News), working in exactly the same way as its

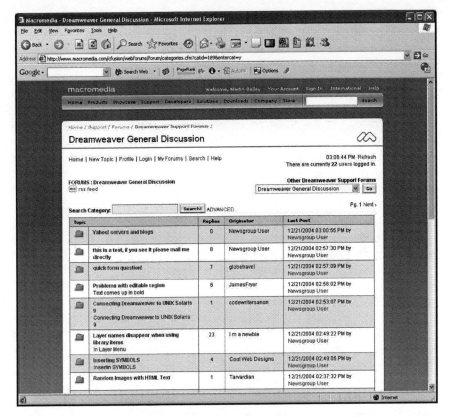

Fig 1.8.7. Web-based discussion groups offer a wealth of information, and are great to pick the brains of experts.

search engine counterpart, which trawls through all of the past and present 700,000,000 newsgroup messages and categorises them in a search engine format – just click on the 'Groups' menu on the front page of their website. If you know specifically what you're looking for it is well worth performing an advanced search (over the simple keyword search), specifying a search period otherwise you're likely to come across information that could be 10-15 years old! Note that Google only searches Usenet news groups and not web-based forums, although a standard Google search might prove fruitful if your keywords are precise enough.

If your newsgroup search did not deliver, then you need to start visiting the web-based discussion groups in your industry. If you find a website that is specific to your requirement that also has a forum, you're more likely to either find the answer you're looking for straight away, or get an answer to any of your posts. A good starting point is trade association websites, followed by industry portals.

For companies with a wide enough user-base, you may wish to consider adding a forum to your own site. Depending on the route you choose to take this is not as daunting as it sounds. The easiest route it to enlist one of the online message board host services, such as **www.boardhost.com**, which for around $10 per month will host a basic message board service. The downside is that you cannot do much to customise the look and feel to match your site aside from adding a logo and change a few colours. If you either have in-house web staff, or are happy to pay a programmer, you can add one of the many excellent freeware or shareware programs, such as wwwboard or phpBB. Most of these can be installed and configured by anyone with general programming (PHP, CGI or PERL) skills in under an hour. Finally, if your website already has a number of customer-oriented, database-driven services online you might want to integrate the bulletin board into the existing structure, perhaps to take advantage of existing username and password details. This is where you will need the help of a professional programmer who can take an existing system and modify it to suit your needs, or perhaps write a solution from scratch.

Discussion groups bring personality back to the Internet; a stark contrast to static web pages and impersonal junk mail – you are talking to real people with real-world problems, which hopefully you can offer solutions to. If your business is suitable, adding a forum to your website can breathe new life into it by quickly gaining repeat visitors. Newsgroups are an invaluable source of human reference, and used effectively can open up new business opportunities, help you to resolve problems that normally would either cost a great deal in time or money and allow you to put a digital finger on the pulse in very specific areas of interest.

Fig 1.8.8. Tools such as Liveperson add an extra layer of communication to your website.

Web-based customer services

In our 24/7 society, customers expect a website to provide services at a time to suit them. Many businesses offer web-based services to compliment or replace traditional services such as telephone support. One example is

Liveperson.com. This service allows companies to place a button on their site which signifies that an operator is available to offer online assistance. When clicked, the browser is connected with an operator with a live text chat link. One operator can service several calls simultaneously and push web pages to the client's web browser. Results show that this can multiply sales conversion rates by 3 times and increase order size by 35% – consumers can verify product information with a 'real person' and place orders during an online chat. This personalises the sales process, much like going into a store. A freeware version of Liveperson, called Humanclick is available at **Bravenet.com.**

Online screen sharing services such as Smartmeeting, Webex and GotoMyPC take this a stage further, allowing complex products or services to be demonstrated to one or more people as if they were in front of the supplier. The days of the sales rep travelling hundreds of miles to deliver a PowerPoint presentation are numbered, as a shared screen and conference call can produce similar results within a much quicker timeframe (which may suit the client better) and vastly reduced costs. Users simply log into a specified location, or follow a hyperlink from an email to be connected to the shared location. Cost are either monthly or on a per-usage basis.

Web Logs (Blogs)
Originally scoffed at by many as geeky online diary rants, blogs quickly became the marketeer's best kept secret. As a word that (at time of going to press) is not in the dictionary, in 2004 it was the most requested online definition, according to E-commerce Times. Web logs are best described as a diary, breaking news outlet, collaborative space or general soapbox published online. In simple terms it is a website where content is added by one or more people, usually in date order, on a regular basis. New content is listed at the top. Users can then leave comments relating to your content. A leading site is **Blogger.com** (owned by search engine goliath Google), which allows free blog sites to be created, literally within a minute or two. Blogs empowers those with absolutely no HTML experience to get their thoughts online. Microsoft, not one to rest on its laurels, hit back with MSN Spaces, which enables users to store words, pictures audio and video within a 'blog site'. Users can update content via email and the resulting site is compatible with RSS (so you could allow your blog to appear on another site or be read offline by an RSS reader).

Fig 1.8.9. 'Blogging' is now a common word. Anyone can create a blog using Google's Blogger service.

The collaborative approach of blogs incites readers to interact with comments on the site (as visitors can place their own comments against each posting, building a thread of opinions), but the major factor is the content itself – because it is normally written on a specific subject, the pages are generally rich in keywords relative to that topic – as a result they are outranking many commercial sites. Many blue-chip companies are now encouraging staff to use corporate blogs, which deliver a wealth of wide-ranging and rich content that search engines are only too happy to absorb. Do not underestimate the power of the blog!

RSS Newsfeeds

RSS is a simple format (based on the popular XML code format) designed for sharing news headlines and other web content. The jury is still out on what RSS actually stands for – some say Rich Site Summary, whereas others call it Really Simple Syndication and yet another name is RDF Site Summary. It is effectively a mini database that, in addition to displaying your news on other sites, can also flow into other products such as PDAs, mobile phones etc. Email newsletters can also easily be updated with RSS. You may, for example wish to place industry headlines on your website or even spread your own content onto other sites. By simply adding a few lines of web code to the page, content can be pulled from the source website. When the source code is updated, all sites that link to it will also display the updated data. A quick search for 'free RSS generator' will point you in the direction of software that will simplify the process of generating the file – all you have to do is upload it to your site and inform the world of its presence.

Connecting to the Internet

For many home or lightweight business users, a standard 56kbps modem is still the weapon of choice for connecting to the Internet, despite the advent of broadband technologies. 'Broadband' is the term given to a high-speed connection, which can be delivered through ADSL (Asynchronous Digital Subscriber Line), Cable modem, 3G mobile data services or satellite.

There are various speeds of broadband available, but they all deliver the same service: an always-on connection. With a dialup modem, you are connected at a relatively slow speed – normally about 5kb per second, and are immediately out of touch with the rest of the world as soon as you disconnect. It also ties up a phone line – a problem for the small business and home user – and is charged per call. With broadband you can leave your email software running and respond immediately when an enquiry arrives. A monthly flat rate charge is generally levied. Video conferencing becomes a reality (especially with free products such as Eyeball, mentioned earlier). A high-speed always-on connection is virtually essential for businesses today – customers expect a timely response, and with broadband you can offer real-time demonstrations, services and support to your customers. One point to watch for is bandwidth capping – some broadband providers may offer a high speed connection but limit the amount of data you can send/receive, either forcing you to pay more if you reach this limit or simply blocking your access altogether. Check the small print before you sign up with any provider.

Legal implications of Internet usage within your company

Remember that email is now generally considered as legally binding as printed or faxed documents. There have been many legal battles caused by incorrectly addressed or libellous emails so make sure that anything you or your staff send is professional. Companies also need to ensure that staff do not abuse their Internet access, and there are many applications that can assist in tracking Internet usage. Abuse may also include using P2P systems to download files (such as music) illegally, using IM software for personal rather than professional reasons and spending time browsing non work-related websites.

Of the thousands of newsgroups on Usenet, there are hundreds that cover less than savoury topics, both in terms of text and downloadable images. If you are allowing staff access to Usenet or web forums it is worth investing in suitable scanning, tracking and blocking software to see what your employees are really looking at. There are also legal aspects that must be taken into consideration. As with emails, your company may be liable for postings on a newsgroup that make false or libellous claims. Newsgroups can trace you using a unique number that every computer on the Internet has – an IP address and there have been countless cases where individuals or corporate bodies have felt the long cyber-arm of the law. If you're lucky you might just get a rap on the knuckles. Repeat offenders either get blocked from the newsgroups or get their account terminated with their ISP (Internet Service Provider). Extreme cases result in lawsuits.

To protect themselves, many of the websites that run forums operate in a 'moderated' method, meaning that each message is vetted before it goes live. There are several problems with this, not least the amount of time it consumes for the site's Webmaster. Any site that does this is also effectively censoring material, thus removing any 'unbiased' label it may be seeking to achieve. Also, by vetting material, they are essentially approving it, also making them liable in the event of any legal issues. It is more commonplace for sites to operate unmoderated, but to require registration, and for messages to be deleted if they break certain guidelines.

Summary

☐ The Internet is a massive resource of information and services. It can be a fantastic tool or an extensive waste of time, depending on how you use it. It can be very easy to spend excessive periods of time trying to achieve the unachievable or searching aimlessly when you're not sure exactly what you're looking for. Ensure that your staff are using the Internet for the right reasons and not leaving your company open to attack (either technically or legally). Make sure that your company's network security is up to scratch, with operating systems, firewalls and antivirus software patched to the latest versions. Find the tools that work for you and stick with them. Try new ones and analyse their suitability for your business. Ask business colleagues and customers what website or other Internet tools they use – as the Internet is so vast the chances are they have discovered something you haven't. Subscribe to an Internet magazine to keep up with the latest websites and technologies.

 Pearls of Wisdom

'Online marketing still works best when it's backed up offline. So make sure your website and email addresses are on all your printed advertisements and literature, especially your marketing collateral, letterhead and business cards.'

Bruce Townsend
Marketing Manager, Actinic Software Limited

1.9

Trade Shows and Seminars

On the CD

- Exhibition material
- Web links

Exhibitions and seminars are excellent methods of putting your products and company directly in front of well-targeted prospects, but there are many pitfalls that force companies into believing that previous events were failures rather than the way they prepared for and exhibited at the show. Attending or hosting events can be a costly business. However, if planned effectively with realistic objectives, they can then yield demonstrable or even dramatic results. There a number of ways that you can ensure that you attend the right events, put on a memorable show and track feedback from attendees. Hosting your own event can also be a viable alternative that does not have to cost the gross national debt of a small country to make an impact.

This chapter is divided into two sections, the first concentrating on preparing for and attending trade shows, and the second on hosting your own seminar.

Section 1: Trade shows

For virtually every market there is a trade show to support it – the problem is working out the best show to attend, especially if there are several to choose from. But before you establish where you will show your wares, you have to establish why you are showing them. The resources relating to a tradeshow should not be focused entirely around the event itself. Forethought and planning prior to the show, followed by post-show follow-up are as important, if not more than the time you spend at the show. Tim Perutz, Managing Director of leading exhibition stand manufacturers Nimlok feels that many exhibitors are left to their own devices by event organisers, which ultimately leads to the show being less successful; *'The trade show industry in general needs to be more responsible to the exhibitor. We need to help educate the exhibitor how to be more effective at the show. Their success is our success.'*

On average a visitor to a show will spend anywhere between 7 and 10 hours at exhibits, and slightly more for retail events. Over half attendees plan to buy products seen at the show within a year of the event, and over 8 out of 10 attendees will be new prospects.

Selecting the right trade show

There are three main reasons that any company attends a show – lead generation, branding and selling of products. In their 2001 reader survey, *Exhibitor Magazine* asked their readers why they exhibited:

29.3%	Our customers are there.
15.5%	Shows produce sales for our company.
12.9%	Shows uncover prospects we would not find otherwise.
10.0%	Shows are a cost-effective way to reach prospective customers.
8.8%	We exhibit for image reasons.
8.5%	Shows reinforce existing customer relations.
7.9%	We want to introduce new products.
5.3%	Our competition is there.
1.5%	We have a long history of participating in shows.
0.3%	We want to reach trade press.

You will probably already have decided which categories you fall into from the above statistics, but before deciding which event you should attend, you need to evaluate your reasons for exhibiting in the first place by answering the following questions:

? Why am I exhibiting at this show?
? What do I want to accomplish here?
? What image do I want to project?
? How does this specific exhibition fit into my broader sales and marketing plans?

Your answers to these questions form the specific objectives needed to be a successful exhibitor. Goals that are set should be measurable and achievable and they need to be realistic. If you are working with an exhibition stand manufacturer, provide them with as much information as you can about the show – although you probably know your industry better than they do, they will know more about general event management and will more than likely know the venue as well. Emma Swales, Marketing Manager for Nimlok says; *'When we work with our clients, the success of their show is equally important to us as the construction of their stand. Based on the customers' understanding of their own industry and our knowledge of exhibition management, we try to provide them information about exhibiting and services that allow them to achieve their goals.'*

Shows that cover your industry may differ in the audiences they attract, so your first port of call should be to contact the organisers to receive an exhibitor pack. This should not only detail a breakdown of the type of attendees, but also a list of exhibitors. When evaluating any trade event you should consider the following factors.

- Do recognised associations back the show?
- Is the show a regular event or a new (and therefore untested) show?
- Is the show limited to a geographical region, national or international?
- What do the audience statistics tell you in terms of relevance, previous/future projected attendance patterns, buyers vs. non-buyers?
- Are the statistics reliable? Does an accredited bureau audit the show?
- Are competitors exhibiting?
- Are there additional promotional or marketing activities available?
- Is there any feedback from visitors or exhibitors on previous shows?

Working out space requirements

This is generally the stumbling block for most companies considering exhibiting for the first time – how do you decide how much space is required? This is not as difficult to calculate as you might think! It can be broken down into a seven-stage equation:

1. Start by finding out how many buyers are likely to be attending the show. The exhibition stats should be able to give you this number. Let's say it is 7,000.
2. CEIR (Center for Exhibition Industry Research) studies have shown that on average 16-20% of an audience will be interested in your products/services. So that gives us at least 1,120 targeted individuals
3. The interest factor will differ depending on whether the show covers all segments of an industry (horizontal) or just one segment (vertical). Statistics show verticals to be 53% with horizontal at 37%. Let's base this example on vertical, which brings the number to 594.
4. We now calculate the likely visitors per hour. If a show is running for three days at 8 hours per day we can on average expect 25 visitors per hour.
5. If a demonstration takes 10 minutes per salesman that gives you 6 demos per hour. This means that you will need around 4 staff.

6. You'll need around 5 square metres (5.5 yards) per staff member, giving us 20 for this example.
7. Finally you need to calculate the space you need for products, which will vary dramatically depending on your business type. You also need to make provision for furniture and promotion material/stand structure. Adding this to your staff space gives you the golden number!

Deciding on a stand location

Once you have your exhibitor pack you'll no doubt have a floor plan of the hall(s). There are many elements that you must take into consideration when booking a location, including:

- Currently available space – if you're booking relatively close to the event, or if it is a popular show your options may already be limited?
- Space requirements – the space you need will most probably limit your choice of locations
- Type of space – shell scheme or space only, and number of open sides. Be sure also to check if there are any obstacles not shown on the floor plan, such as columns, windows, pipes etc
- Competition – do you want to be near to competitors?
- Local attractions/facilities – are there seminars, registrations areas, stairs, restaurants, toilets, telephones nearby that may attract traffic past your stand?
- Are there related shows running in adjacent halls?
- Is the show divided up into categories?
- Are there any restrictions in one place over another (e.g. lighting, storage, height)?

Statistics show that users generally will work their way around the show from the right of the main entrance, although this trend will very much depend on the hall layout and number of entrances. Try to find out (from the organisers or previous exhibitors) if this is the case with your show – this could effect your decision on which space to select!

Planning the event

Before you budget, design, book or promote, you must put a structured plan in place. Invariably you will encounter pitfalls along the way, so start planning at least 4 months prior to the show, or longer where possible. If you are not organising the event yourself, appoint an event organiser who will have overall responsibility for the show. Start by generating an exhibition plan with a list of tasks with deadlines and allocate responsibility, ensuring the deadlines are met. Creating an internal mailing list to circulate updates and reminders will ensure that a constant focus is placed on all aspects of the event.

An exhibition plan should include:

- time scales
- budgets
- space requirements
- stand and graphic design parameters
- on-site services
- staffing levels
- pre- and post-show promotions
- show evaluation criteria
- on-stand data capture
- follow up procedure for leads.

Budgeting for a show

Many companies make the fundamental mistake of taking the space as the cost of the show. In reality this generally works out at less than half of the overall costs. In addition to space cost you need to consider:

- **stand structure** – designing it, building it, insuring it, graphics design, production and storage
- getting it there – cost of transporting all items to and from the show, including insurance
- **promoting the event** – literature and give-aways, pre-show mailing, advertising and sponsorship, hospitality etc
- **at-show expenses** – electrics/AV/computers, carpet, security, cleaning, hired staff, telephones etc.
- **staff expenses** – salaries, additional training, accommodation and transport, entertainment
- **lead management/processing** – forms, badge scanners/pens, mailing, postage etc

Don't forget to read the exhibitor's handbook provided by the organiser, especially relating to deadlines for booking items such as electrics, furniture etc. Often these companies will increase their prices for bookings taken closer to the show. If you are budgeting based on the cheapest prices then ensure you obtain them by booking within the listed leadtimes.

Only once you have all of these figures in mind can you put a real price on your show's costs.

Deciding on a stand structure and design

Many companies make a fundamental mistake when designing their stand

– they forget to tell people what they do. You literally have a few seconds to convey who you are, what you do and what you offer.

Make it clear with graphics and title text the products/services you offer.

It should be made clear that 'structure' and 'design' are separate within the context of this chapter – the design is what the attendee sees – the structure is the 'building blocks' used to construct the basic layout of your stand on which the design (graphics) are hung.

Fig 1.9.1. Modular stands are more flexible for companies attending different size events throughout the year as they can be scaled accordingly.

Companies such as Nimlok offer several product ranges that can be customised to suit any space. These range from roll-up banners that can be put up in seconds, pop-up 'walls' that can be assembled by one person in minutes or complete custom modular systems that can be constructed in several different ways to suit events now and in the future. For larger or more adventurous displays, you may also want to consider their custom design service. This design (pictured) by James Wellstead shows a number of components that can be easily assembled and repositioned to suit the available space. The graphics panels are interchangeable and can be updated at low cost. John Lowery, Design Manager of Nimlok offers this advice; *'Ideally the customer should be thinking of their 1-2 year exhibition objective to allow what is designed now to accommodate product expansion plans for the future.'*

An important element to the overall exhibiting experience is the consideration of logistics. If you are using a roll-up banner or compact pop-up system this is less of an issue, but for an exhibitor using a custom modular solution that can be reconfigured and used all over the world or simply a custom modular stand, they may want to look at companies such as Nimlok that can manage and organise the entire shooting match. Design, build, I & D, graphics, storage, transportation and worldwide services support and capability should be part of the planning process. Options such as rental or split purchase/rental may also be available and should be considered where appropriate.

How you structure your stand at the event will be dictated by your primary reason for attending. We discussed earlier the three main reasons to exhibit – lead generation, branding and product sales. If your stand is a branding exercise then it will be focusing mainly on your core image (normally a logo/brand name), whereas stand-based product sales are likely to require a more store-like layout, with products available for customers to view.

Lead generation is more about inviting the attendee to spend time with a sales person, who will qualify them as a valid prospect for following up after the show (or closing there and then if appropriate) – this type of stand will probably have a demo/seating area, perhaps also with refreshments to allow comfortable discussions.

The stand designs below, provided by Nimlok, demonstrate the various implementations based upon the three main customer requirements. Here you can see how and why the stands differ.

- **Branding.** Wealdstone Engineering wanted to get the message across that they re-engineered the Ford Engine. The stand was designed to clearly promote the Wealdstone name through the use of their corporate colours and name prominently displayed. Additionally, pistons were designed on the gantry to reflect the engineering aspect of the company.

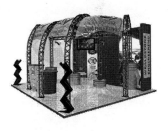

- **Lead Generation.** A cyber café was created for OSIS, which was designed to be open and inviting with eight communication stations to collect prospect details. The height of the stand helps to attract attention from other parts of the hall.

- **Product Sales.** Creative Nails needed to build a retail style environment to display and take orders of product on the show floor. The extensive use of shelving, attractive lighting and the inclusion of well thought-out storage and payment points ensured the stand design allowed for a fast flow-through of customers.

113

Once you have agreed on the main purpose of your stand, you can concentrate on how you want attendees to interact whilst there, which will ultimately dictate the layout. Do you want attendees to move around freely or a more controlled layout, with areas specifically for 'interested' users? Look at previous stand structures of companies that would have similar objectives to you (not necessarily competitors) and see how they structured theirs.

You need to ensure that you allocate space for:

- staff
- products
- seating
- brochures
- PCs or laptops
- lead acquisition (scanners etc)
- giveaways
- secure storage
- clothing and personal belongings (jackets, cases etc)
- hospitality.

As with designing any advertising material, unless you have the design skills in-house, it pays to leave this to the experts. There is no point in spending good money on all of the costs associated with a show if you cut corners on the display itself. Supply the designers with as much of your existing material as possible, along with your objectives for the show so that they can draw up an effective campaign.

Pre-show promotion

The more effort you place on promoting your stand before the event, the more likely it is that the event will be a success. There are many low cost processes you can carry out to achieve this.

- Send out a press release at least ten weeks in advance, detailing what visitors will see at your stand.
- Contact all customers and prospects either in letter format or by newsletter inviting them to your stand – many shows give out free tickets, so why not send them one in advance?
- Back up customer/prospect contact with email marketing just before the show, perhaps also providing useful information such as transportation, links to hotels, show times – make it a useful resource rather than 'just more unsolicited email'.

- Follow this up with telemarketing
- If budget permits, rent previous show attendee mailing lists and mail them with your newsletter/letter.
- Add a line at the bottom of every invoice, delivery note or other documents inviting people to the show, citing your stand number.
- Make sure that all staff mention the show in any conversations with prospects or customers. Provide them with additional information about the show including location, times, how to get there etc.
- Obtain the show's logo from the organisers and add it along with your stand number to your website, linking it to a page of information about your presence at the show – link to the organisers website or put up a form allowing users to request tickets online.
- Add the show logo and your stand number on all advertising at least 3 months prior to the show.

You need to make it clear to visitors what benefits they will gain by visiting your stand, be it through information, special pricing, prizes, give-aways etc.

Selecting the right staff for the show

80% of an attendee's memories of a company's performance at a show will relate to the staff they interact with, so it's important to choose staff with the right attributes. A positive and enthusiastic attitude is without doubt the most important part of the trade show staff's psyche! You can have the best technicians or sales people in the world, but if they are not motivated to attend the show this will come across in everything they say or do. If your product is highly technical, see to it that one or more suitable members of your technical team will be on-hand to 'talk techie' to like-minded 'propeller-heads' and may even help you cover all aspects of a sale at the show, ensuring a quicker deal closure.

There is an old expression that dictates that we have two eyes, two ears and one mouth, and that they should be used in that order! This has never been truer than at exhibitions. Staff should be good listeners, asking only key questions to understand the prospect's requirements. A good grounding of product knowledge is important, although they don't have to be experts – a full understanding of your features and benefits is enough if they have the confidence and charisma to pass on their own enthusiasm to visitors.

Even though you may have selected the best of the staff available, you can still provide them additional tools and tips to improve their chances of success. Encourage staff to stay near the edge of the stand ready to strike up a conversation (let them take it in turns so they stay fresh), and provide them with ideas for conversation openers. 'Can I help you' is almost inviting the visitor to say no, closing the door, so make greetings open-ended – 'What are you looking for at the show today?' Give staff training prior to the show on questions they are likely to face and how to overcome them, and check to ensure they understand the information and commitments you are trying to get from attendees. Emma Swales of Nimlok advises; *'It's critical that your booth staff understands what is required of them and have clear show objectives. Assigning a stand manager is the best way to make sure you stick to the plan.'*

Hospitality and promotional give-aways

Providing a relaxing environment in which to communicate your sales message to customers is pivotal to the success of your stand, so ensuring that all attendees feel that they are receiving five-star treatment should be high on your list of priorities. How far you extend this hospitality will depend on the main stand focus. If, for example you are selling products on the stand, then you will be aiming for a high turnover of attendees – hospitality might extend to a bowl of sweets on the counter. For more in-depth discussions you may have a sit-down area that also offers hot/cold drinks, perhaps extending to snacks. The mix of hospitality and its availability needs to be measured against how long you want attendees to spend on the stand. You must also consider abuse by attendees that are not target prospects; ensuring that refreshments are available in an area specifically for demos or discussions should dissuade them from diving in to help themselves!

People like to receive free gifts, and giving them recognition for visiting your stand can retain brand awareness long after the show. A gift should be an item given selectively, not one that is there for all to take without giving any commitment back. You want visitors to earn the gifts, perhaps by filling in a lead card or watching your demonstration. All gifts should be branded with your logo, and where possible contact details – this need only extend to telephone, website and email unless space allows. By far the best promotional products to give out are wearable items, such as ties, t-shirts etc. Show badge neck straps (if the shows badges lend themselves to this) or carrier bags work well as give-aways for everyone as they act as walking adverts for the duration of the show.

Lead management

There's no point in creating and promoting a stunning stand if you don't handle lead information effectively during and after the event. You have one opportunity during the show to capture all of the relevant information you will need from each attendee, so you need a method that will do this quickly and efficiently. Some shows offer lead management services – you can hire a scanner/printer that will scan a barcode on the attendee's badge that will then give you name, contact details and the interests they selected during registration. While these are good, you may want to capture additional information relating to the clients needs.

A lead capture form will ensure you get the right information each time. Designing a lead card is simple – you can do it in MS Word – all you need is a quick and easy fill-in-the-blanks form. Firstly you need to determine what makes a qualified lead – is the person the right decision maker or will they influence purchase, is the requirement urgent, can you meet their budget etc. Write down a list of all of the questions you want answers to, ideally in some form of natural progression so they prompt qualifying answers – get sales staff to give their input here! Rather than having a line of text to complete for each answer, try to make tick box answers – these are much quicker to fill in and can allow the stand staff to continue talking to the prospect without having to concentrate too much on writing. This is especially useful for quickly identifying hot prospects, so, for example you may want five tick boxes as follows:

- large order, ready to buy
- small order or large order with longer time frame
- small order with longer time frame
- literature or database
- other.

Lastly, leave a box that prompts the user to staple a business card over the space.

Keep the competitive edge – don't give it away

A danger at any event where competitors are attending is for them to gain inside information on your company and products, but there are methods you can employ to avoid this. Make sure that all staff attending are aware of which competitors will be at the show, and where they are located. Try to familiarise yourself with any corporate clothing competitors may be wearing so you're aware when they are close by. Keep bar-room, hotel lobby and other public business discussions (formal or informal) to a minimum – you never know who is standing behind you! You may also decide to keep product literature under lock and key on your stand, or at least out of reach of the casual passer-by, only giving them out to qualified individuals.

After the event – measuring the show's effectiveness

This is where you find out if all of your efforts have paid off. There are several elements you can gauge the success of, the main one of course being the bottom line. The database generated from the show will be accurate, so it is easy to see over a period of time which leads were converted to sales and work out the cost per sale accordingly. Depending on your average sales cycle you may want to run this check three to six months after the show.

If your main motivation for attending a show is to generate new leads, then knowing your cost-per-lead will give you an immediate indicator of the show's effectiveness. Dividing the number of leads by the overall show cost will give you a cost per lead. Further analysis can give you the cost of the demonstrations at the show and hospitality costs.

Over and above these stats there are other methods you can employ to measure a show's impact. Ask staff what their opinion about the quality and number of attendees, how the stand itself performed (e.g. did it make the right impression, was it laid out correctly, were the staffing levels correct etc). You can also survey your customers by phone, mail and through a form on your website to gauge their opinion of the show, in both terms of your performance and in general.

Post-show promotion

Just because the show is over it doesn't mean that the PR machine has to stop rolling. As soon as you have packed up your stand and returned to your office you need to immediately concentrate on the leads generated from the previous few days. Jamie Zavoral-Brown, Sales Manager for Nimlok recommends; *'The speed at which you respond to leads after the show is critical. We would always recommend replying with a targeted letter addressing the level of interest and expectation specific to the notes from the lead card taken at the show. The prospect should receive this within two days of seeing you on the stand. They should then receive a follow-up phone call, with the information going onto your marketing database for future mailing and product updates.'*

Here are the most important post-show tasks.

- Follow up all of the prospects that visited your stand. This is the fundamental flaw that many companies are guilty of. If you don't follow up you may as well not have attended! The way in which you communicate with prospects after the event will differentiate you from your competitors and demonstrate your keenness to do business with them.
- Follow up with your press contacts. Many trade magazines do a post-show review. If the editors did not get to your stand at the show, this is your opportunity to ensure you get the coverage. By providing them with any missed press material and discussing their editorial requirements for

any review you meet their 'need' of demonstrating to their readers that they trekked tirelessly around every stand to give a well-rounded review.

- If possible rent/buy the exhibitor list and mail a 'sorry we missed you, however' letter, perhaps including your latest news letter.
- Send follow up letters to all prospects, where possible using your CRM software to customise content depending on their interest at the show – if the numbers are small enough to manage manually then make each letter personal.

Alternative promotion at exhibitions

If you cannot afford to exhibit at a show yourself, why not approach companies that you might be able to partner with to share space. It may be that you can provide additional interest on their stand and provide a more complete solution to their/your prospects. Splitting the costs in this way can also follow across to show advertising, mailing of prospects etc. Even if you do not attend the event in person, a partnering company may still want to use your products on their stand to complement their own. For the more daring and adventurous among you there are always guerrilla-marketing tactics, as covered in chapter 1.6!

Section 2: Hosting a seminar

A seminar differs greatly from an exhibition – most/all of the attendees are there to see your and your company and the fact they have chosen to attend demonstrates either an intention to purchase or strong loyalty/customer retention. You may know many or even all of them fairly or very well. The preparation and post-event follow-ups, however are very similar to that of an exhibition.

In Chapter 1.6 we discussed the possibility of hosting an event such as a workshop or seminar. Such events need not cost a fortune to organise, whether you are sharing the cost with a partnering company or running an event solo. A seminar could be held to cover one or several topics:

- new product launch
- user group forum, discussing forthcoming products or to gauge feedback on existing products
- joint seminar with one or more non-conflicting companies that share your customer base
- technical briefing (covering technical issues rather than just promoting a product)
- tutorials and 'top-up' training sessions to re-educate customers.

Location, location, location

If your offices are more pit than palatial, or if you work from home, do not fear – you can still hold an impressive event without visitors stepping foot inside your day-to-day premises. This is where working with partners can really pay off. If, for example you sell garden tools and often work or recommend a company selling products that compliment your range (e.g. garden furniture, fencing etc) see if they would be willing to be the venue, assuming that their premises are not similar to your own! If yes, then great – chances are you've found a low-cost venue that will also attract attendees. If not, then maybe you can share costs to hire an alternative venue.

The location you choose for the event, if you are not using your own premises, will also depend on how far you are casting the net to attract visitors. If you are holding a local event (say, within your city) then venue location is not so important – travelling times will be minimal for most visitors. For national or international events travel times are more critical, so try to host it near to major motorway, train or airport routes.

If 'Venue plan A' was not successful, the next option should be to hire a conference room at a business centre or hotel.

Where a bigger budget is available, why not really stand out and go for a venue that will really impress! Hotels, business centres or offices are all suitable locations, but imagine the lasting impression you'll leave in your attendees mind if you invited them to:

☆ a castle or stately home
☆ a boat
☆ a recognisable landmark building
☆ a sporting venue.

An international airfreight company invited its customers and prospects to a seminar and meal on a boat to discuss new services being launched and thank the existing customers for their business. They had a full house (over 200 people) who were not only pleased to be there, but also a captive audience while they relayed their sales message.

Lastly, don't forget to check that your venue caters for those with disabilities – this is especially important if you don't know your attendees too well.

Preparing for the event

Once you've decided on the basic event content, venue and whether you are working solo or with one or several partners, you need to communicate this to your prospective attendees. A simple mail-merged letter to each company is all that is required to get the ball rolling, but if you really want to ensure you get a reasonable attendance this will need to be followed up by telephone or any other contact you are likely to have with the recipient. If your company uses telesales or field sales staff, set them a target of attendees to register (perhaps with a prize for the winner). The letter must cover the 'what's in it for me' mentality, spelling out why it is in the their interest to attend.

The date you set for the event is important. For daytime events try to avoid Mondays or Fridays – few people are in the right mind to be sold to on these days and they can also be the worse days to travel on. Evening events are a little easier, as you could break into the weekend, but you should still avoid Sunday, Monday, Tuesday and Wednesday. Psychologically, people are not so concerned about a late night towards the end of the weekend or on a Saturday night – earlier times in the week are not so appealing especially if they have a long drive to work in the morning. Don't forget holiday seasons. It may be an ideal time for you to run an event when your business is quiet, but there's a reason you're quiet – your customers are sunning themselves on a beach!

By now you have your content, venue, date and list of potential attendees to mailshot. Make sure that you are giving them enough time to allocate time in their diaries – if you set the event for a week after the mailing many people may already have commitments. Ideally you should contact them at least 4-6 weeks before the date, and then follow up the week after. If it quickly becomes apparent that you are not going to get the required numbers, you then still have the opportunity to cancel without causing too much inconvenience.

Preparing pre-event information for attendees
As registrations start coming in, you need to follow this up with more detailed information about the event. This might include:

- a full agenda, detailing times of speakers or subjects being covered
- food arrangements, times and who to contact with any special dietary requirements
- travel and parking information (trains, roads, flights, local airports etc)
- a map of the location and how to get to it from major roads
- local hotel information if attendees wish/need to stay over
- who to contact to arrange for special needs for those with disabilities.

You can help visitors further by contacting a local hotel and negotiating a special rate – most hotels will be interested if you tell them you may require a number of rooms, more so if you are booking in a tourist resort or city centre out of season. If time permits, organise the hotel rooms on behalf of your guests. You could also apply this approach to a taxi firm – especially useful if the event is near an airport or train station.

The event itself

As you could be preparing for an event on subjects ranging from bookkeeping to biochemistry, this book obviously cannot deliver a step-by-step guide for every scenario. What it can do, however is offer a few dos and don'ts for the preparation you'll need to do before the event and what you might want to do during the event itself

- If you are preparing information packs, make sure you have some spare – you never know if someone may want to take away extra information for other staff, or if you'll get surprise additions.
- Have a trial run to make sure you get timings right.
- Try your presentation out on staff to get feedback. Where possible also test it on unrelated people that may be similar to your target audience (perhaps even family members) where they are likely to be able to give you a 'real' opinion. Staff might have too great an understanding of the content to know if it will make sense to others and may even be too afraid to tell you if it does not measure up.
- Provide your visitors with a means to make their own notes, ideally on paper and with pens/pencils branded with your logo.
- People are happiest when they are fed and watered (and not desperate to answer a call of nature) – stop every 2 hours maximum for a coffee break and have water readily available.
- If yours is a standard seminar with users listening to a speaker, make sure everyone turns off their mobile phone before the start – including you! If you are giving a slideshow presentation, it is not uncommon to see a message to this effect at the beginning.
- Funds permitting, give them a parting gift to go away with. Everyone loves a 'freebie'.

If your event is a customer user day, then you may want to make a special offer for those that made the effort to attend. This not only builds good rapport, but also gives users reason to attend any future events. Set a reasonable time limit, and provide the offer in writing for users to take away – don't expect them to remember it.

It is often difficult to gauge how your event has been received. Depending on the type of attendee, it may be worth providing a feedback form to collect information about various aspects of the presentation, speaker and overall delivery. Although not suitable for press events, it is especially useful when presenting to customers who are more likely to provide honest feedback. Design the form with a series of tick boxes (perhaps from Very Satisfied through to Very Unsatisfied). Ask questions such as:

? Did you find the topics covered of interest?
? Did we cover everything you wanted to see?
? Were you happy with the presenters? (Perhaps break this down to each presenter so that you can get better analysis)
? Would you attend a future event?

Add a comments section at the bottom to collect any further opinions.

Post Seminar follow-up

There is little difference in what you do after a seminar from what you do after a trade show. Attendees should all be contacted after the event, to ensure that they obtained the information they wanted and to take any enquiries further. Again, this should be done within a few days of the seminar while it is still fresh in their minds. Any special offers made at the event should be followed up to allow decisions to be made before the offer expires.

Summary

❑ Taking your company and placing it visibly in front of your prospects is what exhibitions and seminars are all about. Both are costly in comparison to telesales and mailshots, with exhibitions being the most expensive, but the one-to-one approach can build a much closer relationship with prospective customers. The presentation of your company at these events can drastically alter people's perception of it, so remember to look at the little details – every effort you put in to making your prospect's experience enjoyable at events will be remembered. Prepare well in advance and don't stop when the event does.

 Pearls of Wisdom

'Follow the four P's – Preparation, People Skills, Productivity and Promotion. Define your plan, execute it and follow up with consistency.'

Tim Perutz
Managing Director, Nimlok Limited

1.10

Advertising

Saint Bernadine of Siena knew a thing or two about public relations, speaking and persuading people to his way of thinking (and religion) – so much so that he became the patron saint of advertising! Sainthood is most likely to be beyond the rest of us mortals, but advertising should not be discounted simply because it costs money. Granted, this book focuses on low-cost methods of promotion but advertising should still have its rightful place in your marketing budget.

Often seen as a necessary evil, advertising is probably the largest regular marketing cost within most companies. Deciding which type of media to use has become increasingly difficult due to the explosion of media types available. Go back twenty years and you were limited to only a few TV channels, even fewer commercial radio stations, a narrower range of printed media and no Internet. Today we have advertising encroaching on every facet of our daily schedules, so deciding where to spend your hard-earned cash is not easy.

One thing is certain – the minute you start your press activities by sending out press releases, talking to editors and generally promoting your company, you'll start receiving advertising sales calls.

Ad agencies – should you use them?

There may come a point in your business where it becomes more cost-effective and beneficial to outsource your advertising workload to an advertising agency. While in black and white the financial costs may initially look frightening there is a lot to be said for passing a job such as this to the experts. Ad agencies employ key talent across all advertising areas and have better access to information and materials than an individual business would normally have. Although the difference between the money you save by outsourcing and the cost of an ad agency is likely to differ you could quickly recoup these costs due to a much more successful campaign.

A good advertising agency will be able to pinpoint the best vehicle(s) to reach your target audience, and then create the idea to be delivered. Kevin Dundas, Chief Executive Officer of Saatchi & Saatchi (UK) said, *'Historically, ad agencies used to handle everything 'above the line', e.g. public media including TV, print, posters etc. Other communication companies would handle 'below the line' activities such as direct marketing, B2B and more recently electronic media but this sends out mixed messages – two sets of branded messages, often of varying quality were going to the consumer. We recognised this in the mid 1990's, even dropping 'Advertising' from our name to focus on "Ideas that through a broad range of media can transform our clients' businesses, brands and reputations.'*

Fig 1.10.1. Kevin Dundas, CEO of Saatchi & Saatchi UK

Ad agencies are suitable for both Business to Business (B2B) and Business to Consumer (B2C), although by their nature much of their business will be consumer orientated. Saachi & Saatchi's Kevin Dundas says, *'The reality is that many people still come to us first for advertising and we will then take a look at their overall brand requirements. Integrated ideas allow one idea to travel. This means for example, that both the trade and consumer are receiving a common brand message across all audiences.'*

Saatchi & Saatchi is undoubtedly the most famous ad agency in the world, handling 60 of the top 100 advertisers worldwide. Its global marketing and creative communications network includes 138 offices in 82 countries. Among the agency's list of multinational clients are Procter & Gamble, Toyota, Visa EU and Carlsberg Breweries A/S.

Tracking a campaign

Gauging the effectiveness of a campaign is paramount. There are several ways to do this, depending on the medium used, but they generally revolve around having unique identifiers per campaign and/or advertising method to allow it to be pinpointed. For example, an advert (radio, printed etc) may give out a special telephone number that forwards to the standard company number, but the number of calls received can be counted. You may choose to divert calls for a campaign to a call centre, or specific staff so that very targeted information can be collected. An Internet banner advert might take visitors to a particular page within your site, which your statistics reports will immediately pick up on. It is also vital that your telesales/field sales staff ask 'where did you hear about us' when talking to new prospects and log this into your prospects database accordingly. Unless you strictly record this information, you will have no way of knowing how effective your expensive advertising campaign was.

There are four mainstream advertising types that we will explore:

- printed media advertising (newspapers, magazines)
- billboards (on buildings, transport etc)
- radio and TV
- internet.

You will probably already have a rough idea which of the above is immediately unsuitable for your business, but have you considered any of the above media types in detail outside of your existing advertising methods? For example, while TV advertising is likely to be unreachable to all but the most affluent business, radio or cinema advertising may be suitable if it can reach your target audience. This chapter only serves to outline the main benefits and drawbacks of each of the main advertising types – recommending a specific advertising schedule to meet with every business type would be near on impossible! Let's take a look at each type in detail.

Printed media advertising

Whether you sell directly to consumers or operate in a business-to-business market, it is likely that there will be several magazines that will be suitable – hopefully you're already receiving good media coverage by sending them your press releases! The question is whether magazine advertising is worth your marketing funds over other advertising forms. The Magazine Publishers of America (MPA) thinks it does, and has released research information that showed magazine advertising to be substantially more effective than TV (40%) and radio (60%) in terms of return on investment.

If your marketing campaign budget allows you to contract several forms of advertising, then magazines should be high on your list. However, they can also bolster other media extremely well. MPA's report also quantified the synergy of magazine and television advertising working together. By analyzing the weekly pairing of magazines and TV at the brand level they created three brand groupings representing three different approaches to advertising pairing. The overall effectiveness of both magazines and TV – and the individual effectiveness of each medium – was the highest when there was substantial overlap in weekly scheduling. This is likely to be the most cost-effective and targeted type of traditional media.

Billboard advertising

If you operate in a B2C marketplace, outdoor advertising using billboards is a strong medium for reaching a wide audience at low cost. This market is split into four recognisable sectors – roadside, transport, point of sale and ambient.

Roadside – consists of panels by the side of major roads.

Transport – buses, taxis as well as transport locations such as airports and train stations.

Point of sale – advertising at supermarkets and shopping centres.

Ambient – more diverse outdoor locations, such as petrol pumps, wash rooms, take-away lids, floors etc

Billboard adverts are particularly efficient across a number of key groups such as ABC1s, younger age groups and main shoppers. Billboard advertising is probably the most accessible medium for the smaller business or secondary brand without the budget for a national TV or press campaign.

This medium has seen substantial growth in the last decade. According to MMS, in 1991, 35% of the top 200 advertisers in the UK were using outdoor advertising – in 2000, this had leapt up to 83%! Entertainment and media products are generally the heaviest users of roadside advertising, with motor vehicle advertising, food, business/industrial and finance taking the next four top spots. This changes starkly for the other three sectors. Maiden, one of the UK's leading outdoor advertising companies state that the audiences most other mediums find difficult to tap into, such as the 'youth' and 'time poor' 'cash rich' are the two major audiences advertisers are buying into when including transport on their media schedule. Meanwhile, point of sale advertising is dominated by food, followed distantly by household products, drinks, confectionary and cosmetics/toiletries.

Fig 1.10.2 - Billboard advertising can produce effective localised awareness

Maiden cites ambient usage as the fastest growing media currently in the UK, mainly due to its ability to surprise – to reach an audience in a place they would least expect. Statistics show however that ambient advertising is most effective when backed up with outdoor advertising in more traditional locations.

Radio and TV advertising

Probably the most wide reaching and costly, these mediums are again mainly consumer driven. Your product will require a quick sale cycle requiring little or no interaction with sales people. They both also offer good brand-building opportunities.

In 2002, the Radio Advertising Bureau commissioned 'Radio Days 3' – research into the listening habits, behaviour and attitudes of radio listeners, which provided information on:

- media consumption habits
- radio listening behaviour
- attitudes to radio and other media

On average, radio is the second most popular medium, behind TV, with a third of consumers' time spent listening to radio broadcasts. This equates to around 2.6/3.3 hours, depending on the day of the week. Interestingly, radio listening often takes place alongside the consumption of other media, such as reading newspapers (38%), magazines (36%), internet (13%) and watching TV (8%).

The advent of cable and satellite TV now means that no two television markets are the same: there are strong local and regional nuances that impact everything from product distribution and consumption to program viewing preferences. Willard Bishop Consulting found that in 1995 it took three TV commercials to reach 80% of a specific target audience – just five years later it rose to 97 ads to reach the same group. Ad agency Doremus concluded in a recent newsletter; *'Short of being embroiled in a scandal it is almost impossible to get your name in enough channels to build substantial awareness.'* In short, unless you can reach your target audience because its niche is covered by only a small number of channels or relevant programmes, then you will probably have to spend a large amount of money to get your message in front of the right prospects.

A sub-set of TV advertising is cinema advertising. Independent studies have repeatedly shown cinema advertising to be at least 5 times more effective in terms of advert recall than a corresponding TV advert. This can be attributed to several factors. Firstly, it has a captive audience – theatregoers have chosen to spend 2-3 hours in a darkened room. The experience is normally shared, with 96% watching with other people and the core cinema audience is under 45, with a third over 35. With the advent of multiplex cinemas, generally with bars and restaurants, the complete experience separates people from everyday events and distractions – research has even shown that cinema commercials are an integral part of the cinema-going experience.

Another major benefit of cinema advertising is that it may be suitable for local businesses – how often have you been to your local theatre and been presented with an advert for a nearby restaurant? If your business targets a relatively small geographical customer base and sells directly to consumers then it may well be advantageous to find out more.

Internet advertising

Since 2000, internet advertising has seen a massive price drop, as people started to realise it would not be the death of other media as previously predicted. Also, the market has become saturated, with every site clamouring for your click-through with ever more intrusive forms of pop-up, nag screen or floating advert. As a result, impressions (showings) to click-through rates are generally under 1%. Pop-up adverts, although intrusive and hated by many yield almost twice as many click-throughs as 'traditional' banner adverts, according to research company Gartner, which it attributes to many users being unsure as to how to close them down. As users and ad-blocking software becomes more sophisticated this margin will inevitably narrow. Windows XP now blocks pop-up adverts as standard.

Many of the search engines, which were previously free to submit your company details to, now charge to even consider your site for inclusion in their directories, without even guaranteeing that you will be listed. There are, however still several large free search engines still out there (the predominant one being Google), so regular search engine submission may still be a cost-effective alternative to either paid-for inclusion. In February 2005, Microsoft launched MSN search. However, it paled in comparison to Google – a search for 'Microsoft' on Google delivered 188,000,000 pages, but on MSN's own search only found 85,251,651. By the time you read this the tables may have been turned – Microsoft are pushing this service hard, with many of their other applications (such as MSN Messenger) suggesting that you set it as your default search engine during their installation routines.

The difference between internet advertising and any other form is that the technology allows your adverts to be much more targeted. For example you can purchase banner adverts that only appear when specific search terms are used on a site that covers your market. Google's Adwords, mentioned below, is a prime example of this. Not only will your advert be seen by users more likely to have an interest in your products, but you only pay for the times that users click on your advert rather than just view it – no other medium offers this degree of accuracy.

If you decide to go the Internet advertising route, search out portal sites for your industry and inquire about pricing to get an idea of the going rate. Depending on the quality and technical complexity of the site, they may simply offer traditional 'advertising per period', per click through or per showing (impression).

Your web statistics will identify traffic coming from specific sites, so you will be able to easily monitor the performance of any web-based adverts. Many sites will also offer you stats from their site, either emailed at regular intervals or available by a Control Panel on their site.

The goliath of Google

If you are waging an Internet advertising campaign, then you cannot ignore Google. It has two interlinked services – Adwords and AdSense. You as an advertiser can create an Adwords account, select keywords and set your spending limit. Your advert will be displayed on the right-hand side of the screen whenever your keyword or keywords are used, but you only pay when someone clicks on your link. Once you hit your predetermined spending limit per day your advert is no longer displayed until the following day. Google ranks adverts by the

Fig 1.10.3. Google's adwords should be your first port of call for online advertising.

cost per click specified by the user and the clickthrough rate – if your advert is irrelevant to users then they won't click on it, and it will subsequently move down the page. Relevant ads will rise to the top at no extra cost, so your ad could be above a competitor if it highly relevant for a specific keyword.

AdSense works in conjunction with AdWords, or to be more precise it uses the AdWords engine. You may have already seen other sites that carry 'Ads by Google' banners, with boxes similar to AdWords? Google allows webmasters to earn money by placing targeted ads on their site, based on the site's content. A website that discusses mobile phones might have adverts dynamically supplied by Google that list special deals on the latest models. This means that your AdWords advert can appear on industry-relevant sites anywhere (within regions specified within your AdWord account settings).

Which medium is right for your audience?

Depending on your market sector there will be many other types of advertising you might want to consider, ranging from advertising on public transport to sponsorship of a sports team. In this advertising saturated world, it is impossible for this book to cover every type of opportunity, so to make a decision on any commitment to advertise you should ask yourself these questions.

? Will this medium reach my target audience?

? Does it offer value for money over other forms of advertising I could use?

? Can I convey the message of my product over this medium as good as or better than other forms of media (e.g. would radio be better than a magazine advert)?

? Is it within my price range? Are there high associated costs (such as advert design for TV)?

To help you make these decisions any company selling advertising will have created a media pack. This contains information and statistics relating to their audience, and will be broken down into relevant sectors such as geography, age group or job title. Ideally, an independent body such as the Audit Bureau of Circulation will audit these figures, giving you assurance of their accuracy.

There are also industry-recognised codes to categorise the social grade, level and occupation of individuals.

Grade	Social Grade	Social Status/Ocupation
A	Upper middle class	Higher managerial, administrative or professional
B	Middle class	Intermediate managerial, admin or professional
C1	Lower middle class	Supervisory or clerical, and junior managerial administrative or professional
C2	Skilled working class	Skilled manual workers
D	Working class	Semi manual workers
E	Low/non workers	Those at lowest State pensioners or widows (no other earner) level of subsistence casual or lowest-grade workers

132

These codes generally are only of use to B2C businesses. If, for example you were booking radio or TV advertising space for a relatively expensive consumer beauty product, you would probably want to target those in groups A, B, C1 and C2, choosing the best vehicle according to their circulation figures.

For the majority of businesses, a combination of magazine and Internet advertising will probably define the extent of their advertising activities. TV and radio tend to focus on consumer products with a fast sales cycle, or as a branding exercise for larger companies. Local radio or TV may be considered if geography is a deciding factor, and because of their limited exposure may also be within lesser budgets although don't forget there will also be high production costs, especially with a TV campaign.

Producing your advert

This is where the creative skills are needed. If this is not your strong point then it's worth paying someone to do this for you. There is no point in spending large sums of money on a campaign only for it to fail because the message was not properly defined and put across to your audience. With most media you only have a few seconds before your audience will switch over or turn the page so unless your advert is purely branding it has to be immediately clear what you are advertising. Here are the top tips to remember when constructing an advert:

☑ Your slogan needs to be short, sweet and to the point.

☑ Don't use too many fonts – stick to the same style you use on other literature.

☑ The same also applies to colours – limit it to two or three dominant shades that don't clash, unless you're going for a particularly garish look.

☑ Make sure that contact details (where relevant) are prominent. On printed adverts the phone number and web address are usually the most important details, so make them bolder and larger than other text.

☑ Humour and/or play on words can be effective ways to grab attention, but keep it clean unless you know your target audience will tolerate risqué humour. Get the user to question what they are seeing or hearing – make them want to find out more.

Negotiating better rates – the 'Agency' secret!

You may have already negotiated a good rate for your advert, but it is sometimes possible to squeeze a bit further! Many media organisations will deal with a company through their ad agency. The ad agency handles all of the negotiations, prepares artwork copy and generally takes the hassle away from you – at a cost. This is the cost that you are already trying to reduce by taking them on in-house, such as advert design. You can doubly save by requesting your 'ad agency' discount, which could be up to 15%. This is a relatively standard commission that agencies receive from publications, partly due to the fact that they are supplying print-ready copy. If you're using DTP software such as CorelDraw or Adobe Illustrator to design and produce your artwork, then you can do the same.

Supplying artwork

To get your agency discount you've got to earn it, and that means giving the advertising company exactly what they want. Every media publication will publish 'mechanical data'. This is the criteria and boundaries with which you have to work within. For example, when designing an advertisement for a magazine, they will provide you with the physical width and height of the advert together with the bleed area – this is the area where any solid colours around the edge will bleed over. If you did not add a bleed area to an advert you will get differences in the quality of the edge of the advert throughout the print run, e.g. a slight white strip around the edge. All this information can be found in **brad** (British Rates and Data), published monthly and available at reference libraries, who frequently sell off two- or three-month old copies at a fraction of the original cost.

Producing an advert for your company has various degrees of complexity depending on the output media. Designing a printed page advert in-house is relatively straightforward, but producing a full TV commercial in-house is something else entirely. Many of the disciplines will be the same, but the equipment and skills required will differ greatly. Unless you are sure you have the skills and creativity to design an advert that will work you should seriously consider outsourcing.

Working to editorial calendars

If you can afford to advertise every month, that's fine. For those that can't or choose not to, it is still worth considering advertising infrequently when planned editorial compliments your products or services. Although you may decide to advertise to bring in much needed business during a slack period, it is worthwhile drawing up a calendar of all the editorial events that may be relevant to your company. If a magazine is running a group test of your products or there is an annual review in which you have submitted a story it may make sense to back it up with an advert.

Whether you initially intend to advertise with a particular publication or not, you should still contact their Ad Sales staff as this can build a very beneficial relationship. Obviously their angle is always primarily to sell ad space, but they also want you to get good value out of their title so will make sure they tip you off when you should be supplying a story or if anything else relevant occurs. As mentioned previously, ad sales and editorial are generally two entirely different beasts and should be treated as such – don't ask ad staff to push your editorial through the newsroom.

Contra-deals and trade-offs

If you have a product or service that is of interest to advertisers then you might be able to cut a deal exchanging products for advertising. This works out much better than a standard payment as you can trade at list price, effectively netting you your profit margin as a discount. It also secures you a new customer and a reference site, with the opportunity of repeat business in the future.

Summary

❑ While a great deal can be achieved through the other methods covered in this book there is little doubt that there should be a place for advertising in your budget. Don't just commit to advertising because the sales guy did you a special one-off deal – you may be throwing your money away if it is not the best vehicle to reach your target audience. One-off advertising is never as effective as a series of adverts, so (funds permitting) look at a longer-term advert series rather than a short hit during a slow spell. Pay as much attention to the advert itself as the medium you are using to convey it. Online advertising allows for immediate exposure and can be quickly modified if a campaign requires it. Google AdWords are a great way to gain immediate coverage not only within the search engine itself, but on sites that a directly related to your specified keywords.

 Pearls of Wisdom

'Find the most motivating truths about your brand and communicate it to your most important consumers in the most single minded and bravest manner. They will respect you for it.'

Kevin Dundas
Chief Executive Officer, Saatchi & Saatchi

Part 2

Marketing
Your Business

£ $ €

A theoretical and practical guide
to cost-effective promotion

Practical

2.1

How to: Write a Press Release

On the CD

- Office Software
- Web links

A well-structured press release is an excellent way of receiving free publicity for very little effort and cost. The length should generally vary from between around 300 to 600 words, or 1-2 pages depending on the subject matter and target media. Before we examine how the release should be structured, let's observe some rules that you should always apply:

Do:

- Make sure you have a story in the first place. Look at it from the Editor's point of view. 'Is this going to tell my readers something of value?' Identify the problem from the perspective of the user, then write the press release in a way that clearly solves that problem.
- Keep asking why! Dig deeper to get more of the story out. If, for example someone makes a saving because of your product – why? Were there knock-on effects that saved them more, and so on?
- Write a short and to-the-point headline. Never try to create something that may be a clever play on words, but leaves the reader confused as to what the subject matter is about.
- Concentrate on making the top few lines of the release tell the main part of the story in one go, with the rest backing it up with more information and quotes from relevant people.
- Write your press release in the third-person perspective. Don't add 'we', 'us' etc, except when writing quotes from staff.
- Try to write in a style that is similar to that of the magazines that you are submitting the release to. The less work an editor has to do to your release, the more chance you have of getting it published. Continue this trend and you will find that editors will increasing run more of your releases as they get to know and appreciate your style.
- Provide e-zine sites with additional material or even a longer press

release if required – some online news sites suggest that the longer the press release, the better. This is because your keyword-rich content will help their site in the search engine rankings, and ultimately yours when they link back to you.

Don't:

- Don't sell. A press release is not an advert! If it is seen as such the chances are that it will never be printed. While you obviously want to say complimentary things about your products, don't just copy text from your product literature.
- Don't use too much jargon. When you have to use technical terms, ensure that you explain any complex terms. Remember, many editors are not actually as clued up about your industry as you may be.
- Don't use words such as 'revolutionary', 'ground-breaking' etc. Editors see these every day, so unless you can justify why your products/services warrant such a term, stick to more direct descriptions.
- Don't make claims that you cannot substantiate. Provide facts, figures and statistics. Provide answers, not statements.
- Don't allow typographical or grammatical errors to creep in, as it will make you look amateurish.

Now that we've got the basics out of the way, let's look at the structure of a press release. As mentioned earlier, templates should always be used where possible, and press releases are a prime example of this. They will generally always be laid out in the same fashion, and sent out with the same methods. Once you've written two or three you'll be able to generate news releases extremely quickly as the format will become second nature. A press release can be broken down into several sections:

- header
- title
- first (leading) paragraph
- main body of content
- closing content
- company contact details
- additional closing information/further resources
- end and word count.

Before we take a look at each of these, we'll start with the format itself. You will normally deliver a press release in three formats – email, web and printed. For printed versions use standard letter or A4 letterhead paper – don't print on both sides, as this will look cheap. Ensure that you have at least 1 inch/25mm margin on the left-hand side, and choose an easy-to-read font such as Arial, at least 10 point in size. The web version will be virtually identical to the printed version, but within the confines of your website's design template. We'll cover the email format in the distribution part of this chapter.

The Header

This is the area above the title, and we normally start by telling people that they are looking at a press release! You should always start the first few lines as:

Press Release
For Immediate Release

Contact details:
[Contact name]
[Company name]
[Telephone number]
[Fax number]
[Email address]
[website address]

Note that this is the contact information that you want editors to use, not the information that will be printed alongside your release – that appears further down.

The Title

This is your hook. You have less than 10 seconds to grab the editor's attention, so keep your title snappy, direct and to the point. You should try to sum up in less than 10 words what the entire release is about. This immediately tells the editor where he is likely to position your story. Include your company name in the title where relevant. If your press release relates to a case study, then focus on the customer's name and the main benefit they have achieved with your product e.g.

'ABC reduces production costs by 25% with XYZ product'.

Take Intel – they make a highly technical product but have to release information in a language that we mere mortals can understand. If we look at one of their releases, taken from their Pressroom at Intel.com we can see that their titles tend to range between six to twelve words and always focus on core facts rather than detail, keeping jargon to a minimum.
    Examples include:

Intel-Based Systems Move Up In Supercomputing Ranks

Intel Extends Pentium® 4 Processor Platform Leadership With Four Advanced Chipsets

Intel Opens $2-Billion New Mexico Manufacturing Facility

As soon as you read this you know exactly what the story is about and whether it is of interest to you. Don't try to make it into something it's not, as any editor worth his salt will quickly discover this, which will only harm your reputation. A good title will not need to be edited, so try to envisage the title that you would like to read if your press release were published.

The first paragraph

Aside from the title, this is the most important part of your release. Confining the content to three or four lines, it should contain the 'who, what, when, where, how and why' of your release – in short the first paragraph is a condensed version of the rest of the release. We start by listing our location – for US companies this will be City/State and elsewhere should be City, Province/County and Country (if the release is to be distributed outside of your country). Add the date, and then start with your opening paragraph. Keep it factual without using jargon – even the most technical of companies will never add jargon into its first paragraph. If we go back to Intel.com, we can see that they have tackled a technical issue using hardly any jargon, summing up the entire content of the release in a single sentence

> *SANTA CLARA, California., Oct. 7, 2002 – Intel Corporation today delivered four new desktop chipsets that bring advanced levels of performance, reliability and flexibility to PC users who demand a richer digital media, gaming and broadband experience.*

They succinctly explain what they have done, what it will mean to their customers and why it was needed.

The main body

Now you can start getting into the detail. Your title has summed up in one sentence what the story is, and the first paragraph has set the scene a little further – now you have to put some meat on the bones. This is where you substantiate any claims/statements made in the preceding text. Again, don't forget that you are writing a release to advise users of how you have or will solve a problem that they are interested in.

If we again revisit the Intel press release and take the first two paragraphs of the main body of their release, we can see that they now get deeper into the detail, but still in general terms that can be understood by most readers involved in the subject matter.

142

The enhanced Intel® 850E chipset and the new Intel 845GE, 845PE and 845GV chipsets are available in PCs starting today. All of these chipsets will support Intel's groundbreaking Hyper-Threading (HT) Technology**, which enables software programs to run as though there are two processors available with only one processor physically in place. HT Technology will be introduced later this year on desktop PCs with the Intel Pentium® 4 processor at 3.06 GHz.

'We're very proud of these new chipsets," said Louis Burns, vice president and general manager of Intel's Desktop Platforms Group. "Not only will they dramatically enrich a PC user's experience today; they also provide the platform foundation for our upcoming HT Technology, which can deliver up to 25 percent more performance for many mainstream consumer and business applications."

It is always good practice to back up technical claims with a statement by an identifiable person from within the company. This also gives you the freedom to make the language a little more personal – press release content must be quite clinical, but a quote can be used to express opinion as well as helping to push the main message home. For example, if a press release reflects sales performance, you may include a quote from your CEO/Managing Director talking about past/future performance and how the company is placed to perform well, but you would not write this type of text outside of a quote unless it was a statement of fact that could be backed up by statistics.

Closing content

Every written document you produce should always have a definable start, middle and end. In the case of a press release, the closing content advises the reader (not the editor) where they should obtain further information. The size and structure of your company will depend on the information you publish. Intel chooses not to list a phone number on their press releases, instead directing readers to the press room on their website where the only contact option is a fill-in-the-blank form. Although this is not exactly editor-friendly, the nature of their business and exposure in the marketplace means that they have to channel enquiries into a manageable format.

Smaller businesses would be better adhering to a more approachable format. Give users a phone number, email and website address. If your release is being distributed outside of your country remember to add the country code on the phone number, however if you are only distributing in your own country you can disregard this. You cannot go far wrong with a closing paragraph of:

For more information contact CONTACT NAME at COMPANY NAME on +XXX XXX XXXX, email info@companyname.com or visit www.companyname.com.

End company information

After closing the press release you should also include a short brief about your company to give editors an idea of your position in the industry. Keep this down to two or three sentences and focus on:

- the industry sector you cover
- number of years trading (unless you are a start-up company)
- existing customer base (if relevant)
- awards or accreditations
- any other basic statistics about your business.

This paragraph would appear at the bottom of every release, so once you've written it you can just cut and paste it onto each release. Keep it factual and remember to check it occasionally to ensure it is still up-to-date!

A sample section may look like:

COMPANY has been specialising in INDUSTRY TYPE since 1978. With a customer base of XXXX, COMPANY sells its range of XXX products through a network of resellers throughout Europe. Its products include YYYYY, which offer AAA, BBB and CCC features.

Try to keep the features limited to simple, short descriptions without jargon.

Additional content

It is always worthwhile making photos/screenshots available to editors, especially when publishing your release online. Ensure that all images are of a high quality and zip them into a single file. Add a line to the closing content to state that pictures are available for download from your website, and publish the full URL – editors don't have time to hunt for the files. Ensure you also list the size of the file as not everyone is blessed with a broadband connection, and most pictures tend to be quite large, even when compressed. A simple line as below will suffice:

Download hi-res images at www.companyname/press/file.zip – 3MB (approx 10 minutes at 56kb)

Note: Adding the download time is optional, however you should always remember that many people might not quickly recognise that a file may take a while to download. Also, as many editors work remotely, they may choose to download the pictures the next time they are in the office. Therefore providing them with a rough indication of how long it is likely to take shows additional courtesy and forethought.

Quick calculation guide:
A standard 56kbps modem downloads at roughly 5 kilobytes per second. Therefore:

- 100kb will take approximately 20 seconds
- 500kb will take approximately 1 minute 40 seconds
- 1MB (1000kb) will take approximately 3½ minutes.

The end
Once you've added your closing paragraph, the end of a press release is simple. As strange as it may seem, you need to tell the editor that they have reached the end by adding:

--- *END* ---

Underneath this you should also add the number of words. Select all of the title, first paragraph, main and closing text, and then perform a word count – in MS Word this is performed by clicking on Tools and Word Count. Then write:

XXX words.

Sample press release
Now that we have the basic understanding of a press release structure, let's build a press release using these principles. We'll base it on a fictitious computer hardware company that has recently released a new graphics card featuring a new fast, upgradeable chip (see overleaf).

Press release
For Immediate Release

Contact Details:
Lisa Smith
Eyeglaze Graphics Ltd
117 New Street
Anytown
United Kingdom
XX73 2KW

Tel: +44 (0) 299 124 1433
Fax: +44 (0) 299 124 1444
Email: sales@eyeglaze.co.uk
Web: www.eyeglaze.co.uk

Eyeglaze announces Blind Havoc™ TS34 chipset upgradeable graphics card for business users

Anytown, UK - 1st June 2005 - Eyeglaze Graphics Ltd has announced the release of a new range of upgradeable AGP graphics cards targeted at the high-end PC business user. The Blind Havoc™ range of cards is powered by the new TS34 graphic chipset, ideally suited to graphical intensive application, such as desktop publishing and video editing.

Utilising new core architecture, the TS34 chipset is equipped with high speed RAM that allows a data throughput of 6GB/second. Several configurations of memory are available - 128MB, 256MB, 512MB and 1GB using industry standard memory chips, allowing users to upgrade as required. All Blind HavocTM cards support standard resolutions up to 1600 x 1280 in 32-bit colour.

A unique feature is the inclusion of a PGA (pin grid array) socket to house the main TS34 chipset. This allows the chipset to be removed and replaced as new models become available.

Performance at high resolutions is what sets the Blind Havoc™ apart from the competition. With a WinMark™ performance benchmark figure of 4521.5 it is 23% faster than the nearest priced competitor. This allows users to run their graphically intensive applications at higher resolutions without compromising on

---

speed. Gamers will also benefit greatly from the TS34-powered cards, as the graphics card automatically processes many tasks previously handled within software.

Said Sadie Bennett, CEO, *"We believe that the release of the Blind Havoc range places affordable power into the mainstream desktop market. Both gamers and power users can benefit from the additional processing power it delivers. As it takes standard memory, users also have an upgrade path in the future. In addition to this, Blind Havoc is the first graphics card that can be upgraded like a motherboard, with the chipset being upgraded like a normal CPU. This brings the cost of upgrading down in the future and therefore gives much more value for money."*

The Blind Havoc™ range of graphics cards is available from all major computer outlets, or is available to purchase online at www.eyeglaze.co.uk.

Eyeglaze Graphics Limited specialise in developing high-end graphics processing cards for IBM compatible computers. Based in Anytown since 1993, Eyeglaze now manufactures and distributes products to 35 countries, shipping 300,000 units last year. Its range of graphics card offer solutions for general office PC, gamers and high-end business requirements.

For more information contact Eyeglaze at +44 299 124 1433 or email sales@eyeglaze.co.uk. Product box shots are available to download at www.eyeglaze.co.uk/press/blindhavoc/

--- End ---
401 words

So here we have our finished release. We can see that the title has the main story content in just twelve words. The first paragraph then concentrates on explaining what the product is in a little more detail, and points out to whom it is suitable. Note also the use of 1.5 line spacing to make it easier to read. As press releases generally are only one or two pages long this is not too much of a waste of space, although it would be tiresome if this book were printed in the same format.

As the release is now completed, it is a good habit to stick to a standard naming format for all of your press release filenames, and to also place them in a constant location for everyone to access. When you refer back to it in a year's time, the filename will be an immediate reminder of the content without even opening the document. Normally the date, followed by a couple of keywords from the release will suffice. In the example above something like PR_0103_ts34.doc would be suitable. Also include zip files (using popular file compression programs such as WinZip) of any images you may be making available with the release.

Summary

❑ Press releases are the life-blood of your media presence. Remarkably, many companies do not even bother informing the press of their activities, wasting a golden opportunity for free publicity. For a task that only needs to take a couple of hours of your time (it doesn't even have to cost you for mailing if you distribute by email) press releases can generate immeasurable results in terms of exposure and brand recognition – it should be a regular part of your marketing activity. By adding a press section to your website you also increase the changes of traffic through keyword searches from search engines.

2.2

How to: Distribute a Press Release

On the CD

- Office Software
- Bulk email Software
- Web links

Once you have written your editorial masterpiece you will no doubt be keen to spread the good word to the masses. This brings us back to our resources chapter – have you prepared your database of press contacts yet? If you did a thorough job, you will no doubt have come across editors that have told you (possibly quite forcefully) that they only look at mailed press releases rather than emailed ones. (You'd think you were doing them a favour providing it in electronic format!) In any case, it doesn't hurt to both mail it and email it. Fax is an alternative, but you will quickly find that editors get annoyed after receiving every press release in triplicate.

If you have yet to create your list of editorial contacts, start by rounding up every magazine related to your industry. Either in the first few or last few pages you will normally find an area that lists the address and contact details of key staff to the title – look for either Editor or News Editor, then enter their name, address, telephone, fax and email into your database. Also do a search online in a few of the major search engines – use keywords relevant to your industry to find online portals that may also take news. Don't forget trade organisations as they often send out newsletters to their members.

Step 1 – Compile your list of contacts to mail and email
From within your database software you will now need to extract the details of the people/companies that you want to send the press release to. This will generally need to be in one or two formats, printed and/or digital:

- You will need to use the export facility within your database to extract all editors' names and email addresses for import into your email software (unless you are using address books in Outlook Express or similar). Most software packages will allow you to extract specific records within a given criterion, which in this case will be all records that relate to the relevant trade media. The format that you will most likely export this information in is known as CSV – comma separated values. It is a text file that can be viewed with Notepad, with each line representing a record and each field separated by a comma. If your software gives you the option to select which fields you want, then you only need name, and email address.

- You will also need to print mailing labels of all editors and publishing houses (or export names to import into whatever print mechanism you intend to use to produce labels). This should be relatively straightforward in most contact management systems as they will have a variety of pre-defined label templates for this task. If you're using Microsoft Access, it has an easy-to-use label wizard – you simply select the manufacturing product code of labels you are using (e.g. Avery J8160), select your data (which could be a Query that selects the information you want) and click print… This can then be saved and re-used in the future.

At the end of this you should end up with a few sheets of labels and a CSV text file with your contact names and email addresses.

Step 2 – Update your website

Whenever you send out a press release, and especially if you intend to make images available for download from your website, ensure that the first place the release appears is online. Nothing annoys editors (and anyone else for that matter) more than clicking or typing in a link appearing on a press release that does not work. Ensure that there is a mention of it on your home page in case an editor does not type in the full link. Also make sure that any graphics used in the release are available for download in high resolution so that the editors can immediately help themselves.

Step 3 – Send out the printed press releases

Print out your press release on standard letter-headed paper, with at least 1.5-line spacing between each line. Don't forget to proof read it before printing dozens of copies – sometimes mistakes that were not apparent on-screen will often jump out of the printed page. If possible, get someone else to look over it as well. Use only one side of each sheet – your release should not be more than two or three sheets. Do not staple pages together – use paperclips if you feel it is important to keep them together, and then use a full-size envelope to mail them.

Step 4 – Send out the email press releases

How you do this will differ depending on your choice of software and your experience, although the format will generally remain the same. Let's start by defining the standard format. Create a blank email with a title line of PRESS RELEASE, followed by your title. Then write a relaxed email along the lines of:

> *Please find below a press release from [COMPANY NAME] relating to [short description of release]. Digital images are available from our website. Please contact me either by return email or on [TELEPHONE NUMBER] if you require further information.*
>
> *Kind regards,*
> *[YOUR NAME]*
> *[JOB TITLE]*
> *[COMPANY NAME]*
> *[WEB ADDRESS]*

Cut and paste your press release underneath.

Golden rules:

- Never send press releases as attachments – many editors work remotely and have slow connections.
- Never email pictures unless specifically asked to do so (for the same reasons) - instead ensure that the press release has a hyperlink to where the editor can download images. If you've placed your images as a zip file on your website it is best to provide an editor with a hyperlink to the file rather than emailing a large file which their mail server may even reject.
- Do not mark your message as high priority unless you have major news.

If you are using a standard email client such as Eudora, Mozilla Thunderbird, Outlook or Outlook Express to send out your emails, then ensure that you send your press release 'blind carbon copied' - in other words, don't put the email addresses in the TO field! You do not want every editor to know that every other editor has also received the same release. Use the BCC field to blind carbon copy each recipient – use the help within your email software to enable BCC if it is not already visible.

Bulk Email software

Another alternative, and my personal favourite, is to use external programs for handling email-shots. This is exceptionally useful if you maintain all of your email addresses in a main database then export them out of that as described earlier, and also ensures you don't clutter up your daily address book with email addresses. There are several free/trialware programs to do this, such as Infacta Groupmail (previously known as Aureate Groupmail). You can easily maintain many groups of email addresses, verify emails are valid, then create and distribute an email-shot to hundreds or even thousands of recipients. Another benefit of bulk email is that it can be configured to send each email personally e.g. like you've sent it using the TO field to each individual recipient, which is a much more personal approach.

Fig 2.2.1. Infacta Groupmail is a great way to handle email-shots to prospects and customers.

Using Bulk email software is incredibly easy – just import your email addresses (usually from a CSV file that can be extracted from your main database), write your email and click Send. Infacta Groupmail can send thousands of emails in seconds.

Step 5 – Follow Up

This should only be done if you have sent out a release of major importance to your industry – you simply would not have the time to follow up every single release you send, and editors would soon tire of your enquiries to find out if they received a relatively minor news item. If you do need to follow up, keep the conversation short unless they need further information. Simply call, introduce yourself and company and ask whether they received the release in question, perhaps prompting them with the title of the release. If they did, check to see if they need any further information or images – if they don't then that is the end of your call, so don't drag it out unnecessarily.

Summary

❑ With today's databases and CRM systems, integrating with email and the ability to easily extract specific records for producing mail shots no longer instil the fear that they used to. A mailing to several hundred contacts can be printed and posted by one person within only a few hours. If you added any web-based magazines you could find that your release is live within hours. Traditional titles can take weeks or even months to run articles -articles I have submitted have appeared almost a year after submission. Remember to keep press releases flowing – it is the best form of free advertising you can do.

2.3

How to: Perform a Mail Merge for a Mail Shot

On the CD

- Office Software
- Web links

With today's office software packages, performing a mail merge to produce a customised mail shot is simple. The more structured your data is within your database the more personal you will be able to make your mail shot.

The Mail Merge facility found in Office suites such as Microsoft Office, Lotus Smartsuite and Easy Office, or contact management packages such as ACT! or Goldmine, allows you to quickly print mailing labels, envelopes, form letters etc.

Example 1 – Mail merge from a word processor

For our first example we will be using Microsoft Word. With this type of mail merge you can create your own data source or use data from multiple applications like a Microsoft Access table or query, a Microsoft Excel database, or even your Exchange or Outlook address book.

A mail merge comprises two or three main components.

- The **main document** contains the basic information – text and graphics. The main document also determines the format of the resulting merged document – for example, a 'form letter', envelopes, or labels.
- The **data source** contains the variable information – for example, a list of names and addresses.
- The **merged document** combines the main text and the variable information. You may decide to merge directly to output rather than creating a separate file that is subsequently printed.

The main document contains the basic text and graphics that will be common to every page of the merged document. In the main document you will insert 'merge fields' to indicate where you want the variable information (e.g. the recipients' names and addresses) to appear. When you merge the information in the data source with the main document, the variable information replaces the merge fields with the individualised information. The result is the merged document, which contains the combination of basic text and variable information.

The data source contains the information that varies within each page of the merged document. The most popular data source to access from Word is a Microsoft Access database file (*.mdb). However, Word also recognises several other formats, including Microsoft Excel worksheets, Microsoft Outlook contact lists and comma-separated variable (CSV) files.

Different Word processors (including different versions of MS Word) have different methods of performing mail merges, but the principle is always the same.

For this chapter we will design a simple mail shot using our fictitious company Eye-Glaze Graphics Limited to a selection of their existing customers that have previously purchased graphics cards to advise them of a new release. We have used Microsoft Word and Access, although most merge functions work in a similar fashion, so once you understand what the software is trying to do, it should not be difficult to produce the same results using a different software package.

Step 1: Write your letter

If you're writing a standard format letter, simply write this as you would normally write it, but without any address information or addressee name. Also, if there are any parts of the letter where you intend to embed text from your database leave these blank as well. For our example, let's say that we intend to merge the name and address details, together with the first line of text, which will mention the previous product purchased and the month and year. An example might be:

> *Our records show that you purchased a TS32 PCI 16MB card in October 2003. We hope that you have been satisfied with its performance and are delighted to announce the release of the TS34 upgradeable graphics card.*

In the first line we will be embedding the TS32 and October 2003 from three separate fields within the database. The rest of the letter will simply detail the benefits of the new product over previous ones, and most of this text can be recycled from your press release and product literature.

Step 2: Check your database integrity

You need to run through every record that you intend to select data from to ensure that all relevant fields contain information. If they do not, then you should add data that will make sense when embedded into the mail merge. For example, if you don't have a person's name against a company record, put a relevant title such as Purchasing Manager in the Last Name field, and leave the Salutation and First Name fields blank.

	CompanyName	Address	Address	City	State	Zip	Tel	Fax	Email	Web	Con	Conta	ContactLastnan	CardPurchase	MonthP	Year
1	Accrington Computers Ltd	12b High	Fullerto	Nantfc	Huntfords	ZH4 2AR	0321 565	0321 565	info@		Mr	Albert	Bennison	TS31 PCI 16ME	August	2003
2	CBA Design Services Ltd	PO Box	London		W1		0207 989	0207 989	sales@				Purchasing Man:	TS32 PCI 32ME	Septemb	2003
3	Tuscany Systems Limited	Unit 36	Tottenh	Londo		N17	0208 636	0208 636	info@	www.tu	Mr		Grimsdale	TS26 PCI 8MB	January	2003
4	Fortitude Computers Ltd	Fairview	16 Fair	Leeds	West Yo	LE99	0113 233	0113 233			Ms	Sue	Newson	TS16 ISA 1MB	August	2001
5	Concord Data Systems Ltd	16 Gaze	Halifax	West		HX 00 9ZZ					Mr	John	Spalding	TS32 PCI 32ME	August	2003

Fig 2.3.1. Getting information out of products such as MS Access is simple, using standard mailmerge functions

The screen above shows a table within Microsoft Access showing the fields that we wish to embed. You can also merge from queries, so you could write a query to filter only users from 2003 onwards, or users of the TS31 cards etc. Note the second record, CBA Design Services Ltd – no contact was available so a title has been placed in the Last Name field.

If there was no information available about a previous purchase (e.g. no information in the last three fields) then you could add a word or phrase that would fit in for each. For Card Purchased it might just be the word 'graphics', and in the date field you could place 'the past'.

Step 3: Insert your merge fields

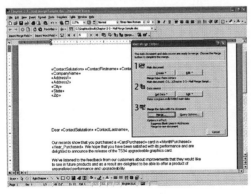

Fig 2.3.2. MS Word's Mail Merge wizard is a simple 3-step procedure.

Now that you've created your basic document you can now link it to your database. Start up your merge process (in MS Word 2000 this is accessible under Tools then Mail Merge). The simple wizard takes you through the three stages of creating the merge.

The first window prompts you to select the main document type. We're creating a Form Letter here, so select this option. You'll be prompted whether you wish to use the current document or create a new one – select the current one.

Now you need to select your data source. Make sure that the correct data source type is selected (e.g. Word, Excel, Access – in this case it's Access) then select your database file. You will be prompted to select the table or query that contains the data you wish to merge.

Once your data source is selected, you need to tell Word where to insert the relevant fields. Word should automatically display the Merge toolbar, but if not, click on View, Toolbars and Mail Merge to display it.

Inserting a field is simple – place the curser where you want the field to be inserted, click on Insert Merge Field and select the field name from the pull-down list. The field names match those within the Access database, so it should be pretty obvious which field is which. If you want to preview how your document will look with live data inserted you can click on the Preview Merged Data icon (which looks like <<abc >>) - this will allow you to scroll through each record from the database and see how the letter will look with the merged data.

Step 4: The final merge

To produce your final document for printing, open the Merge menu again and select the Merge button. Another menu will appear, asking you where you want to merge the document to – this might be either directly to a printer, a new document or email, where you can subsequently select the email field from your database to send each message to. In this case we can select Printer, stack up the printer with paper and leave it to run.

The possibilities with mail merging are endless. With ODBC functionality (Object Database Connectivity) you can link to spreadsheets, databases and even your accounting software, create queries that extract very specific information on each company, then produce thousands of personalised documents ready for mailing. You don't even need to draw the line at letters. As many word processors double as basic or even intermediate DTP packages you could design brochures with prices unique to each customer. As ever the information you can get out of your data systems is only as good as the information you store in them, so make sure that you are collecting and categorising as much information on your customers in as workable a format as possible.

Example 2 – Mail merge using Contact Management software

If you are using a contact management application such as ACT! or Goldmine, it is a little more streamlined to create a mail merge, although the processes are similar to the first example. Here we will use Act to show the various stages of merging record information with a pre-written letter.

Step 1 – Select your records (perform a lookup)

ACT! has a powerful database interrogation facility, allowing you to quickly create a 'lookup' for a specific set of records. This includes general searches on items such as company name, contact, phone, city, zip, status and sales stage. You can also create custom searches on any other field that you create. So, for example, if we had created a field that specified a product type that this customer had selected, we could run a lookup that gave us the results of only the companies that had purchased one particular type of product. Once you have selected your lookup type you'll see the number of records available to view in the top control bar change to reflect the results. Scroll through a few records to verify that this is the correct set of records that you wish to mailshot. ACT! also allows you to specify groups to which a contact may belong, and you can specify an entire group to mailshot when running the mail merge wizard.

Step 2 – Write your letter

This is pretty much the same as the first example. Click File and New – you'll be presented with a popup dialog box with several options. You can either select ACT! Word Processor Template or Microsoft Word Template – we'll use MS Word. When the application opens you'll immediately be presented with a list of the available fields to merge. Scroll down the list, double clicking as you find relevant fields – these will be inserted into your document as bracketed pieces of text.

Now simply write your letter as normal, placing any relevant merge fields directly where you want the merged text to be placed. Once complete, click File and Save – you'll be prompted to save your file with a .ADT extension.

Step 3 – Merge your data

Now we run the mail merge wizard. Click on Write, then Mail Merge – the first screen of the wizard appears. As we've just created a lookup we can just select Current Lookup and select Next, although you can also opt to merge the current contact only, all contacts or a specific group. We are now prompted to select where we want to send our merged data to – in this case we'll take the default option of Word Processor. The final screen prompts you to select the template you created above. Clicking Finish will run the mail merge and present you with a Word Document containing your merged data, ready for printing.

Example 3 – Merging from online databases such as SugarSuite

If you are using an online CRM system such as SugarSuite, the procedure is not dissimilar to the first example. You will still need to merge the data using MS Word's mail merge facility. However, instead of merging data from an Access database, you will merge it from a CSV file. All online systems have an export facility, so export your data into a CSV file to start with.

Once you have a CSV file there may still be some work to do on it before you can use it. Some CRMs just allow you to dump the entire database to CRM, so you might have to filter the data before you have your final sub-set of contacts. If this is the case you could do this simply in a spreadsheet – simply open up the file and sort the column that has the attribute you wish to filter. For example, if you have a 'record type' field, and you want to remove 'dead leads', just sort by this field, then scroll down until you locate all of the relevant records – select them and delete them. Your database is now ready for merging as per the first example.

Summary

❑ Mail merging is a very effective method of creating a one-to-one personalised message to a large amount of people. If your database is up-to-date and information is categorised and stored separately then the possibilities are limitless. Today's contact management and database systems are very easy to use and give virtually anyone the power to achieve results that would have taken days or even weeks to perform twenty years ago. If you can get a CSV formatted file out of a database then you can easily create a mail-merged document.

2.4

How to: Write a Newsletter

On the CD

- PDF Software
- Office Software
- DTP Software
- Web links

Newsletters are a great way of keeping your customers and prospects informed of new products and events surrounding your business. As with every other piece of marketing literature, once you've designed a standard format template, future newsletters can be designed and produced very quickly. You don't need a high spec PC running the latest Desk Top Publishing software – MS Word will allow you to design a quite acceptable document, although your design options will widen if you use one of the higher-end packages such as CorelDraw or Adobe Illustrator.

Step 1 – Decide on your content

A newsletter is not just for pushing your current product range. It can include a variety of different subjects, including:

- extracts from case studies or recent sale success stories
- special offers
- 'How to' guides, showing users how to make the most of products
- information on staff recruitments or promotions
- future expansion plans or product road maps
- company events, such as open house days, trade exhibitions etc
- recent press coverage
- industry information that may not directly relate to your services, but that is useful and helps to show you as an expert in your field (such as tips, tricks, industry news etc).

Don't start writing your articles just yet until you've worked out how much space can be allocated to each story. Just make a note of the stories that you may want to include.

Step 2 – Define your format and print method

The size of the newsletter will depend on your budget, the number that you intend to distribute and the amount of content you have to include. A small business can probably easily fill a single or double-sided sheet of paper but would struggle to fill four pages. Refer to the list of stories you made in Step 1 – you should have an idea of how much space each story will need without being too drawn out.

With today's offices generally having access to inkjet printers, mono and colour laser printers and possibly duplex (double-sided) printing or copying facilities, this gives a wide scope of options for producing low quantities in-house, but this is limited to single or double-sided sheet sizes only. Also, the cost of ink or toner makes it only suitable for lower quantities. With inkjet printing you should also only use the speciality papers to achieve the best quality – standard photocopy paper will just look cheap.

It is relatively straightforward to work out a cost-comparison for in-house printing versus lithographic printing. If you've decided that you'll need 1000+ or need more than a single side, then go straight for litho printing. Otherwise get a quote for 500 and 1000 newsletters to be printed from a printer then add up all of the internal costs of ink and paper. You should also consider the time it will take to physically print on your printer, especially if you're using a colour inkjet. And lastly but by no means least put a value on your own time. The following table shows a breakdown of the benefits and drawbacks per method.

Inkjet	Mono-colour laser	Lithographic
• Ideal for small runs (100 - 200)	• Can use standard photocopier paper	• Cheapest method for larger quantities
• Best quality only achieved on more expensive media	• Many lasers have low-cost duplex options	• Gives the best quality finish on a wider choice of paper types
• Limited to single-sided printing unless you buy expensive double-sided paper and manually print both sides	• Ideal for slightly higher quantities (200 - 800)	• Not cost-effective on smaller runs
• Slow printing method	• Colour lasers may still not be cost-effective in comparison to litho printing for higher quantities	• Not limited by paper size - can produce multiple page newsletters etc

Step 3 – Create your title area

To differentiate yourself from everyone else that sends out 'The ABC Limited newsletter', create a title for your newsletter. Ideally this should be something that ties in with your industry. A manufacturer of industrial PCs and software produced a newsletter called 'The Industrial Times', whereas a CADCAM software company produced one entitled CAMpaign. This will quickly become recognised by your customers as a part of your branding.

You don't have to be a wiz at graphic design – a standard Tabloid newspaper title format will suffice if you don't have the means or will to create anything more elaborate, but if you are using colour you might as well make the most of it and design a title graphic that will leave a lasting impression. Just beneath your title you could add a strap line detailing what the newsletter covers e.g. 'XYZ's furniture update' or 'ABC's news and views of the ZYX industry'. Stick to your corporate colours, and if you have a corporate graphic logo try to include this within the title or design.

To the left or right of your strap line you need to add a date – what you add will depend on how frequently you intend to produce newsletters. If realistically you cannot guarantee that you will have enough time or content to produce them regularly, then simply put 'Issue 1', otherwise put the month, or two months (e.g. Oct/Nov 05) or the Quarter (e.g. Q4 2005). It is better to be pessimistic and opt for quarters, or even issue numbers instead of per month, as customers will quickly see the newsletter as dated.

Step 4 – Adding your content

The amount of space you have available will dictate how much text and the number of pictures you include. On a single page newsletter, you can comfortably cover two or three main items, with perhaps a side column of short pieces. Where you have more space to play with, you can expand on your content.

To get the right layout, just open any newspaper! Here's a rough example of a standard single page layout. There are two main feature articles, each with an image. The text in each of these would span two columns. The left-hand column could contain five or six short pieces, each just three or four sentences long.

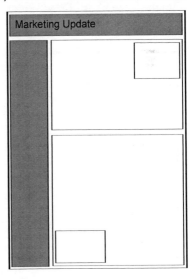

Fig 2.4.1. A basic newsletter template structure.

Where relevant add links to direct pages on your website at the end of each story (this can be in a smaller font). You can also put email links to relevant contacts.

When using pictures for this type of media you must have higher resolution photos than those used on your website. If you import pictures that have been used on your website you will probably find that they are too small and therefore have to be enlarged. In the process of doing this, you'll find that the quality will dramatically reduce and the pictures will become 'blocky'. Ideally you will want pictures that are 300 DPI (dots per inch) which match or beat the physical size that you want the image to appear on the page. Pictures taken with a 2-mega-pixel camera or higher will be more than adequate.

Step 5 – Add your company contact details

At the end of the newsletter you need to ensure that your contact details are clearly visible, although hopefully there will already be direct links to pages on your websites and relevant staff's email addresses. A line of text that simply says 'For further information on any of the above items please contact us on xxx xxx xxxx' will suffice. Underneath this, place your full company name, address, phone, fax, email and web details. The phone number and web address should be in a larger font than the underlying contact details, as these are the main methods that you are most likely to receive responses by.

Step 6 – Produce your newsletter

Before you send the artwork to a printer, or press the Print button, check, check and recheck! Get someone else to run over it to make sure that it all makes sense – if possible choose someone that is outside of your organisation that is detached from your company, products and services. They will therefore be able to see the newsletter in a similar light to your customers.

Once you're happy with the final draft you are ready to start producing. If you're printing in-house, then fill your printer with paper, press the print button and leave it to run. If you're sending it to a printing company then you have a couple more checks to make before sending the file over.

Lithographic (or 'Litho') printers work in four colours – CMYK Cyan, Magenta, Yellow and Black – they use K for black and B for blue. They need to produce four films, and subsequently four plates with each one having the information relating to that colour. You therefore need to provide them with a file that they can use. When obtaining the quote, tell them what software you are using to create your artwork – hopefully they will be able to take the file without you having to make any modifications. Alternatively they may be able to give you some recommendations as to what you need to do to get the file to them in a format that they can use. Below is a brief description of some of the file formats and more technical options that may be requested by printers.

- **Adobe Acrobat** (Portable Document Format). This is fast becoming the most popular form for document distribution. There are many low-cost programs that allow you to create Acrobat files from any application. If you are producing your file in MS Word and the printing company cannot accept it, is the next best thing.
- **CorelDraw File**. One of the leading PC DTP packages. If the printing company cannot accept this file format CorelDraw offers a wide variety of export options.
- **EPS File** (Encapsulated PostScript File). Many DTP packages will allow for export to EPS files.
- **QuarkXPress File**. The preferred format for Apple Mac users.
- **TIF file**. This is sometimes also referred to as a 'flat' file, as all of the content has been flattened into one layer. You should only use this format if your printing company cannot accept any other format and you know how to check and separate colours correctly. For example, if you have black text you must ensure that it is pure black, not a mixture of other colours, otherwise text will appear slightly blurry on the page after printing.

Remember to print off an inkjet proof along with your disc/CD-ROM so that the litho printer knows what the artwork should look like. This is especially important if you are exporting your artwork to a different format so your printing company can read it – applications can sometimes have a tendency to corrupt information when porting from one format to another. If they are using the same software, ensure that you are both running the same version, or they are running a more recent version that you – newer versions will normally be downward compatible, but if you have a newer version of the software than the printing company, the chances are that vital information will be lost or they may not even be able to open the file.

Step 7 – Distribute your newsletter

This is the easy bit – send it to everyone! By everyone, this includes customers, prospects, suppliers, editors and even key staff within your own company. Run labels from your Contacts Database to cover all live records. Make sure that a copy is included in shipments, invoices and any other material that is received by customers or prospects. Have a stack of newsletters in reception and make sure that external sales staff have a supply to either hand or mail out.

Send your newsletter at the beginning of the week – it is more likely to be read in the middle of the week rather than on a Monday or Friday when people's minds are elsewhere.

Step 8 – Repeat the above regularly

Once you've started producing a newsletter, make sure that you continue. Customers will get used to the regularity of receiving your newsletter once every month or so and it will instil in them the fact that your company is reliable, stable and still here. You are also building up a library of material that can always be referred back to where any point previously covered needs expanding on. In Step 3 we covered adding a date or time period – make a note in your diary to ensure that this deadline is met.

Summary

❑ Customer perception of your business, both in size and reliability is a very important factor in ensuring their continual loyalty. By demonstrating that there are constantly positive events and developments occurring in your company, you drive home the 'feel-good' factor of dealing with a reputable organisation.

2.5

How to: Write a Case Study

A case study is an excellent method to promote your company, and is extremely recyclable! Not only can you design a brochure that your sales staff can use regularly, but it can also appear on your website as a downloadable brochure and, more immediately can be used as a press release. Once you've written one case study, this will give you both a design and content template to regularly replicate the procedure extremely quickly. Case studies can be any length, which of course will be determined by the complexity of the content, but as a rule a single-sided sheet will suffice.

Why should an existing customer agree to a case study?

As well as being a good advert for your company, a case study is also an excellent promotional vehicle for your customer too! If they are in a B2B environment it also shows their customers that they are ahead in their field to such a degree that their suppliers want to use them as an example. They will also be thankful for the free publicity you generate. Here are the top reasons you can cite:

- It's free!
- Once you've designed your format, it should only take 1-2 hours of their time – you may even be able to do it over the phone.
- The case study is likely to appear in your industry press, copies of which you can provide to your customer.
- Your customer will get a brochure (either printed or electronic) which they can use to promote themselves.
- Their details will appear on your website, which in turn is another route to their own site! (This can actually boost their rankings within search engines!)

A company that is either associated with a strong brand name or is well known themselves may refuse to allow a case study to be written about them. They will no doubt have a co-ordinated marketing effort that this may not fit into, and they also want their customers to be concentrating on their brand – not yours. Also, companies working on secretive projects, such as defence may not be in a position to allow a case study on them to be printed. You may be able to get around this by offering to write the case study anonymously, although this does limit what you can do with the case study once complete – it wouldn't for example make a good press release but you could still use it on your website, in newsletters and other direct communications with customers.

What you should ask your customer?

Before you even start talking to any existing customers you need to compile a series of questions to ask. They need to dig at all areas of your product and service to the customer, and will of course differ depending on whether you are a product or service-based company. Once you have compiled these questions, revisit them after writing your second or third case study to see if you've missed anything. Save the document and keep it in a central location on your PC or network server for future use.

Although the questions below will give you the basis of a relatively well-rounded story, you should always analyse the answers you get and ask 'why' - if there is an answer to be had then dig deeper. For example, if you've supplied a product and the company says, "It saved us 30% time" ask why. Pinpoint exactly where the savings were made, as this is the detail you need to substantiate the overall statistic. Perhaps give details about why the problem existed in the first place to further clarify the solution. Keep digging until you have a complete, detailed justification of the point in question.

In general the question areas will break down as follows:

Company or user information

At some point in your case study you need to describe the customer using your product so that the reader can compare himself or herself to them. If your products/services are directed at the individual, this description will differ from describing a company. When you have a broad portfolio of case studies you will know which are most relevant to each individual/business and can handpick them to ensure that they see information that they can identify with.

For case studies focused on a business you should collect information such as:

- Number of staff

- Turnover (some companies may not disclose this)
- Year the company was founded (useful if it is a longstanding and respected business)
- Description of their line of business (get them to provide this so that you use the 'official' description)
- Equipment they are using that may be relevant to your product/service
- Company web address (everyone likes some free publicity)

For case studies focused on individuals, the information you collect will be related much more to the product you are discussing as opposed to simply giving a description of a business size and style. For example, if you're writing a study on cosmetics or beauty products, you may only want to note the person's job just to demonstrate what kind of physical environment they are working in. If you sell garden products then a description of the time that the user spends in their garden (e.g. playing with children etc) will allow the reader to empathise more with the case study.

What system or product were they using before?
This may not actually be used or indeed be of relevance. Generally it is not good etiquette to write the company or product brand that a customer was using before yours. You can suggest, infer, and hint but you should not fully disclose. How do you feel when a sales guy slates his competitors to you? To many it will appear that his product is weak as he has to resort to kicking his competitors rather than selling on his strengths. Knowing where you are strong over your competitors makes this a useful enough document without making it obvious who the competitor was.

How did they hear about your company/product?
If a customer heard about you through recommendation then this may be worth including. Find out why the initial customer recommended you, as this may not only give you additional statistics to include but may also lead onto another case study. Maybe they read an article, or perhaps even a previous case study?

Why were they in the market to change products/services?
While you should not namedrop, there's nothing to stop you mentioning all of the failings of your competitor, or at least the problems that forced the user to come to you. These might include poor product or support, expensive upgrade or maintenance costs etc. if possible try to put a ballpark price comparison if relevant, e.g. 'It would have cost £xx to upgrade so it was more effective to buy YY product instead.'

What was the deciding factor for the customer to choose your product/service over your competitors?
More than likely this will be a similar answer each time – price or service. It still does not hurt to spell it out.

What products/services did you deliver?
This is where you detail exactly what you provided. You may also need to specify that you supplied this over and above other solutions you offer – what need did that specific product fill.

Was the implementation/installation process easy/easier?
If one of your products benefits is that it is easy to get up and running then it is worth getting a user's perspective on this. A non-technical company is likely to be more interested in a product that requires less technical support from others to get operational than others.

What were the immediate benefits?
If you delivered a product, most likely you can pinpoint one or several benefits that would have been immediately apparent from initial use. Try to quantify these with as many statistics as possible. For example, by installing XYZ the user saved XX time or YY money. Examine the different types of customers you have and map out areas where they generally achieve savings – these are the questions you need to ask each case study customer. Aim to have at least two or three good statistics – these should either be percentage or ideally financial where possible.

Was any training/after sales service required?
If your product or service requires training or additional support this is where you can demonstrate your strengths over others. Focus on ease of use, shorter training times, lower number of support calls, time savings etc.

Have any additional or long-term benefits come to light?
How often have you bought something to perform a task and found after a while it solves another problem you weren't expecting it to? The same may apply to your product, so it's worth asking the question. One good example was a case study for a software company that controlled a manufacturing plant. As a result of streamlining through the software the company could standardise on single sizes of material, which gave them additional purchasing power. This only became apparent after a few months. Another company using the same software product received a software update, delivered free under maintenance, which improved their machine's performance so much that they reclaimed 2½ months' machining time per year.

Did the product/service deliver the enhancements the user thought it would? Where did it exceed?

This is where you go for the jugular with your 'killer app' - talk about features that no one else has. This question will probably generally get you the best quotes to add to the bottom of your case study.

What plans for expansion does the user have in the future and how does your product/company fit into this?

Here's where you can show that a long-term relationship has been forged not only with your product, but also with your company. Maybe they need to buy more of your product, or intend to build on what they have using your product as a foundation.

If another customer were to ask your customer why they chose you, what main reasons would they give?

This is a fantastic question, and while it may seem a little tactless to ask your own customers this you will be surprised at the positive answers you'll get!

In addition to text you will also need images to include on your case study. These should be digital (3 megapixel and above will be fine) and might include the following:

- Picture of their building (may be useful to give perception of size of organisation)
- Pictures of products being used or the results of the product/service supplied (e.g. customer products). Rather than using standard library pictures it is better to show the product 'in-situ', although if the customer has some professional shots these may stand a better chance of being used by editors looking for 'sexy' pictures. Your customer may be happier with you using shots that they have already approved for distribution

Writing the case study

Now that you have your collection of answers and images you now need to go about getting it into a palatable order. You should start by sifting through the user's answers and making a list of around ten features/benefits – this acts as a good ground for the rest of the study, and the bullet points can also usually be used somewhere on the brochure to good effect.

The order of the main text content within a case study will generally be the same:

The problem

The starting paragraph about the company, their previous product/

service, and problems they encountered together with why they chose your product.

The solution
The next paragraphs focus on what you supplied and why you supplied it. Go into detail about the benefits that the user has achieved since their purchase, using the statistics you collected to qualify statements wherever possible.

The closing paragraph
This is where you summarise why their choice of purchase was a wise one and detail where your product/services may be of benefit in the future. Save the best user quote for inclusion in this paragraph.

Designing your case study template
We're nearly there – all we need now is to define the look and feel of the case study with a template. This can be broken down into a set of regions that will always include the same content, be roughly the same size and colour etc. This is probably the hardest part to get right, but once you've done it once, all future case studies will be produced in 1/10th of the time. It is quite feasible to write up new case studies in under an hour once you've done the first few, as the style and structure becomes second nature.

A case study is a brochure, not a letter and therefore a good eye-catching header is necessary. This could span the top 40mm of the page and might include a picture of the building or person, a title of the product supplied and customer name and location.

Note: It may not always be wise to feature photographs of people. By their very nature, people will move jobs, and in doing so may render your case study less effective, or in extreme cases useless. While it is okay to quote the user, only add photos of them if it is deemed necessary for your industry or product. When adding quotes from staff, obtain them from key individuals as high in the organisation as possible – they are more likely to stay with the company and not switch jobs.

We mentioned bullet points earlier – it is worthwhile allocating an area in one part of the page to include the main bullet points as a list of benefits. This allows the reader to quickly skim through and still understand the main reasons for purchase. It is also very useful for editors if they choose to re-write content for a news story and want to refer back to a benefit list. The page can also include a small box with company information and a few key quotes from individuals (everyone likes to see their name up in lights).

Once the text is in place you need to add some graphics to liven the page up a little. Your header, main text and side info bar should already be in place now, so simply insert one or two more relevant images and wrap the text around them. If the pictures need explaining, place one or two lines of small text underneath. You shouldn't need more than two images, but if your product demands more, why not create a row of small images across the top or side?

The bottom of the page should include your logo and contact information. Ensure that your web and email addresses are also listed. If you sell through resellers, add in a small white box where a reseller can overprint or adhere their own details. If you use a product such as Adobe Acrobat Professional you can make the reseller box editable so that they can easily type in their details and print it themselves.

The case study is written – what next?
The first step before you can do anything is to obtain final approval from the customer. It is not uncommon to send a case study to a customer only to find that you've missed a crucial element of the story, or made a mistake. I've known of one situation where a company took a case study to their MD for final sign-off and he flatly refused permission – the person who had originally agreed it had not checked with him. So, send the case study in PDF format for final approval, and ask for a confirmation email in return – this covers you in the event of any back-tracking by the customer.

Once you have final approval, several opportunities immediately present themselves.

- You can immediately email the PDF to your prospects (making sure the file's not too large!). This gives you a genuine reason to contact them with something that may be of interest and/or use.
- Place the PDF in a case study section on your website. Most search engines (including Google) can read PDF content, so will happily harvest the content and direct new traffic your way.
- Send the case study out as a press release. If you generate these frequently, consider allocating a case study exclusively to certain magazines – this builds a stronger relationship with the editor and almost guarantees that you'll get greater exposure as they know that every Tom, Dick and Harry is not going to be running the same article – if you do grant exclusivity hold back from adding it to your website, but sending to prospects should be okay.

Example case study:
In the press release chapter, we wrote about the fictitious Blind Havoc graphics card for PCs – here we've created a case study for an organisation that has decided to standardise on the range. A PDF version of the case

study also appears on the CD-ROM.

All future case studies for this company would use the same header, right-hand area and text size/format. Image size and placement would change to differentiate each study, and the top header strip could perhaps be colour coded for different products.

Note that a background tint of the product also appears underneath the top paragraph. This gives the benefit of showing the product without taking up additional space.

Summary

❑ Case studies are an excellent form of drip-feed marketing. They give you a regular reason for a press release, an ever-increasing arsenal for your sales team and website, and your customers will thank you for writing about them in such a positive and dynamic way. Many editors prefer case studies to general product news stories – it makes readers think that they wrote the articles, not the supplier. Once you have a template drawn up you can generate new case studies extremely quickly. Adding case studies to your website also adds valuable content that is rich in keywords, making your site likely to rank higher for very specific searches.

CASE STUDY

PRODUCT: EYEGLAZE BLIND HAVOC TS34
USER: XYZ ENTERPRISES INC

XYZ Enterprises, based in Townsville, United Kingdom manufacture a range of kitchen cabinets and constantly require greater performance from their development and sales PC's. As users now expect to work in a 3D requirement, a greater workload is placed on the graphics card. Commented Andrew Slater, CEO of XYZ; *"Although our computers are relatively new, our existing graphics cards still could not keep up with our software. The demos in our showroom did not look as slick as they could do. Also, our developers complained of slow redraw times and flickering graphics. We didn't want to buy new computers, so wanted to investigate how we could improve performance at minimal cost."* XYZ decided to look at replacing the graphics card in one system initially to perform benchmark test and, after checking several magazine reviews chose the Blind Havoc TS34 with 1GB of Ram.

Installing the card provided no problems, with fitting and driver install taking less than 5 minutes. What was immediately noticed was the speed at higher resolutions. Added Slater; *"We generally run at 1280 x 1024 as the performance degradation at high resolutions was too great, but now we can run at 1600 x 1280 in 32 bit colour without a glitch."*

Virtual kitchen tours now have much more realism as textures and lighting effect can be added

During sales demos users are taken through a 3D interactive version of the kitchen of their choice, allowing them to walk around a virtual reproduction of their own home. As a result of the inclusion of the Blind Havoc card not only have the existing demos been improved, but a higher level of detail can be applied. *"We are now adding much more detail to the tours, such as surface textures and lighting effects. We've even added pots and pans on the stove with additional steam! It's details like this that really help customers to visualise the end product."*

Since installing the card in their showroom PC, XYZ have seen a marked increase in both general interest and sales. Demos take less time to set up as users requirements can be planned quicker in the 3D environment, and the overall experience is much more enjoyable for the user. Added Malcolm Blair, Sales Manager; *"It almost became an event for one family who visited our showroom recently. A lady originally visited our showroom a week before and was so impressed that she brought the whole family back. We closed the sale there and then. In the first month we saw sales jump by 20%, many of which we clearly attributable to the slickness of the new demos."*

XYZ currently has 25 showrooms throughout the UK, each housing at least two demo suites, together with the development centre, which hosts twelve developers. Slater has committed to upgrading the entire network within six months, citing that the sales growth they have already enjoyed has already covered the cost. "Given the overwhelming reception that the new card has received, both internally and external it would be false economy not to upgrade. Seven showrooms, totalling 12 units have already been upgraded. We also plan to upgrade the graphics processors in the development Pc's as new they become available."

ABOUT THE USER

Staff:	85 through UK
Market:	Kitchen design
Units sold:	12
Config:	TS34 with 1GB
Platform:	Intel PC
Web:	www.xyzent.co.uk

MAIN BENEFITS

- Painless installation, with card being immediately recognised and drivers installed automatically
- User can now run at higher resolutions with no degradation in performance
- User has an upgrade path, as processor and memory can both be upgraded in the future rather than replacing the card altogether
- Demos have been graphically enhanced to bring a new level of realism and take less time to set up
- Sales have increased by 20% as a direct result of the improvement to presentations because of the new level of graphic performance
- Much more cost-effective than upgrading an entire PC

COMMENTS

"Developing our graphical environments is a much easier, more pleasurable experience now - the Blind Havoc makes the whole experience fluid because of it's sheet speed"

Ian Plimmer
Developer

"This makes our own product look so much better in front of the client - one sale justifies its cost."

Malcolm Blair
Sales Manager

Eyeglaze Graphics Ltd
117 New Street, Anytown
United Kingdom, XX73 2KW

Tel: 0299 124 1433 **Fax:** 0299 124 1444
Email: sales@eyeglaze.co.uk **Web:** www.eyeglaze.co.uk

Local Distributor:

EYE GLAZE

Fig 2.5.1 A sample case study template for Eyeglaze.

2.6

How to: **Build a Website in HTML**

On the CD

- Web Design Software
- Graphics Software
- FTP Software
- Web links

This chapter could in fact be a book in itself! You should only contemplate writing a site yourself if you have the time to do so, and have a basic understanding of HTML (HyperText Markup Language – the code used to write web pages), or if you cannot afford to have a website professionally written.

IMPORTANT: If the ability for users to purchase products from your website is an initial requirement you should read Chapter 2.7 on adding e-commerce to your site, as this may change the method and products you select to build your site. This chapter is dedicated to building a basic, functional website that will display static information.

A half decent website does not have to cost a large sum of money if you can build it in-house. In fact, it doesn't have to cost anything at all, aside from the cost of hosting it (under $100 per year) and the time to write it. This chapter concentrates on building a small, functional site to promote a range of products/services and provide users with general product and company information. Whether you're building the site yourself or simply trying to scope the project, an understanding of the basics of a good website is essential.

Clarification: What a HTML-based site can and cannot do

No doubt you've already used the internet to book a flight, check hotel availability and maybe pay a bill. Sites that offer these services are generally 'dynamic', meaning that they are hooked into back-end programs and databases to provide live information. This chapter covers the designing and building of a simple, static site, capable only of displaying predetermined information. While you will be able to create a site that has fill-in-the-blank forms that email you information, don't expect to be able to provide your customers with live links to your in-house inventory or accounts systems. Any form of functionality other than basic data capture generally requires a scripting language such as PHP, ASP, CGI, Perl or Cold Fusion and potentially costly programming services unless there is an off-the-shelf package that does the job. Note that you could implement an off-the-shelf package (such as Actinic e-commerce) into an existing HTML-designed site quite easily, which is covered in Chapter 2.7.

Working out what you want from a website

It is important not to lose sight of why you are building your site in the first place. As when defining any communication medium you should ask yourself:

- What type of visitors are we hoping to attract? The content required will be obvious if you are targeting mainly existing customers
- How are many of our customers accessing the site? Are they likely to be on a slow or fast connection? If you don't know, play it safe and build a fast-loading site that will work well for a standard modem
- What functionality do we need? Is it purely to provide information in either HTML or downloadable format (such as PDF)?
- Who will need to update site content? If only one person is building and maintaining the site, this simplifies matters, although there are many good tools available such as Macromedia Contribute that allow staff to update specific content without damaging any of the main site design and structure.

Before you decide to go down the 'build it with HTML' route, check out chapter 2.8 to see if a Content Management System (CMS) will fit your needs. Many CMS systems offer enough breadth of structure to provide most of the features you'll need plus a few more besides, and can do this without you knowing HTML. If this is the case, you could be up and running with your own site in less than an hour, but you will be restricted to the functionality that the CMS offers unless you know a developer with enough skills to customise the base system to your needs. For personal sites, a CMS system may be enough, but for most commercial sites a HTML or dynamic site will be required.

There are a variety of HTML web design tools available that you can use to build your site, both freeware (such as AceHTML) and commercial products (such as Adobe GoLive!). For this exercise we are using Macromedia Dreamweaver MX.

GOLDEN RULE: CONTENT IS KING!

The more valid and useful content you can add to your website, the better the perception will be of your company. Make a list of all of the documents you currently mail out to customers, including any fill-in-the-blanks forms – anything you mail out should also be something that a user can download. This could include accounts forms, service documents, newsletters etc. Also write down the reasons why customers/prospects call in – can any of these questions either be answered on the site or could online forms provide users with an alternative method of asking the question?

Step 1 – Map out your site

Before we even get close to the keyboard we need to go back to the drawing board – literally. Take a piece of paper and draw a box at the top of the page, labelling it home. Now you need to draw several boxes underneath relating to the main sections you intend to have on your site. These are invariably similar and will generally consist of 'About Us', 'Products', 'Services', 'News', Events/Shows, Site Map and 'Contact Us'. You should now have something like:

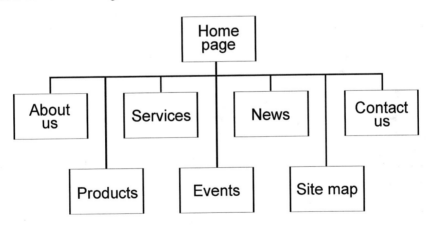

Fig 2.6.1 A basic website structure

Note: For space reasons only Products, Events and Site Map are positioned below the other categories.

Now we need to add any secondary navigation. This is a set of additional links on each of the pages above. Some pages, such as About Us may not have additional links, but your Products page may have many sub-pages.

Let's also assume that Products and Services each have three sub-pages, and About Us and Contact Us have none. News will expand as new press releases are added online, as each release will be an additional sub-page – for the moment we've illustrated this with three press releases in line with Products and Services. We now end up with the following diagram:

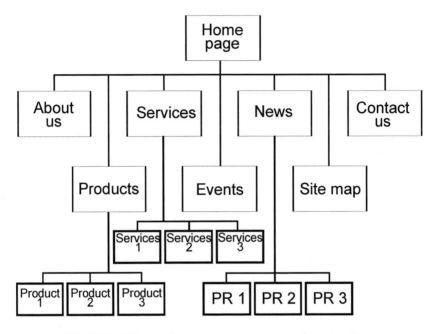

Fig 2.6.2. We now have a deeper level of navigation, allowing for a greater amount of content.

We now have a good navigation map of our website. Try to remember the three click rule – users should be able to get to any page on your website within three clicks.

Step 2 – Creating a design template

Once your site is mapped out, you will have defined the main navigation points that will be common to all pages. Websites can quickly grow into dozens or even hundreds of pages, so it is important to maintain a common look and feel across the site. This is why templates were invented. All good web design applications allow you to design a standard template page (or pages) with fixed and editable regions. When you create a new page based on the standard page or template, you can only edit the regions specified, normally where the main body of text will appear. If you decide to change the template, for example to add in another menu option, every page based on that template is automatically updated, saving you hours of time and removing the possibility of error.

We need to start defining the basic look and feel of the site. Where will the menu be placed? Where will your logo sit? The colour scheme will generally be determined from your existing literature, but should be confined to two or three colours. Get another sheet of paper and sketch out where you want the constant elements to appear on every page. These will consist of:

- company logo
- menu buttons or text
- main content
- copyright information.

Golden rule: Never use light text on a dark background for the main body of your pages! It is very difficult to read.

Normally a logo will be positioned either in the centre or top-left corner of the screen, with main navigation either vertically down the left or horizontally across the top. This leaves the majority of the page free for content. Below are examples of the two most common layouts. The grey area signifies the non-editable region that would be part of the template. The white area is where your main content will appear on each page.

Fig 2.6.3. Two standard page and menu layouts.

The simplest method of creating the above is to use 'tables'. This allows you to create a re-sizeable grid of boxes that you can put content into. The examples above show tables with either two rows or two columns.

An easy alternative – ready-made templates

If you have a fair grasp of HTML and graphics packages (such as Adobe Photoshop), you may want to examine some of the many ready-made templates that are available either free or for a relatively small fee (normally under $50). Sites such as **www.elated.com/pagekits/, freelayouts.com** or

boxedart.com allow you to download an HTML page with pre-designed graphics and rollover button images that change as the mouse is moved over them. Most also include the source Photoshop files to allow for easy customisation.

To use a pre-defined template, simply download it and place it in your site's directory on your hard disc. Open the file in your HTML editor and remove the sample text and graphics in

Fig 2.6.4. Ready-made templates can save time and provide you with 'ready made creative flair'.

the main area of the page. Save the page as a template then specify the main area to be an editable region. You can then either create new pages based on the template or open an existing page and apply the template. If you have the basic to intermediate skills required but your artistic design skills are lacking then this is an ideal way to create a classy, professional site without the hard work. If you don't have the skills, then perhaps use these sites to find ideas.

Tables vs CSS (cascading style sheets)

CSS is fast becoming the standard not only for specifying typeface colours and sizes within certain areas of a page, but is also being used in preference to laying content out with tables. As a seasoned web designer, I can recommend you stick with tables for the time being. This is still the standard method used by many designers and will remain so for the foreseeable future, so you're in good company. Designing a site using only CSS will be difficult for all but the most skilled designer and requires a high level of HTML experience. You should, however use CSS to control how text is displayed on your site, as this does reduce the overall page file size and makes the site easier to update.

Example: Dreamweaver template

This template, taken from the **marketingyour.biz** website, has a vertical side strip, with each main section represented by text, which ensures that it is search engine friendly. (This is covered in more detail in a later chapter) The site logo appears across the top, with a copyright notice at the bottom.

The main white area is where all content will appear. When a new page is created based on this template the user can only add text into the white area – exceptionally useful if several people add content to a site, either with Macromedia Dreamweaver or Macromedia Contribute.

Let's assume you're going to create a table with the navigation on the left. You would select the table tool, creating a table with one row and two columns. This can either be set to a specific pixel width or to fit the screen

Fig 2.6.5. The Dreamweaver template for www.marketingyour.biz

width. The screen in Fig 2.6.5 shows one such table within Dreamweaver, with our top level navigation embedded. Granted, it doesn't look very pretty at the moment as we've not created any styles, or applied any colours.

Note: At this stage you are not linking the navigation text anywhere as you have not created the pages to link to! You are simply designing the layout.

Before leaving the template remember to specify the main editable region.

To frame or not to frame?

Framesets consist of several pages on one screen. For example, have you ever visited a website where, when you scroll down the screen the left menu stays in position but the text on the right scrolls? You're actually looking at two web pages – this is a frameset. The screenshot on the right shows three frames – a top, left and main frame. As the main frame has content too large to display scrollbars are automatically added, but note that they only scroll that frame, not the rest of the page. As the user scrolls down the top and left frames are still visible, giving easy navigation around the site. The term 'frameset' applies to a collection of pages that are controlled by one document.

Many people find frames a convenient way to build a site, but frames have several drawbacks, not least for being very unpopular with search engines. The problem is that if a search engine visits your site and bookmarks the page, when a user finds your page via the search engine it will only display THAT page, and not the entire frameset. This generally means that your menus are not displayed so the user has no way to navigate off the page. Frames do have some advantages e.g. if you want to seamlessly embed pages from another site but still show your menu bar, frames would be the best way to achieve this, but unless you are adamant that you want frames it is better to base all of your pages on a template.

Step 3 – Create a style sheet

A style sheet is code that is either embedded in your template or, preferably, a separate file (with a .css extension) that contains design settings for various parameters of your website. To keep within the constraints of this chapter we will concentrate on creating a style sheet to set the main fonts we might use for a simple site.

You can create a style sheet in Notepad – it's just a text file – but a web design package will generally have provisions to make the task much easier.

The great thing about style sheets is that you set a font size, colour and style once, and then just specify within the web page what style the content within a relevant section is to be applied –

Fig 2.6.6. A basic template, created with a two-column table and left-hand menu.

Fig 2.6.7. Never use frames unless you absolutely have to, and even then complain bitterly!

this makes the site very lightweight in terms of code, and consequently easier to maintain. Change the parameters in the CSS file and the entire site updates instantly!

Dreamweaver provides a simple way to create the main styles that you'll need, which are:

- general font styles
- hyperlink styles
- heading styles.

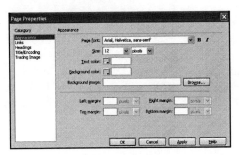

Click on Modify and Page Properties to bring up this screen. You can then use the categories listed in the left to view and modify various parameters of your page. Once you've specified your font face, size and colour, Dreamweaver will create the styles and embed them within the page.

Fig 2.6.8. Creating a standard style for all fonts on a page is easy with the Page Properties box in Dreamweaver.

You'll end up with code similar to the following within the <HEAD> section:

```
<style type="text/css">
<!--
body,td,th {
font-family: Arial, Helvetica, sans-serif;
font-size: 12px;}
a:link {color: #0000FF;}
a:visited {color: #0000FF;}
a:hover {color: #FF0000;}
a:active {color: #0000FF;}
h1 {font-size: 14px;}
h2 {font-size: 12px;}
h3 {font-size: 12px;}
-->
</style>
```

The above code is telling the web page the following:

- Any general text within the Body, TD and TH tags (which pretty much covers most areas) will be 12 pixels high in Arial
- The a.link, a.visited, a.hover and a.active lines specify the colour of hyperlinks at the various stages e.g. when you hover the mouse over a link, when you click on it etc.
- The size of three types of heading – you can specify up to 6

Of course, there are many more parameters that you can add to a style sheet. For a full description of CSS visit www.w3.org/Style/CSS/

The above code is only a couple of hundred bytes in size, and could safely be left within the page, but it is good practice to keep CSS code in a separate file. Not only does it make it easier to update (without updating every page that is linked to the template containing the styles), but once a browser loads the separate CSS file, it is cached and not loaded again for the duration of the visitors stay on your site. This makes your site faster to load and reduces the amount of bandwidth you use – important for busy sites and for visitors on slower connections.

Creating a separate file is simple – just cut and paste everything inside (but not including) the <!-- and --> sections of the above code and save it in a separate file called styles.css (or whatever you want). Now amend the top line to be:

```
<style type="text/css" src="styles.css"></style>
```

Note that you still need the end </style> tag, but this now appears immediately after the above tag, e.g. you're deleting everything including the <!-- and --> tags. If the styles.css file is not in the same directory as your HTML file or template, ensure that this is reflected in the path.

Step 4 – Add your content
Start by creating a new page for each of your main pages based on the template you created, and naming the file relevantly e.g. About Us should be about.htm etc. When naming products or services pages, use their name as part of the filename, as this helps with search engine rankings. Use hyphens (-) instead of spaces as well – many web servers will have problems with filenames containing spaces.

Note: Your home page should always be called **index.htm** or **index.html** – there is generally no distinction between the two suffixes, but all web servers specify index as the starting page for your site and will look for it automatically (some also use **default.htm**, but you cannot go wrong with index.htm or index.html). Ensure that you always use lower case characters as well. So, when you go to Google.com, it's actually loading google.com/index.html – you just don't see the page name, as this is the default page loaded if none is specified. You may come across some sites that have .php, .cgi, .asp or .cfm instead of .htm – this will not be relevant to you unless you are using one of these languages (and if you are, you'll know about it and therefore won't be surprised!)

The internet has certainly shortened everyone's attention spans, therefore when adding information about complex products try to split content into sections, or even different pages. Keep all of the main information on each product page, and then add a sub-menu near the top that gives the user the option to dig deeper as required. You can also scatter links throughout the site where suitable so that the user can get direct access to the right information – but remember the three-click rule!

Below is a general list of pages you will need to create:

Index page (Home page)

This is the front door to your website and will contain a brief overview of what you do, with links to main areas of interest. Ensure that all of the relevant keywords that you want people to find your site with via search engines appear in the text on this page, as it is invariably the first page that search engines will hit. See the chapter on search engine optimisation for more information.

Products/Services

For many of the product- or service-based pages, this will simply be a matter of copying and pasting text and images from existing literature. However, you may wish to break up information over several pages. For example, technical products generally have an overview page, followed by one page per main feature, and then a technical page that details all of the in-depth information that some may wish to read. Mobile phone manufacturers are just one good example of this – why not visit other sites to see how they break down information? Browse a few and see which ones stick in your mind as being easy to use and supplying content in an efficient and pleasing manner. Once you identify what you like you can begin to structure your content layout.

About Us

The 'About Us' page should contain brief content relating to the market and region that you serve, plus a company history and any accreditations you may have. You can include photos of your premises. Include key staff members if personal contact is a part of your business, but ensure that the site is updated if staff leave!

News

Usually this will consist entirely of links to your press releases, with an opening paragraph. To brighten the page up, consider featuring the latest article at the top of the page, including a picture and opening paragraph. If you do not intend to add regular content to your website then leave this section out – there's nothing worse than visiting a site that has 3-year old news on it. You can also include case studies in this section, or perhaps have them as a main section in their own right. For companies that generate a large amount of press releases, create an archive section by year so that people can back-track to older content without it clogging the content that will be of interest to most people.

Events/Shows

If your company hosts in-house or on-site events, or also exhibits at trade shows, then a 'forthcoming events' or calendar page is essential. This also gives you good reason to place fresh content on the home page, which can link directly into this. You could link this to an online form to allow people to register to attend the event. Many trade shows give exhibitors free tickets for their customers, which can be offered as an incentive to register.

Contact Us

In addition to your company name, address, phone, fax and email, include a feedback form if possible – give users the opportunity to supply you with as much information as is reasonable without taking too long to complete. There may be some technical issues with getting this working that you cannot undertake, so if you are new to web design, skip the form for now – anyone with basic editing skills could take a look at Matt's Script Archive – www.scriptarchive.com/ - this site offers an excellent 'form to email' script.

Site map

This is perhaps the most important page. The site map should link to all main and sub sections of your site. It does not need to link to every page, but should allow quick access to pages that would need 2-3 clicks from the main navigation menu. This page is particularly important for search engines as it gives them immediate access to all areas of the site.

Once you've created a page NEVER rename it – if you do a good job with search engine submissions in the future, the last thing you want is for visitors to find your site via a search engine only to hit a dead link because you changed a name. If pages have to be renamed, make sure that you have a custom 404 error page (covered further on in this chapter) set up, so that users have a link to a site map or search facility. Never use spaces, upper case or non-alphabetical characters in a filename as some servers are very specific about what they will recognise as valid – Index.htm will be seen as different from index.htm on a UNIX server.

Step 5 – Adding graphics

A text-only site can be extremely drab, but by contrast an overly graphical site can not only be confusing on the eye but also can take ages to download and be difficult to navigate. While you may be fortunate enough to have a high-speed internet connection, many of your site visitors may still be struggling with a standard modem. This is where you need to take note of image sizes when placing them on your website. As a rule of thumb, your web pages in total (this is the HTML page and all the images on it) should download in less than 10 seconds on a standard modem. At 56kbps (kilobits per second) modem speeds this is about 5KB (kilobytes) per second, giving you a rough limit of 50KB per page. This figure is not cast in stone and is only a guide – if you feel that many of your customers have broadband Internet access, then you can be a little more generous, however it is always good practice to keep your graphic sizes small.

Below is a breakdown to memory sizes. Note that although officially 1kilobyte is 1,024 bytes, it is common practice to round this down to a round 1,000. The same applies to all other memory denominations.

1KB (kilobyte)	1,024 bytes	one fifth of a second download at 56kbps
1MB (megabyte)	1,024 kilobytes	about three and a half minutes download at 56kbps
1GB (gigabyte)	1,024 megabytes	over two days download at 56kbps

The best way to get a good mix of graphics and text is to try to think of your 50kb as advertising space that costs you per kilobyte – ask yourself if the beautiful animated 10kb 'Email Us' icon you picked off one of the free graphics websites is really worth 20% of your page file size. You can be more relaxed about page size the deeper the user goes into your site. They will be prepared to wait a little longer for a page to download if it is likely to contain the information they are ultimately after.

There are two static graphic types that you will use on your web pages – JPGs and GIFs. As a general rule of thumb JPGs are best for pictures and

GIFs are best for text or simple colour graphics. In applications such as PhotoShop, you can reduce the number of colours that a GIF includes, sometimes without visibly reducing the quality of the image but drastically reducing the filesize. There is a third graphic format – GIF89a – also known as animated GIFs, which are usually used to create banner adverts. They work in a similar fashion to 'flick books' - selections of images are flicked through at a pre-set frame rate to create an animation. PNG is another format you may come across, and while supported by most browsers it is not really used that much anymore.

Jumping Jack Flash

You may also have heard of Flash or Shockwave, both Macromedia products. These are much more media-rich than standard graphics, allowing full animation, sound and interaction – there are even Flash games on the Internet. They also have another major benefit – they 'stream'! If a Flash 'movie' is 250kb, taking a minute or so to download via a standard modem, the image may start to play after only a couple of seconds. Then, while the rest of the image is loading in the background the Flash movie will continue playing. You might, for example use Flash to create an interactive tour of a product, which could also include narration and video. Sony Ericsson (**www.sonyericsson.com**) has used this to good effect when launching new phones – users can see the phone interface on-screen and interact to get a feel for how the product works. Standard HTML does not offer this form of flexibility.

If you want a more media-rich website than plain HTML, then Flash is the best-supported product available. There are thousands of websites such as **www.flashkit.com** and **www.flashmxlibrary.com** that offer free tutorials, flash animations and 'components' - small applications that plug into Flash to allow you to create complex effects with very little effort. Visiting one of the many Flash discussion forums, or even Macromedia's Exchange forums will put you in touch with thousands of developers that can give advice if you get stuck. Flash also handles video very well for web distribution.

There are some minor drawbacks – Flash sites can be expensive to develop unless you can do it yourself, and some users may not have the correct software plug-in installed to view your site, although there are technical workarounds for this that will detect if Flash images can be played and reroute users to a standard page instead if the Flash software plug-in is not detected. Basically, unless you know what you're doing or can afford it, Flash may not be a viable option but if you have the requirement, skill and/or finance, Flash can add valuable and eye-catching content to attract visitors to your site. Also, as Flash now integrates with Macromedia's Cold Fusion server platform, you can hook Flash content into back-end databases to deliver interactive rich media with live data.

Step 5 – Amend your template links

Now that you've created your pages, you can re-open your template page and link all of the menu options to these pages. Start by selecting the 'Home' link and link that to your index page. Then select the 'About' link, and so forth... Once done, save your template and all of your pages will automatically update. Now all of your pages will work and be linked together!

If you're using graphics instead of text, remember to add in 'alternative' text. Many users on slow connections choose to turn off graphics in their web browser, so the text specified in the 'ALT' part of an image tag is displayed instead. In most web design software you will simply open the properties window of the graphic and enter text in the ALT box. This also has the useful side effect of displaying the alternative text as a 'tool-tip' when the mouse is hovered over an image. The image below shows the Properties dialog box within Macromedia Dreamweaver for an image with the alternative text of 'Information'. You should always have an ALT tag, even if it is only ALT="", as this will ensure that your code is W3 compliant.

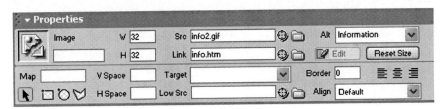

Fig 2.6.9. Adding ALT tags is essential for an accessible and search-engine friendly site.

Golden rule: Always link your logo back to your home page and ensure that your full company name appears in the ALT text for the logo. Most people will instinctively click on the logo to return to the home page and search engines will also use this information as part of their ranking process.

Step 7 – Creating a custom error page

One way to avoid users coming across a '404' - the error displayed when a web server cannot find a page the user is looking for – is to create a custom error page. This can tell the user that you cannot find the page, but then offer useful links to areas that might help them find what they are looking for. This could include links to your site map and site search (if you have one).

Creating a custom page will differ depending on the web server you are using, and if you are hosting with a standard ISP, your first port of call should be the technical section of their website. Do a search for 404 and see if you can find a page relating to the creation of custom error pages. If that draws a blank, then either pick up the phone, send an email to their support desk or visit their online forum (if they have one). No doubt someone will have asked this question many times before, so there should be a standard response.

In many cases, the standard response will be to either create or amend the .htaccess file. This is a standard text file read on many UNIX/Linux based servers. If your web space already has one of these files, then take advice before amending it. If not, you can do no harm in testing to see if this method will work for you if no .htaccess file currently exists. Start by opening Notepad and add in the following line:

ErrorDocument 404 /404.htm

Now save the file as .htaccess (yes, nothing BEFORE the full stop). You'll have to select the dropdown menu to select 'All files' to allow you to save the file without the .txt extension.

The next stage should be done within your web design software. Create a blank page using your standard template. Add in whatever text and links you want to appear on the error page – as you are using your template, users will already have access to your standard menu system. Now save the page as 404.htm and upload it to your web space along with .htaccess.

Important: You must now 'detach' the 404.htm page from its template and recode any links to absolute paths. For example, if you have links to index.htm, you have to change it to http://www.yourdomain/index.htm. When some web servers call the 404 page they call it from the exact location of the page that the person was trying to access. So, if it was at www.yourdomain.com/press/, the 404 page would contain a link to index.htm that would not work if the 404 file is 'looking' in the wrong folder. You will therefore need to hard code links for hyperlinks, graphics, CSS style sheets and Javascript calls.

To test the error page, enter your web address and a page that you know does not exist. Ensure that you also test subfolders as well, to make sure that all hyperlinks and graphics are loading correctly from their hard-coded locations. Your custom error page should now be displayed.

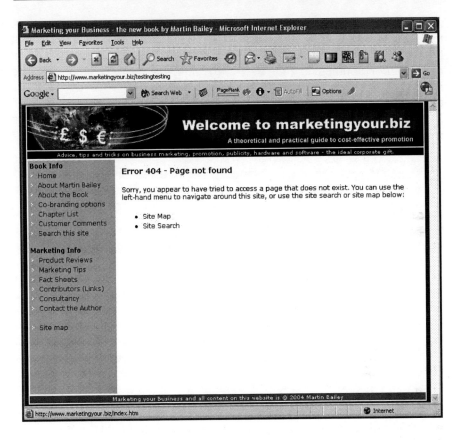

Fig 2.6.10. The custom 404 page on www.marketingyour.biz

For Windows-based web servers, the approach is also quite straightforward, assuming you have access to IIS (Internet Information Services). Create your 404.htm error page as described above, and then open IIS (under Control Panel, Administrative Tools). Right click over the relevant website and select Properties, and then go into Custom Errors. Scroll down to 404, select it and click Edit Properties. Now browse to your newly created file and click OK – that's it. Test as described above and you should now be rid of the standard non-descriptive 404 error page forever.

Step 8 – Adding more functionality to your site

There are a variety of low-cost or even free features you can add to your site with the minimum of web experience. These might include online polls, guestbooks, e-cards, affiliate programs, calendars, forums and site search tools. The Bravenet website (**www.bravenet.com**) has hundreds of free tools, but you may also want to review the resources appendix at the end of this book to see websites that offer specific resources. One downside of many free resources is that they may limit the customisation and are normally co-branded with adverts and links to their own services, but there are plenty that are not.

Here are some ideas of additional functionality you can add to your site with little effort, skill or cost:

- The Zoom search facility from Wrensoft allows you to add a customised search to your site with no branding. The free version is restricted to 50 pages – enough for the majority of small projects. You'll need to remember to update the search index when you add content though

- Add a free forum to your site. There are dozens to choose from, but one of the easiest to get working is YABB (**www.yabbforum.com/** - yet another bulletin board), which only requires Perl scripting services on your web space rather than PHP and MySQL support. To get it working, all you need to do is edit the relevant configuration file, insert your server settings and upload the files. (This information is normally little more than your FTP settings, which directory the forum is stored in and the 'path to PERL' on the server – your ISP can provide this)Everything else is controlled through a web-based control panel. Design customisation will require a little knowledge of HTML. If frequented by enough people, a forum can add an excellent community spirit to a site, plus provide a valuable source of information for new visitors

- Online polls can give you great feedback and information from visitors. Again, they'll generally need Perl or CGI to be running on your server

- Free news feeds can provide up-to-date industry-specific news on your site without you lifting a finger. Many sites offer an RSS feed that you can easily plug into your site, but beware – you may inadvertently be carrying news relating to competitors!

Step 9 – Checking your site for accessibility
Accessibility is the term relating to whether your site is compliant with certain standards to assist disabled people that use the internet. At least 10% of the population in any country has disabilities ranging from visual, auditory, physical, speech, cognitive or neurological. Couple this with a population that is living longer, which sometimes results in users with a combination of accessibility issues, e.g. change in dexterity, poor eyesight or hearing etc, and you could potentially be alienating a growing percentage of your site

visitors. There are several steps you can take to avoid this.

- Add clear and descriptive ALT tags to all graphics and image maps.
- Provide an auditory description of any visual track of a multimedia presentation – these should be synchronised for timing-based presentation.
- Ensure that you use CSS (Cascading Style Sheets), which allow for more efficient page transmission and site support.
- Use heading tags, making sure that you use them in the correct hierarchical order e.g. H1, H2 etc.
- Ensure that texts and graphics are understandable when viewed without colour, and check that foreground and background colours provide sufficient contrast.
- For data tables, identify row and column headings. Provide summaries for tables using the 'summary' attribute of the TABLE tag.
- Ensure that pages can still be read correctly without the style sheet attached – this can happen if style sheets are turned off or not supported by the browser.
- For scripts and other non-HTML technologies, make sure that input is device independent.

A full guideline is listed on the World Wide Web Consortium's website at **www.w3.org/TR/WAI-WEBCONTENT/**. There are also plug-ins for many of the leading web design tools, such as Macromedia Dreamweaver to assist you in creating more accessible sites.

Step 10 – Testing your site

A web designer once told me that if his daughter and mother could use a site he'd designed then he'd done a good job! Before serving up your creation on an unsuspecting public, open your site to a test audience, perhaps by putting it on your local area network or in a separate location on your web server. Don't shy away from asking non-technical people to test it, as you don't know how technically experienced the visitors to your site are likely to be.

Sometimes the most obvious oversight can be very costly in terms of loss of potential business, as this example shows. One business that regularly runs free seminars offered links on every page of their site to entice visitors to sign up, but the take-up was poor. Inversely, their brochure request form was hidden away on the 'Contact Us' page. They added a small graphic of their brochure with header text saying 'Brochure and demo CD request'. As a result they went from one or two enquiries per month to almost one a day.

Top testing checklist

- Don't forget to check the spelling and grammar on each page, and make any amendments immediately your test audience advises you of any mistakes. Most good web design software has a site-wide spellchecker, so make sure you run this regularly. Note the differences between English and American English – if your site is specifically more from one audience than another then tailor the language accordingly.

- Switch off the display of graphics in your browser to see what your site looks like to text-only viewers. In Internet Explorer, you can do this by clicking Tools, Internet Options, Advanced and un-tick Show Pictures. Now test your site again, ensuring to add alternative text to any pictures or logos (this is the ALT tag that appears within the <IMG> image insertion tag)

- Check your site at various screen resolutions, such as 800 x 600, 1024 x 768 and 1280 x 1024. You can change your screen resolution using Display Properties under Control Panel, but your options will be limited depending on the hardware in your computer. When creating a site with tables, you can specify the table to fit either a fixed width or percentage of screen – using percentages does allow a site to automatically resize, but can dramatically change the layout. (If you used a fixed-width table, then you will know that your site looks fine in all resolutions above the width of your table). Try to ensure that your site looks best at 800x600

- Check your site in Internet Explorer, Netscape Navigator (now defunct but still used), Mozilla Firefox and Opera. The chances are you already have IE running, but you can also install Netscape Navigator by downloading it from **www.netscape.com**, Firefox from **Mozilla.com** and Opera from **www.opera.com**. Macromedia Dreamweaver MX has a 'Preview in Browser' facility, which allows you to select which browser you want to test your site in. While IE and Firefox are quite forgiving with code, older versions of Netscape can make a site appear nothing like the original. Your web logs will be able to tell you what browsers are being used

- Most web design packages have extensive code error checking capabilities. Not only will these help to identify code that is not compatible with certain web browsers, but it will also help pinpoint broken links, coding errors and orphaned files (e.g. files that are no longer linked to any page on your site)

- Use online HTML validators, such as **http://validator.w3.org/** to check your site against the latest industry standards

- Validate your style sheets with the online CSS validation service at **http://jigsaw.w3.org/css-validator/**

- Check your site on different computer formats. Apple Macintoshes can also give a website an entirely unintentional new look, while Web TV may not be able to do your graphics justice. If you intend for portable devices such as PDAs and smart phones to view your site, limit the use of non-HTML technologies (such as Java and Flash). If you don't have access to other computers, why not try your local library or an internet café? Alternatively, post a message to a relevant online forum asking for comments. Internet magazine forums are an ideal place as they are often frequented by industry experts

- Check the file sizes of the main pages with all graphics – if you got the graphic sizes right, then each page should be under 50kb if you are optimising for the slowest audience

Step 11 – Getting your site live

Once you've tweaked your site to perfection on your own computer, you need to transfer it to your web space. Although you may come across terms that you've never heard of before, once set up, you can normally update your site at the click of a button.

Note: Before actually uploading your site, head onto Chapter 2.9 and optimise your site for search engines!

To place your site on the Internet you will need the following:

- web space and a domain name with 'FTP' access (this is normally supplied as standard)
- file transfer (FTP) software (unless your web design software has this feature)

Web space and domain name

You can purchase web space and domain names through an ISP (Internet Service Provider) - the chances are that you may already have space if you have signed up for an email address. You may also already own your domain name. If not, they are not expensive to buy (around $10-30 per name) and you can buy as many as you wish, then point them at the same space – this is useful if you want to buy your product name (www.productname.com) as well as your company name (www.companyname.com). You could compare this to buying an easy to remember toll free number, which points to your main telephone number.

Many companies buy domain names relating to all of their products and point them at the main company domain name to make sure that if a user is trying to guess the web address through one of their product names they still get to their site. For example, typing www.windowsxp.com will take you to the product page on Microsoft.com.

Domain suffixes
One confusing issue with domains is the number of suffixes available. In addition to .com and each country code extension (.co.uk, .fr, .it etc) there are now many more suffixes available (.biz, .info, .tv etc). Unless you have the funds to do so or competitors are likely to buy similar domains and point to their website, stick to the .com and, if relevant the country code suffix domains. Alternatively (as with this book – **www.marketingyour.biz**), obtain a domain name that compliments your business or online presence by using a suitable suffix. If the domain suffix can be made a memorable part of the whole name this may be a good alternative if the .com you are looking for is not available. Note also that search engines rank a site based on the relevance of the domain name, so if your domain name includes keywords that users are likely to search on, then you are more likely to attain higher rankings.

Calculating how much space you will need
A website that consists of only a few pages with an average amount of images may well fit onto a single floppy disc! If you've gone by the 50kb page size rule mentioned previously and you have 10 pages, then that's just 500kb. Adding large files such as PDF versions of brochures, zip files of graphics for press releases or movies is likely to take the most space on any site. You can check how much space your site will take up by opening My Computer, locating the folder that contains your website, right-clicking over it and selecting Properties – at the bottom of this window you will see a total file size for all the files and sub-folders in this folder. As most ISPs will give you a minimum of 20-30MB this will not be a problem for the majority of new sites. You can purchase more space later, and the worst that generally happens is that your ISP will suspend you from uploading more than your limit until you upgrade the account – they won't take your site offline.

Note: When it comes to your web space, don't be a cheapskate! Never use free space, or space that comes with your home ISP account – you'll probably find in the terms and conditions that you are not allowed to use it for business purposes. It may also have annoying pop-up adverts (we've all see the annoying Yahoo and Tripod sites) and will no doubt have a very unwieldy domain name.

FTP Access and Software
If you're using Macromedia Dreamweaver or an equivalent commercial

package, it will include everything you need to get your site online. If not, you'll need some File Transfer Protocol (FTP) software. There are plenty of free or shareware (try before you buy) products available from sites such as **download.com** or **tucows.com** – try WS_FTP or Cute FTP. In many cases you can even use Windows Explorer, however it does not have some of the more advanced features you may need (such as synchronisation, CHMOD commands etc).

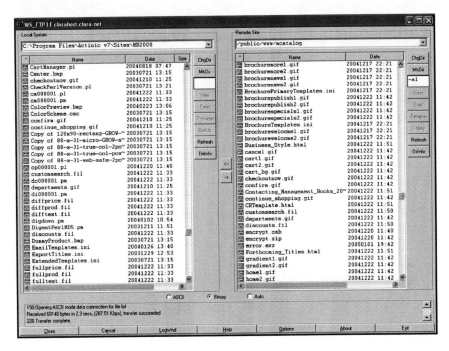

Fig 2.6.11. Most HTML editors have FTP capabilities, but separate FTP software may offer greater functionality.

Regardless of whether you use Dreamweaver or a separate piece of FTP software you will need at least three pieces of information to access your space:

- FTP address
- username
- password.

When you design your website, you can set up the FTP information to allow files to be easily transferred at the click of a button.

There may be additional information, such as a host directory or port, however if this is relevant your ISP will supply it along with the above information, and it will only be relevant if you cannot connect using the information above. If you are working from an office you may also require firewall and proxy settings. Your network administrator will be able to provide this information. Ticking the 'Passive transfer' box is always worthwhile, as this solves many connection problems that occur when a firewall is involved. Dreamweaver has a 'Test' button that will immediately tell you if it has problems accessing your web space.

Instead of you simply uploading files into the root directory that you immediately connect to, many ISPs will give you FTP access to one level above where the web browser actually hits. For example, when you FTP in you might see a folder marked \cgi-bin and another marked \www, \html, \htdocs or any other name that could signify that this is where your HTML files might live. If this is the case you will need to specify this within Dreamweaver so that it knows to synchronise at the subdirectory level. Just enter the directory name in the Host Directory field within Dreamweaver's Remote Info screen.

Whether it is built into your web design tool or is a standalone program, FTP software works the same. Once connected to your server you will be presented with two panels – one shows the information stored on your local hard drive, and the other shows the server. Good FTP software (including Macromedia Dreamweaver MX) will have a 'synchronise' facility that compares the time stamps of local and remote files, then uploads or downloads the most recent version of each file to ensure that both match. This can, however be a dangerous tool, so only use it when you are sure that no-one else is amending code, and that all of your pages are just static HTML (e.g. no dynamic databases or scripts) otherwise you or your colleagues may inadvertently overwrite new content.

Step 12 – Letting others add content in the future

It may be that you wish to continue developing the site while allowing others to add and maintain content. This can be fraught with problems, not least the possibility of others overwriting your code as mentioned above. There are several online and offline tools available that allow users with little or no HTML experience to add or modify pages. Macromedia Dreamweaver has a baby sister in this department – Macromedia Contribute. The web designer maintains the look and feel of the site in Dreamweaver, but allocates editable regions that other staff can access through Contribute. He or she then issues 'keys' for Contribute users, who can then use the software's built-in web browser to access pages on the site, clicking Edit to gain control over the content. Contributeworks in a very similar way to a word processor, so if someone is reasonably familiar with Microsoft Word they will easily be able to master Contribute! Once done, the user clicks 'Save and Update' and the website is immediately updated. The web designer can then synchronise his copy with the live version to ensure no data is overwritten.

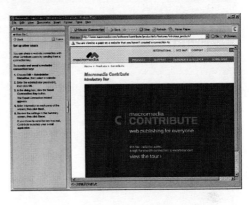

Fig 2.6.12. Macromedia Contribute allows 'non-techies' the ability to edit sites developed in Dreamweaver.

As mentioned at the beginning of the chapter there are completely online CMS tools that allow users with limited web skills to maintain web content. While many of these are easy to use they lack the flexibility that many sites may need. A viable and powerful alternative to Macromedia Contribute-powered site is Typo3, which uses PHP scripts and a MySQL database to build and maintain a site purely through a web browser. This open source program is actually free, but is also quite complex for the beginner. Installation is similar to that of CMS systems such as PHP-Nuke, covered in detail in chapter 2.8; however where Typo3 differs is its comprehensive array of site-building options. Its user level security is also as good, if not better than many of the standard CMS systems available, giving you the flexibility to specify who can change what on your site. While you can build a good site with Typo3, you would be doing it purely online through a web browser. Typo3 actually builds and stores the site within the SQL database, whereas Contribute allows users to modify raw HTML that was created in Dreamweaver. If you already have a HTML-based website that you want others to update, Typo3 is not really an option, but if you are starting from scratch it is certainly worth considering. You can test the system yourself using their demo site at **http://demo.typo3.com** (see overleaf).

Future-proofing your site
Just because your site works well now, that does not mean to say it will continue to work in the future, even if it is only a collection of static pages. The World Wide Web is constantly evolving, with new standards emerging

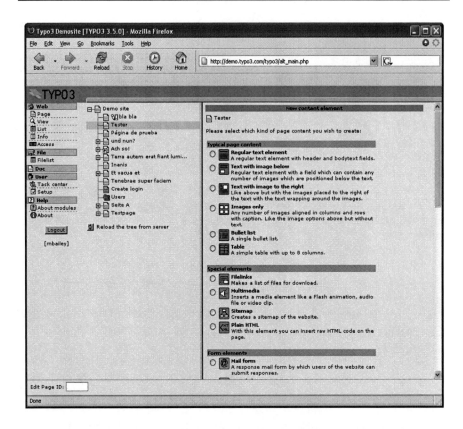

Fig 2.6.13. Typo3 offers a free online website creation and collaboration tool, but watch out for the steep learning curve.

and old standards being phased out. For example, tables and font tags will ultimately be replaced with CSS (cascading style sheets) - where will this leave your site? When Windows XP Service Pack 2 was released in September 2004 it caused web designers no end of problems as the new security measures in place automatically blocked plug-ins and scripts that delivered genuine functionality but were seen as security threats. In many cases, entire menu navigation systems simply disappeared! Admittedly users only have to click on a bar at the top of the screen, but non web-savvy individuals who only know that they should not click on items that they don't understand cannot distinguish between an overprotective computer and a genuine threat.

While Internet Explorer still has a vice-like grip over the browser market,

Mozilla's Firefox is gaining ground, so make sure that your site works well in both. Using templates will help to minimise the pain as for the majority of your page content you will only have to check/modify one page. It pays to subscribe to an internet magazine to keep an eye on new standards and the problems that other designers are coming across because of them.

Summary

❑ Remember, a website is never finished, unlike any other media you develop – it continually develops and grows. Before putting your site live don't forget to optimise it for search engines. The CEO of one of the world's largest internet development companies once told me: *'Whatever you do, get something live now. You can add to it as you go, but if you try to put live a completely finished site with all the functionality you want, it will simply put you months behind your competitors.'* Wise words! Split your site up into stages and concentrate on getting the Stage 1 site live.

❑ Where feasible, allow others to add and maintain content to ensure that your website is the first port of call for new information – spreading the load will help the site evolve quicker. With a basic site built, optimised and up and running you can start submitting to search engines, advising your customers and generally get your brand established online.

❑ Stay abreast of web technology by subscribing to one of the many Internet magazines available. In the UK, .net magazine is one of the best, with a dedicated 'web builder' section that has provided me with many useful snippets of code and information over the years. Ensure your site conforms to the latest web standards.

2.7

How to: Sell Your Products Online – Adding Ecommerce

On the CD

- E-commerce Software
- Web Design Software
- Web links

If you have products that lend themselves to being sold online, then you will want to add this facility to your site. These will generally be off-the-shelf products with a quick sales cycle that can be sold either over the counter or over the phone.

Products that might sell well over the web include:

- books, CDs, DVDs
- games and toys
- electronic hardware and software.

How you write your site will depend very much on your e-commerce requirements. If you're writing your site from scratch, and have a lot of information to add that would be outside of your online store, make this the first priority and only start working on integrating e-commerce once your basic site is live. Failure to do this WILL result in a delay of weeks or even months before your site goes live.

The product or method of development you select will depend on your requirement, technical capabilities and budget. There are four main routes you can take in building your online store:

- small cart embedded into existing pages
- offline catalogue that is generated and uploaded
- online catalogue maintained through a web browser
- custom-built solution.

Solution 1 – The small cart

It is a myth that e-commerce is expensive to integrate at every level – obviously the more functionality and customisation you require, the more bespoke the solution and costly the development will be, but adding a basic shopping cart to a small number of products has never been easier. There are several companies that allow you to process payments online, with PayPal being the most well known (mainly as they are a part of online auction giant Ebay). PayPal has a facility that not only gives you the option to add 'Buy Now' buttons against products, but they also have an entire shopping cart facility. They even generate all of the HTML code required to add these buttons to your site – all you have to do is cut and paste it! When a user makes a purchase from your site, PayPal handles the credit card transaction, takes a small percentage (around 3%) for their services and places the money in your PayPal account. An email is sent to you with the customer's order and invoice/shipping details and you can then transfer the funds elsewhere, or use them to buy products on other web sites, including Ebay auctions. The customer also receives an email confirming their order.

Adding the PayPal shopping cart to your site

Firstly you need to create a PayPal account (this is free). Visit their website (**www.paypal.com**) and follow the prompts. It is worthwhile reading the help files online to get a good understanding of how PayPal works. Now go into the 'Sell' section of their website – this offers a variety of tools, but you'll be interested in one of the following:

- shopping cart
- single item purchase
- donations
- subscriptions.

The process for creating the relevant code for each of the above is similar, so let's assume you have 10 products on your site, either on their own pages or on one single page. The most suitable product to use would be the shopping cart. This would allow users to buy one or several products using a traditional shopping cart approach.

You can add a shopping cart facility to your existing site in minutes using the tools on PayPal's website.

1. Once logged in, click on the Merchant tools and click on PayPal shopping basket.
2. You now start to create your first product. Fill in all the product information you require, such as item name, product number, price and currency. You can also define other options, such as shipping and sales tax, and option fields (such as colour, size etc). PayPal also has the flexibility to customise much more of the user's shopping experience – you can assign different button images or design your own, specify

success and cancel pages, and include shipping address info and additional user comments/notes.

3. Clicking on the Create Button presents you with a screen with two boxes of code. The first box contains the 'Add to Cart' code. Select all of the text in this box, right click and select Copy. Now open your web design software, open your product page (you may need to do this in 'HTML view') then paste the code where you want your button to appear.

4. Go back to the PayPal page and select all the 'View Cart' code and copy it. Return to your web design software and paste it where you want the View Cart button to be. Normally this would be at the top or bottom of the page. If the page is more than a screen in height it may be better to place it in both positions.

5. You are now ready to test your page. Clicking on the Add to Cart button brings up a pop-up window that will now list your product and give you the opportunity to specify a quantity. Closing this window does not lose the items already in your shopping basket. When you've finished shopping clicking on View Cart will bring up the same window and allow you to proceed to the checkout, where payment and shipping information can be entered.

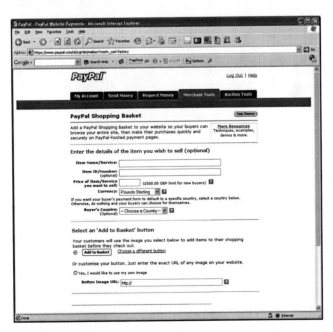

Fig 2.7.2: Creating a shopping cart icon within Paypal's website.

The above example has placed online purchasing for one product only – to add more buttons you will need to repeat step 2 & 3 nine more times to create the ten products required.

More advanced users will be able to modify the code in their web pages to create new buttons without going through this procedure – all you need to do is copy the existing 'Add to Cart' code elsewhere on your page and amend the contents. This brings down the time to create new buttons to literally a few seconds. There is also a free extension for Macromedia Dreamweaver that automates the process, and PayPal integrates with Macromedia Contribute, so others can add and update your store if required. Furthermore, many e-commerce solutions such as Actinic and Zen-Cart, covered in this chapter, also integrate with PayPal.

PayPal is a great solution if you have a small number of products or have the skills and resources to manage a larger stock range. However, you may reach a critical mass and need to move onto a full catalogue solution. When this occurs, you will have to re-key your product range into the new system as there is no way to export your product list into an importable format.

Solution 2 – The offline catalogue package

There are hundreds of shareware and commercial products available that will offer you the next step for e-commerce and this book cannot do them all justice. The word 'Offline' makes reference to the fact that you build the product database on your PC, and then upload it to your website. The server handles the shopping cart and checkout transactions only.

With most of these applications, you will have to bear in mind that you may effectively have to control two web sites – your existing one with the basic company information and your online store, controlled by the e-commerce software. This is not as frightening or as work-intensive as it may seem once the system is set up, but the real challenge lies in integrating the new software to look and feel like the rest of your site. In fact, it may even be easier to modify your existing pages to look like your store pages!

Will you need to run two sites?

Actinic may even be able to replace your need to develop and maintain the other pages of your site. The ability to create 'brochure pages' is included, so you could create About Us, Contact Us and other pages from within the catalogue software. The downside is that these are limited in design structure, so if your other pages have any level of complexity you may have to compromise a little on design or content. Therefore replacing your existing site altogether is likely only to be suitable to those that mainly want an online store. More recent versions of Actinic Catalog and Business have resolved some of the previous restrictions.

Of the many commercial packages available, we will take a look at Actinic Catalog, a low-cost (approx £400/$660) that not only gives you an easy interface to build your store offline, but also takes care of order management and stock control, and can be integrated with many existing credit card payment partners. There are also several other modules available, such as links to Sage accounts and a separate Order Manager (where the site owner only wants to process orders). Actinic Catalog also has a big brother – Actinic Business – designed for sites that require a more complex pricing and user structure. You can configure a wide variety of discounts (such as per user, 'buy one, get one free', buy 2 of A and get B half price etc), and then give users unique passwords to access the site to view and order at their reduced prices without everyone else seeing them. You can easily upgrade from Catalog to Business if required in the future – this only requires the purchase of a software 'key' to unlock the additional features.

One limitation of stores built in this fashion is that they are not 'dynamic'. When visiting stores such as Amazon, the page is built based upon your previous and current buying/browsing patterns. If you bought a book on gardening, Amazon recommends similar books or might recommend some gardening products. This practice is known as 'cross-selling' and is the online equivalent of saying to your customers 'would you like fries with that?' Sites that are built offline and uploaded are static – while you can manually set up alternative products it does require some effort, both initially and as the site develops.

Adding an Actinic Catalog to your site

Building the catalogue and adding the content is the easy part – customising the look and feel, then getting the whole thing online is where the skill comes in and it may be a better use of your own time to pay an expert to do the latter for you, allowing you to concentrate on getting the content right. Actinic does ship with dozens of templates, all of which can be quickly colour co-ordinated, so if you're happy to work with one of their standard layouts all you need to do is drop in your logo – this is covered in more detail further on.

Step 1 – Get the right web space

Actinic uses a language known as CGI scripts to handle the processing of your web store, and the server that your website is hosted on will need to support this. Most commercial ISPs support it to some degree, but it is worth checking before wasting time trying to solve a problem that is unsolvable due to a non-existent service. Actinic provides a document that you can email to your ISP's support desk to confirm that they can do what you need, and also provide you with the settings required to get your site up and running. It is worth asking your ISP if they support Actinic – if they do then they should be able to immediately provide the settings you'll need.

Assuming that your existing provider is suitable, or you have subsequently moved your site to another host, you will need to re-assess the amount of web space you have. Nowadays 50MB is the norm, but if you have a product range of thousands, this will be quickly eaten away. This may not be something you need to worry about straight away, but make a note to keep an eye on the space available. One problem with Actinic is that when you delete a product from your database it does not delete any associated images, so these will remain on your web server forever unless you make a point of deleting them remotely. For companies with a relatively static or slow-changing product range this will not be a problem.

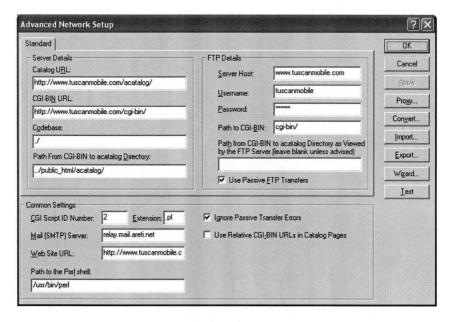

Fig 2.7.3. The Actinic Network setup screen requires basic information to get a comprehensive store online.

Step 2 – Configure Actinic's Network Wizard
In the same way that you added FTP details to your web design or FTP software in the previous chapter, you will also need to add this information

to Actinic. A handy wizard is included that takes much of the pain out of configuring Actinic to talk to your website, however additional information is needed. If you sent Actinic's technical information request form off to your ISP they should have provided you with the necessary data. Once you've run the wizard (and the tests all respond positively) you are actually in a position to upload your site and take orders, but it will not yet blend into the rest of your site.

Step 3 – Customise the look and feel of your pages

This is where your HTML skills (or those of a friend or consultant) will come in. The aim here is to make your store pages look like the pages on your existing site, and include navigation to relevant pages so that users cannot tell the difference when browsing between the two. As mentioned previously you may decide to turn this on its head – Actinic is supplied with a plethora of predefined themes that will require little in the way of customisation, except for adding your logo. You can change the themes as many times as you want without destroying the product information you have added to the catalogue, but if you customise the underlying HTML code, subsequent theme changes will overwrite this – only experts need be concerned with this!

If you decide to customise Actinic to look like your existing site you should pick a theme that is closest to your existing design, then open the Template Manager. There are two views available, a graphical view and a tabular view. The graphical option shows all of the areas of a page – clicking an area brings up the relevant slice of HTML code, which you can then tweak, test and revise. The tabular view gives you access to the same information, but through several screens of buttons, linked in a flow-chart fashion following the order of pages. You may also want to change some of the graphics to be more in line with your current look and feel – this involves only copying them from your existing site into the Actinic site directory.

Changing site colours to match your corporate identity is easy. All of Actinic's template graphics can be tweaked using the 'Color Scheme' menu. Chose from one of the dozen colour schemes, then tweak it further using the swatches on the right side of the screen. Once saved the entire Actinic site is updated in seconds to reflect your selections.

If you decide to opt for one of Actinic themes, and are not using Actinic to replace your existing site you'll then have to change the look and feel of the main site to match the catalogue. This is not as scary as it sounds, especially if you used a single template to create all of your pages. Depending on your level of experience you can even use one of Internet Explorer's more hidden tricks to do most of the work for you. Preview your Actinic site in your web browser, then select File, Save, and select Save as

Fig 2.7.4. Actinic can change the colours of all template schemes easily using a single dialog box.

Complete Web Page – place the files somewhere within your existing website's location on your PC. Now open the page up in your web design software and strip out all the content in the middle of the page where your main content would normally appear. You will have to get your hands dirty and strip out some additional code that Actinic adds in (such as the box that displays the number of items currently in your shopping basket), but to anyone with a general knowledge of HTML, this will not prove too much of a problem. Now for the masterstroke – save this page as a template, specify the main area as the editable region, and then apply this template to all the other pages. You've just converted your entire existing site to the new Actinic template!

If you do need to dig a little within the Actinic templates (easily identifiable within the \Site1 folder as files starting with Act_), there is a free plugin for Macromedia Dreamweaver that allows you to view one of your catalog pages and identify which part of a template is used to build a particular element of a page. Every Actinic page consists of data pulled from dozens of sub-templates, so this is a handy utility for quickly identifying which files you might need to edit to change a specific area of a page.

Step 4 – Adding your products

Creating a store within Actinic is simplicity itself. Once the software is installed, you are presented with a dummy set of products (pictured on the following page) that demonstrate the various product configurations you can have – you can safely delete these once you have familiarised yourself with constructing them. All products are built into a navigation tree; similar to the way you would navigate through Windows Explorer. You start by building your root categories – these are the first options your user will see when they enter the store.

Taking the example shown, this would give you:

- Basic Products
- Products with a range of options
- Products with optional extras
- Products built from add-ons
- Select items from a list

If we take the 'Products with a range of options' category, you will see a sub-category and two products:

- Choice dependent pricing (sub-category)
- Pair of men's walking boots
- Set of fragranced candles

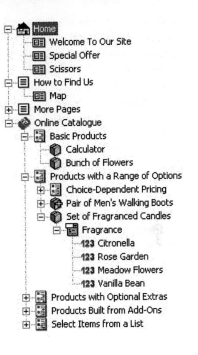

Fig 2.7.5. The Actinic catalogue tree

Building a category consists of right clicking over the place you want the category to appear (in this case at the root of your online store), selecting Product Group and filling in the information in the popup window. Adding products follows a similar path, but this will be a more time-consuming task, as you will no doubt want to assign more information to your products. The tree structure pictured right shows an example of how Actinic displays products and categories.

If you already have your product information stored in another database such as your accounts software, there is a much easier way to get this information into Actinic via an export/import feature. If you can extract all of the necessary information from your source database in standard CSV (comma separated values) format you can then easily insert the entire product range into Actinic using a wizard to map fields form the source file to their correct destination. You will, however have to re-sort the products into their relevant categories afterwards, although this is a substantially lesser workload than re-entering all of your products. A long-term solution to this is also available – if you can create another field in your source database you can store information relating to where you want the product to appear in your catalogue, so that when you export your data this information is passed to Actinic, and all of the products will simply drop into the right categories.

Images can easily be associated with products, but you should try to maintain a standard size for all graphics – 150 pixels width by 200 pixels in height would be a good maximum to set. An excellent tip for adding images to a large catalogue is to visit your suppliers' web sites and take the images for use in your own, but make sure you have permission to do so. Associating the graphic with the product within Actinic Catalog is as easy as right clicking over the image, selecting Save As and placing it in your Actinic site directory. Then, within Actinic, you open up the product information box and associate the graphic with it. It is worth also saving a smaller thumbnail image, as this can be shown during search results.

You can preview either a single page or your entire catalogue at any time to see how your product pages look. Try to limit pages to about two screen lengths by splitting them into sub-categories. Not only will they load quicker but by breaking down your products into distinct categories users will find what they want quicker and search engines will rank the page higher as it will invariably contain a higher concentration of relevant keywords.

Step 5 – Uploading and testing your store

If you've got to this stage, all the hard work required to build your store is over. Uploading a site within Actinic requires only a single mouse click on the Up arrow icon in the toolbar (pictured on the following page). Actinic will then busily chat with your web server, check which files have changed and upload them to your site. Depending on the size of your site and the speed of your connection this can take anything from 30 seconds to a couple of hours (in very extreme cases). Once done you can test your store by typing in your web address and adding /acatalog/ at the end of it – this is the folder that Actinic places your store in.

Fig 2.7.6. The one step to getting your entire catalogue online

Although this stage is technically simple, it should not be passed over quickly – this is where you must test your site to make sure that the user's browsing and buying experience is as simple and informative as possible.

Another important item to check is that Meta tags are added to each category within your catalogue. Meta tags are relevant keywords that search engines use to gauge the relevance of your page and are covered in detail in the next chapter on website promotion. These are not visible when people view the web page, but search engines will compare them against the visible content on the page. You can add the relevant words by opening the category within Actinic, clicking on the Meta tags tab and adding in keywords that relate to the products within that category that users might key into a search engine. These will generally be many of the words that describe the products on the page itself.

Step 6 – Modifying your existing site
Assuming you are not using Actinic to handle all of your pages you will now need to link to your catalogue from your existing pages. This is where you thank your lucky stars that you used a template! Just open the template, add in a button or text link called 'online store' or whatever you choose, hyperlink it to www.yourdomain.com/acatalog/ and save the changes – all of your pages will be updated.

It is also advantageous to add key products to your home page to drive traffic directly to these pages. As Actinic does create rather long web addresses the simplest way to do this would be to insert the picture of the product into your home page, open Internet Explorer, find the product within your live catalogue and copy the URL in the address bar. Now paste this into the hyperlink field within your web design software.

As mentioned previously it is worth noting that Actinic Catalog and Business does now have a comprehensive brochure page option, so it may be better to ditch your current site and pull the content into Actinic. For the HTML-savvy amongst you, it's easy to add raw code into a brochure page, so all you are using Actinic for is to generate the menu and basic outline of the page – you have complete control of everything else. By using brochure pages you'll eliminate your need to effectively use two software products to maintain two sites.

Solution 3 – The online catalogue solution
This solution is similar to Actinic in that it is suitable for large numbers of products and can be customised and maintained relatively easily. The difference is that it is a purely web-based solution that stores your products in a database kept on the server. For this section we will focus on Zen-Cart – an open source (and therefore free) comprehensive shopping cart solution. You may also want to consider OScommerce, another open source

project, which Zen-Cart is based upon. There are several CMS systems that have reasonable shopping cart systems available, and these may be better if you wish to create a site that has a shopping cart as only one of several facilities on the site. See the following chapter on general CMS systems.

Zen-Cart can be installed on any server running MySQL and PHP, both of which are open source and common services supported by most ISPs. It offers most of the features found in other products such as Actinic Catalog without requiring software to be installed – products are added through a web browser.

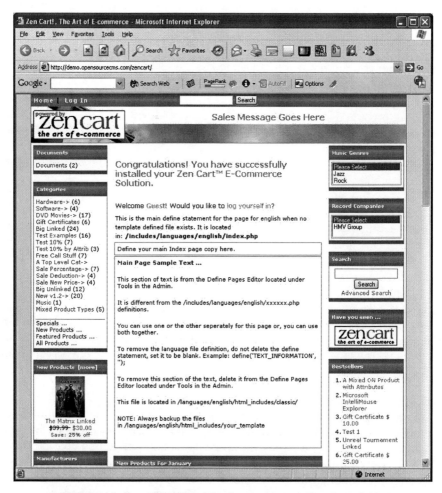

Fig 2.7.7. A standard Zen-cart front screen after installation.

Step 1 – Obtaining Zen-Cart

This is the easy part! Go to **www.zen-cart.com** and follow the links to the download section. This normally takes you to a link to the Sourceforge site (home to thousands of open source applications). Select the most recent version and download it from the nearest server location. Unpack the files to your system locally and open the install.txt file that is located in the root directory.

Step 2 – Uploading Zen-Cart

Assuming that the installation method has not changed radically since the time of writing, the next stage is to transfer the files you downloaded to your web space. The install.txt file will tell you precisely what to do. If Zencart is going to contain your entire website, then upload it to the root folder, but if you intend to have Zencart only as a part of your site, then create a subfolder and upload it there. The upload could take over an hour, even on a high speed connection due to the number of small files that are being uploaded and error checked through the standard FTP upload process. Depending on your web server you may also need to change the permissions of some files and directories to 'writeable' - this is normally referred to as 'CHMOD-ing'. Check the installation documentation for additional information on this.

Once done, run the installation script, located at www.yourdomain.com/zc_install/. This will take you through a wizard, prompting for relevant information on each screen. The most important information to enter correctly is the text relating to your MySQL server access – this will have been provided by your ISP and will consist of the MySQL database name, username and password (which in many cases will be similar to your FTP login details). Once you have set this, along with your other main site preferences, you're ready to go!

One of the strengths of Zen-Cart is that it integrates with a popular open source forum system – phpBB. This means that your users will have one username and password to access both areas on your site, not only making their lives easier but giving a better overall impression.

Before proceeding to the next step, it is wise to follow the security precautions documented in the installation guide. This suggests deleting the installation files (stopping someone from overwriting your system with the default settings) and changing the permissions of specific files. This is very important if you do not want to leave your system open to abuse from chance hackers.

Note: One of the options allows you to insert demo data into the system – only do this if you have an easy method of deleting the data from the database later (by means of a tool such as phpMyAdmin) otherwise you will have to manually delete this, which will probably take hours! If you need to play around with a system, why not use the sample system on **www.opensourcecms.com**, which is reset every two hours.

Step 3 – Administering your site

If you've got this far without any errors, then it's safe to say that you are over the most complex part. All that needs to be done now is for your site to be set up the way you want it. This can be a time-consuming process if you want to give your visitors a professional impression.

- Before you enter any data, consider the graphics you will use for your products and categories. Work out a specific size (something of around 100 x 60 pixels for category images will suffice, but change this to suit)
- Start by entering as many of the manufacturers of the products you sell (in the Catalog I Manufacturers section at www.yourdomain.com/ [zencart_folder]/admin/). Zen-cart allows users to search by manufacturer, or see other products by the same manufacturer when viewing each product
- Before adding in your products, ensure that you have your currencies and countries configured. If you sell worldwide, then you can leave the countries as they are, but if you are limiting your sales to one or a handful of countries, then delete the ones you don't want. Add in all of the currencies you wish to use, along with the appropriate exchange rate – you will need to keep this updated or you could lose out if the rates take a tumble.
- Configure your taxation requirements.
- Configure your shipping and payment methods.

Now you can start to add in your categories and products. Try to provide a comprehensive and logical hierarchy of categories that will not restrict your products but without being overly complicated. Remember, you can create subcategories later and move products into them if required

Step 4 – Changing the look and feel of your site

Within the Admin section of the site, the Tools menu contains the majority of the options you'll need to modify the site. Zen-Cart has a number of templates available, and these can be further customised with a little skill. Visit **www.zen-cart.com** to gain access to dozens of free templates, as well as additional modules and functionality.

Start by selecting the template you want to use. The 'Template Selection' option displays the currently installed templates. Adding new templates is a simple case of downloading new ones from Zen-Cart's website, then uploading them to the templates sub-folder of your web space. Click on Edit within Template Selection, choose your template from the dropdown menu on the right, and then click on Update. You can now preview your chosen theme.

Once you've got a theme you like you'll need to add in your logo. That's as simple as overwriting the Zen-cart logo with your own. If you want to do more customising expect to dig into the code a little, but as Zen-cart relies heavily on CSS this does make life a little easier – just change the one style sheet file to make site-wide changes.

The site should now have the general corporate identity you want, but may still be displaying information that is irrelevant. For example, maybe you don't want users to be able to select products by manufacturer if you are the manufacturer of every product. If you don't sell music you'll have little need for the music genres box. Thankfully all of these can be toggled on or off, and the position and sort order of the box can also be changed.

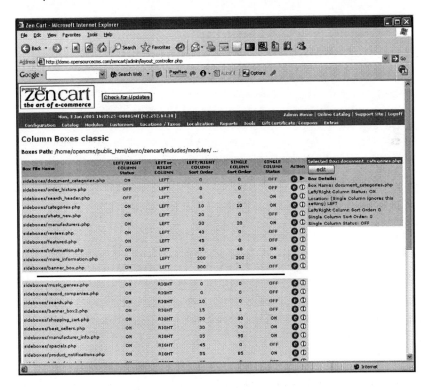

Fig 2.7.8 Moving, enabling or disabling column boxes is simple in Zen-cart

Carry on working your way through the extensive menu system to tweak your site as you need to. Zen-cart offers many features that you'll want to use, but some that you won't, so don't be afraid to switch off features that you'll never need. Other areas you'll need to consider/configure might be:

- pricing policies and discounting structures
- emails sent to customers
- cross-selling by product type, genre, manufacturer etc.

Zen-cart is more complex to set up than offline solutions (see below), but then again it is a more comprehensive solution. Taking the time at this stage to structure your products and site correctly will pay dividends in the long-term by providing a robust site that provides visitors with a positive shopping experience that makes it easy to find products.

Zen-cart vs Actinic – which is better?

The answer to this lies in several questions.

- **?** How comprehensive or complex a site do you need?
- **?** What are the skills of those that will be maintaining the site?
- **?** Do you want/need the ability to cross-sell with every product, and how automated do you want this process to be?

Zen-cart does have advantages over Actinic, essentially because it can generate pages live as customers are on the site, changing the browsing and buying experience based upon its databases. If a user is looking at a particular movie, Zen-cart can automatically display other movies in the same genre. On the front page it can also show a 'Most Popular' product list that is dynamically generated. The downside to this comprehensiveness is complexity. A novice might find Zen-cart perplexing to install and daunting to configure at first glance, but the price tag of zero might just be enough to tempt many onto the e-commerce ladder.

As Actinic is an offline-based product (in the sense that pages are built offline and orders are downloaded and handled within Actinic) it does have strengths over Zen-cart. It can be linked directly into accounts systems such as Sage or interfaced with other systems such as MRP (material requirements planning). But for many it will be the ease of entry into e-commerce. It is quite feasible for someone without any web knowledge to build and upload a respectable store within hours – that same person would fare very differently with Zen-cart.

Another point to consider is the search engine friendliness of your site. Actinic generates static HTML pages, whereas Zen-cart will build pages as they are requested by the user, generating long URLs which some search engines cannot or will not follow (although Google can spider dynamic sites).

Still not sure which one to use? Then why not try them both before you decide? There is a 30-day trial of Actinic on the CD accompanying this book, and you can test Zen-cart (both the store and the admin screens) at **www.opensourcecms.com** – note that this site is reset to a 'virgin' installation every two hours, and other users might be dabbling with the settings at the same time! Alternatively, if you have a server that supports PHP and mySQL, you can install and test it at your leisure.

Solution 4 – The custom-built site

A custom-built solution should only be considered if any of the following apply.

● You have a stock list of tens of thousands of parts that an off-the-shelf product cannot handle.

● You cannot categorise or configure your products to fit within the framework of an off-the-shelf product, to the degree that visitors to your site would not be able to find or easily price the right product. An example of this might be a power cable supplier that sells several different core thickness of cable at several voltages in several lengths – in paper form this could be displayed with a simple table but within a product such as Actinic each column in the table might need to be a separate product.

● You need the system to show absolute live information, thus requiring your web server to be connected live to your stock control database – this could actually be done with the previously mentioned Zen-cart if it were hosted on a server within your company and your stock control system could write directly to the mySQL database.

● You need a complete end-to-end solution whereby orders placed on the website are seamlessly fed into your Sales Order Processing system and processed without human intervention, perhaps also with automatic accounts checking for customers who have a line of credit with your company – this could be partially achieved with both Actinic and Zen-cart (but only if Zen-cart were hosted internally and additional modules/interfaces were written). You would need to decide whether the extra level of automation is worth the cost of a complete bespoke solution.

Here we are using the label of 'custom-built' to mean a full online catalogue that may also communicate automatically with your existing product and sales data systems and is tailored to specifically fit your product and business model. There's no beating about the bush – this level of customisation is not going to come cheap. Firstly, you are likely to need your own server, costing several thousand dollars. This may need to be hosted in-house to allow it to be securely linked to your live database, requiring a high-speed permanent Internet connection to your offices (normal ADSL or cable may not even be acceptable under the ISP's terms and conditions, and also from a technical standpoint as they generate a unique IP address for you every time you switch on the computer, making it unsuitable for hosting your own web server). And this is even before you start to have applications written using one of several server-side languages such as ASP, Cold Fusion, PHP, Perl etc. You will either need to contract or fully employ one or even several staff to build and maintain the system, or hire an outside company to develop the application for you.

This book cannot even begin to cover every eventuality of a custom built solution, and if you're reading this last section with seriousness then your requirement is going to be pretty unique. If you need to scope the job for development, then the best way forward is as follows.

- Create your fundamental requirement list in as much detail as possible along with a flowchart of how the site will work both from the customer's perspective and interaction with existing systems and software. Provide mock-up screens showing how data will be displayed and captured.
- Examine the security issues – can someone hack your web server and obtain customer information?
- Ensure you select a server-side technology (such as ASP, PHP or Cold Fusion) that can be supported in the event of your supplier going out of business.
- Define a staged project plan to see whether you can get some functions live first – if, for example you can allow customers to get their product and pricing information before online ordering can go live this will at least reduce the number of calls your sales desk receives. Before you go live to all customers test the system with a select few so that bugs can be ironed out.
- Ensure that adequate internal resources are allocated to drive the project forward. Also, make sure that this project receives sponsorship from management at the highest level – failure to achieve this will result in it taking second place to other work, ultimately hampering or even dooming the project altogether.

Summary

❑ If you don't have an online store, you are missing out on an exceptionally cost-effective sales process. The longer you leave it the more you are potentially losing.

❑ Setting up e-commerce need not cost the earth if off-the-shelf packages such as Actinic or Zen-cart can fit the bill, as they deliver immediate shopping cart functionality with relatively low technical requirements in comparison to bespoke systems.

❑ PayPal offers a simple solution for small online stores, and can also deliver a swift means of taking credit cards through other e-commerce systems.

❑ Bespoke systems can offer the ultimate in functionality and automation, but be prepared to have deep pockets!

2.8

How to: Build a Web Portal/Content Management System

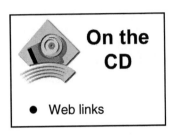

On the CD

- Web links

This chapter can serve two very different types of audience – those that are looking for a site built with the minimal of exposure to web code, and those looking to build a comprehensive site with a wide range of content, features and services, e.g. a web portal. Both sites are generally built and maintained with the same tool – a Content Management System (CMS).

Note: There is little on the accompanying CD relating to this chapter (apart from links) due to the constant development of CMS systems. They are constantly being updated, patched and even superseded, so do your homework before choosing the software you'll use to build your site, as you will be stuck with it for some time!

A web portal is commonly referred to as simply a portal, and is a website that offers a broad array of resources and services, such as forums, search engines, news, online shopping etc. AOL was one of the first web portals, but many search engines followed suit, Yahoo being a notable example. Predominantly, the content that generally keeps visitors coming back is downloads, news and forums. Many web portals focus on niche markets, becoming authorities in their selected field. They are the one-stop-shop in their industry.

You may already have a company website, but feel that you can provide a wider range of information to a larger audience within your business sector through a separate, perhaps differently branded site. If you have the time, skill and resources to build it, a portal can generate revenue, sales leads and a certain level of kudos for your company and yourself. Alternatively you might want to rebuild your existing company website into a much larger resource, and open up the publishing of content to a wider team of staff internally.

225

Where the term Content Management System (CMS) comes into play is the method by which administrators add new material to the site, plus the link of all content within the site (for example, linking news stories to a certain company etc). A CMS system normally consists of the content management application (CMA) and a content delivery application (CDA). The CMA allows the site author to manage the creation, modification and deletion of content from the site, while the CMA compiles this information and updates the website. In other words, the CMA is the back end that you use to add content, and the CDA is what your customers will see.

What content and services should a Portal offer?

The answer to this will very much depend on the individual, so ask yourself which sites you go to for specific things (such a news, sports, hobbies, technical information etc) and consider why you go there. The answer is simple – you go to these sites because you can get what you want easily, and the site offers the breadth of information for your chosen topic, with fresh content added frequently.

At the very least, your portal should offer news stories along with a search system. There are a variety of other features you can offer:

Calendar: List of forthcoming events and exhibitions, perhaps linking to the event holder's website.

Trade Associations or important organisations: Details of relevant trade organisations and important companies serving your industry.

Magazines: List of trade journals for your industry.

Books etc: list of relevant books, videos, DVDs, CDs, perhaps even drawing content from Amazon or similar providers.

Discussion Groups: Online forums, allowing users to ask questions to 'industry specialists'. This is the biggest draw for many sites. Live chat systems are also popular, although as none of the messages are stored there is less content stored. Many sites see much of their traffic from search engines that have spidered and stored messages in forums.

Surveys/Polls: Not only a great way to get people to interact with your site but also an excellent source of information. You could even send out a press release with your survey results – great PR with very little effort!

Technical articles: How-to guides or in-depth articles about specific subjects. Again, these are great crowd-pullers as they contain great 'search engine fodder'.

Classified Ads: Allow people to advertise products or services on your site.

Auctions: Allow people to sell their products online. (Unless you are in a niche market you might have problems competing with the mighty Ebay).

Downloads: Any relevant software or information that can be distributed electronically.
Subscription services: Allow people to subscribe to receive a newsletter.
Online store: Allow people to buy products or services online.
Site Search: All the above sections tied together through a single search screen.

Portal revenue streams

You can generate revenue from a variety of methods, the most obvious being banner advertising. Adding random or fixed banners across a website is commonplace, although with everyone clamouring for advertising spends, it's unlikely to be your biggest revenue stream unless you have a respected site/brand. It is worthwhile signing up to Google's AdSense service, covered back in Chapter 1.10.

The next option is through selling products/services on the site. If you have a books section on your site, it would be relatively straightforward to sign up as an Amazon.com associate, gaining a percentage of sale value for every product purchased as a result of a link on your site. Amazon has several levels of both affiliation and integration – you can offer a 'search Amazon' facility, link directly to specific products or pull content directly from their site, with the different options offering a sliding scale of revenue from resulting sales. There are numerous different affiliate programmes available, some of which may be specific to your industry, so a quick search on Google might be worth a try.

For portals offering an online directory service, a 'Yellow-pages' style approach can be adopted. Basic listings can be added for free, with enhancements being paid for (such as bold listing, link to website etc). Classified ads work in a similar way – basic listing for free, or pay for enhanced exposure.

Busy auction sites can also produce good income through the sale of listing enhancements and auction fees. A percentage of sale value is automatically charged at the end of each auction. Listing enhancements might include bold listings, inclusion of one or additional pictures and top placements in a chosen category.

With many CMS systems offering e-commerce plugins, you can easily add an online store to your site. If all you require is the ability to list products and provide a basic shopping cart facility, then most should suit your purpose.

The architecture of a portal

As with building any web project, there are two main options to select –

whether you opt for an in-house developed solution or select an off-the-shelf CMS product. While a home-grown system will give you exactly what you want, it will require a great deal of skill, time and energy to build and maintain. An off-the-shelf product is likely to have most of the features you need and will allow you to get up and running almost straight away.

In-house developed

Although this chapter is mainly geared towards pre-developed CMS-based sites, there are many outstanding portals that are written from the ground up in either HTML or using a scripting language. While it is entirely possible to build a site from straight HTML the downside is that maintaining relevant links manually across multiple pages can be a nightmare. For example, if you have a directory of companies on your site, and then link each news story to the company's directory page, plus place a link on the directory page to each story, you have to manually add a link to at least two pages each time you add a story to the site (which you will also be performing manually). If you decide to develop a site from scratch in-house, you will almost definitely want to have a database-driven solution. Using this method means that you can attach a unique identifier to each story to signify which company it relates to. Dynamic pages can then be built that will list all stories relating to a specific company. The table opposite describes the main differences between a 'flat' HTML and database-driven site.

So you've decided to go the database route – which database solution do you opt for? MS Access, SQL Server, or MySQL? Also, which server platform will you adopt? Windows, Linux, Unix etc? Which server-side language will you use? ASP, Cold Fusion, PHP etc? The answer to all three of these questions will be dependent on your in-house technical expertise and to a lesser degree on your hosting arrangements. In short, if you don't know one of the above languages well, or don't have a great deal of time or money to devote to this project, forget about writing something – go for an off-the-shelf solution.

Off-the-shelf CMS systems

Although there are many commercial CMS systems available, the focus of this book is cost-effective marketing, so for this chapter we will investigate some of the more 'economical' products. There are a literally dozens of free (Open Source) programs available that will allow you to build a comprehensive portal with little or no programming knowledge, such as PHPweblog, PHPNuke (pictured below), PostNuke, PHPSlash, Sips, PHPWebsite and NewsPro. Most of these will require web space that can run PHP code and a MySQL (or similar) database, which are standard

Standard HTML site	Dynamic database-driven site
Benefits	**Benefits**
• Quick to setup	• Site updates and maintains itself (adding one piece of info updates other areas immediately)
• Requires standard/basic web hosting services	• Much richer functionality and user experience
• Can use products such as Macromedia Contribute to allow others to add content, keeping costs low	• More likely to generate traffic/revenue because users will want to come back
• HTML is more search engine friendly	
Drawbacks	**Drawbacks**
• Large sites can be difficult to manage	• Slow to start as structure has to be built before a single page can go live
• Lack of functionality without massive workload (e.g. linking all stories about a company to their company details, ecommerce etc)	• May require more advanced hosting services or even your own server, which can prove costly
• You may end up having to port this over to a dynamic site later on anyway	• Development and support costs will be higher
	• Some construction methods are not so search-engine friendly

services offered by most ISPs. There are some very useful reviews at **www.opensourcecms.com** – if you are considering a system of this type, then you can also test-drive most of the popular systems here.

We mentioned Typo3 – a high-powered CMS – back in chapter 2.6. While this will deliver much the same in terms of functionality and design as a PHPNuke or similar site, the learning curve to get there is substantially steeper. If you are considering a CMS then it is worth investigating, but spend a few hours reading the documentation, try out the demo site and even download and install it yourself if possible. While you will find it more complex than the 'Nuked' sites of this world, it may be that it gives you the level of detailed control and structure needed to build your required site that can easily be maintained by a team of people.

One very positive trait that the Internet has spawned is that of community spirit. The open source developer network is thriving, and as a result there are hundreds of plug-in features available for products such as PHP-Nuke, developed by organisations and individuals alike. While the standard products have plenty of functionality there are many free 'modules' you can

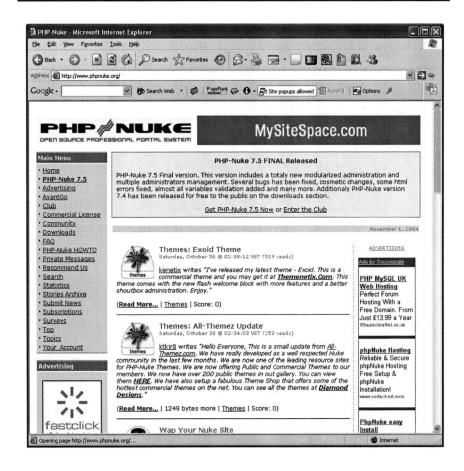

Fig 2.8.1. PHPNuke is one of many low cost/free CMS systems available

plug into your website with minimal technical knowledge. These range from online recipes, games, weather modules, e-commerce systems to even 'joke of the day' modules. PHP-Nuke is also 'skinable', meaning you can download any one of hundreds of different site templates, commonly known as themes. Changing the look of every page of your site is as simple as selecting a template from a dropdown menu in the administration pages and clicking OK.

A criticism of many CMS packages is that they all look very similar – indeed, many of them are based upon the same core system. They all have two or three columns, with similar menu systems and similar navigation.

Also, as many CMS's don't include decent image handling tools, most sites include few or even no graphics with their associated content. When you start to evaluate CMS systems you will immediately pick up on how many seem to be clones of each other, even though there is an abundance of free downloadable themes to customise the overall look.

Building a site with an Open Source CMS system
The main benefit, as mentioned earlier, of an Open Source CMS of this type is 'speed to market' - you could have a system up and running within a few hours of reading this page. Setting a site up is relatively straightforward for anyone with basic HTML and FTP skills. Here's how:

Step 1 – find your web host
You'll need a web host that can offer both PHP and MySQL support. Buy at least 100MB of space, or more if you intend to allow users to upload files to your server. This should not set you back a great deal – on average about £100 per year.

Step 2 – Download your script
You'll need a copy of your chosen CMS system. Getting this is easy – simply go to the vendor's website and follow the links to the download section. At time of writing PHP-Nuke has started charging a negligible ($10) fee for downloading, but all of the others mentioned above are free.

Step 3 – Configure your script
Most CMS systems will have a CONFIG.PHP file (or similarly named) that will require some minor configuration. You have to tell the system where it is going to reside (your server address), your username and password, and your MySQL database name. They may also ask for a database table prefix – this prefixes all of the database table names with a predetermined word, which is useful if you want to remove the system later or if you use other applications within the same MySQL database. Open the relevant file in your favourite HTML editor. Normally the required sections will be clearly marked out by comment sections, or mentioned in an associated 'INSTALL' document.

Step 4 – Upload your scripts
Use an FTP program (such as WS_FTP LE) to upload your files to your web space. Note that you will also have to change the permissions of certain files and folders. Your CMS will need to modify certain files and folders during normal operation, and by default this will be disabled, so you need to tell the system that certain files can be read, written to or executed as a script. This

is known (on Unix servers) as 'CHMOD-ing' the files. Within WS_FTP LE this simply consists of selecting the file or folder to be changed, right-clicking, selecting CHMOD, and then ticking or un-ticking the read/write/execute permissions you wish to apply.

Note: Although the total size of the files you're uploading will only amount to about 30MB they could take several hours to upload – this is because the FTP protocol verifies data for each file uploaded, and there are hundreds (if not thousands) of very small files. If you are using a Windows server and have command prompt access you could upload the zip file and unzip it remotely.

Step 5 – Run the install script
Many scripts have an install script that will create all of the relevant tables within the MySQL database. Follow the instructions within the installation documents. These screens are normally very straightforward, and may ask for the same information you placed in the config.php file. Depending on the CMS you are using you may not need to perform step 6, as the installation script may have done this for you. You will know if you need to perform this task if the demo site is not displayed when you type in your website address.

Step 6 – Importing your table structures into MySQL
Within the source files you downloaded there may be a directory marked SQL. This will contain a file that details all of the tables and fields that will need to be created within MySQL. Your ISP might have a control panel that you can use to import this data. Alternatively you can use the invaluable open source program called PHPMyAdmin (pictured opposite, available at **www.phpmyadmin.net**), which gives you a slick web interface for controlling and backing up your databases.

Step 7 – Test your site
Once you've imported your database tables, uploaded your source files and made the necessary permission changes, you are ready to test fire your site for the first time. Point your web browser to the root directory where you loaded the scripts to – if all has gone well you should be presented with a working dynamically generated front page.

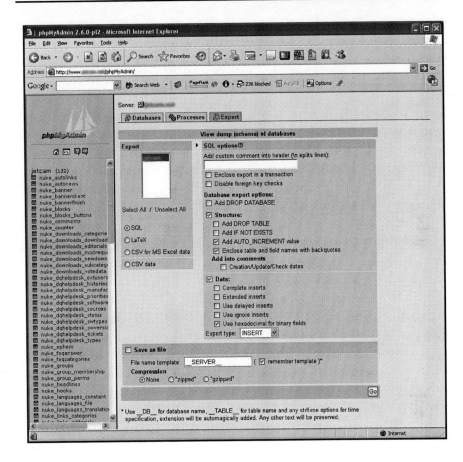

Fig 2.8.2. phpMyAdmin gives an easy method of accessing, building and maintaining mySQL databases – think of it as Access in web browser form!

Step 8 – Go to the Admin section of your site

At this stage you can be relatively confident that the hard part is out of the way. You can now take time to configure your site and get it looking the way you want it. In the administration section (PHP-Nuke's admin section pictured right) you'll be able to create the various categories that will relate to your site's content, set up users and permissions, create your forums, set up online polls and change the site's colour scheme. You can also upload other modules and plug them it seamlessly. It is important to understand the terminology used on the site for specific objects; namely: blocks, content, news, sections, categories and topics. While many of these interlink they offer various ways of segregating your content so that users can quickly find them within relevant parts of your site. Get this right and you'll build a framework that will make your site a joy to use. Get it wrong and you'll end up re-categorising all of your content a few months down the line.

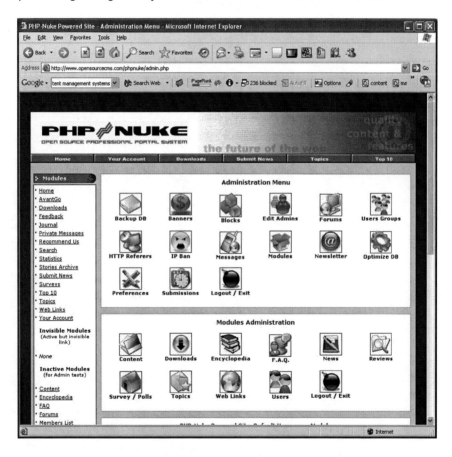

*Fig 2.8.3 The PHPNuke screen provides a simple interface
to design and maintain your site and its content.*

Step 9 – Secure your site
Much has been written on potential security issues that surround some Open Source CMS sites, with PHPNuke specifically coming in for criticism. While some of it may lie at poor coding within the CMS itself, the majority of

sites fall foul of hackers and defacers because they didn't close all of the right security holes. Make sure that your site is secure by following these simple rules:

1. Add a password to the admin directory of your CMS. Your web host might offer tools for applying password to a directory. This will add an extra layer of security to your system.

2. Check the CMS vendor's website for updates. There may be security patches available. Make sure you're running the most up-to-date code. Also search the forums to get any further advice on tightening security – learn by other's mistakes!

Fig 2.8.4. Password-protect important directories.

3. Make sure you change only the write permissions you need to on your server. When you're CHMODing the files on your server, only change the files and directories as directed.

4. Change the standard username from 'admin' to something different. Choose long passwords that include letters and numbers. Some hackers employ programs that will keep hitting sites with different usernames and passwords to gain access. By selecting a non-standard username and long password, you drastically reduce the possibility of hackers getting through (unless they are happy to allow their programs to run literally for days or weeks as the program relentlessly tries millions of permutations).

Step 10 – Add your content

Now that you have a well-structured empty shell it's time to populate it with your content. Although this will probably be quite a time-consuming task, thankfully it is a simple one. Just go to the Admin section, go to the relevant module or section and enter or paste in your text – it's that simple! Where you are adding in news items, you'll be prompted to enter text within specific fields, such as Title, Sub-title, Header text etc. You'll also need to specify the category for your item so that it is correctly catalogued.

As mentioned elsewhere the old adage of 'content is king' is still true. The more content of interest that appears on the site to your target audience, the more value your site is, to both 'real' visitors and search engine spiders. The best thing about having a database-driven site that allows users to interact is that it quickly builds up a following. Forums can generate thousands of words of content every day without your lifting a finger. Allowing users to comment on articles that appear on your site gives the site more personality (and yes, more content!).

Summary

❑ While a home-grown system may cost more and take longer to develop, you will get more of a unique site for your money. Open-source CMS systems can be very 'samey', but if the value of your site is in the content then users will generally forgive the lack of design creativity.

❑ Building a site out of raw HTML will quickly become unmanageable as the site grows so a database-drive site is a must if you want to offer users the functionality they desire without committing too much time to maintenance.

❑ A well-structured CMS system will deliver a powerful and fully-functional site that can easily be maintain by someone with little or no HTML coding experience. Off-the-shelf open source programs are freely available that can be up and running in a matter of hours.

2.9

How to: Publicise your Web Site

On the CD

- E-commerce Software
- Web promotion and analysis tools
- Web links

Building a good website is one thing – getting people to visit it and to keep coming back is entirely another.

There are a variety of ways that you can build awareness and subsequently regular traffic to your site. These can be broken down into two areas – online and offline techniques. We will start with the offline techniques, which are mainly common-sense but often overlooked.

Offline Promotion

'Offline promotion' is defined as the various methods of promoting your website without actually using the Internet, or more to the point, using your existing customer contact methods to get your web address in front of their eyes. This could take many forms, the most common of which are:

- Adding your web address to your letterheads and business cards – this is the most common oversight of many businesses, and the first place your customers are going to look if they want to find your web address.
- Placing your web address on the side or rear of all commercial vehicles. While it is acceptable for a van to have a logo emblazoned across its side, it might be wise to keep a slightly lower profile on executive vehicles. A 40cm x 10cm window sticker might suffice.
- Reminding your staff to ask customers/prospects if they've seen the website, and directing them to relevant content during conversations, such as advising of downloadable brochures or forms if requested. Ensure that staff themselves know what is on the site.
- Printing web and email details on all invoices and quotations.
- Adding your web address to any merchandise given out at exhibitions or seminars.

- Ensuring that your web address appears on all advertising material.
- Mentioning your web address in all press releases.

All of the above are extremely low-cost methods of keeping your domain name in front of customers and prospects. If you are prepared to pay for additional exposure there are plenty of magazines in all industry sectors that now carry one or several pages of 'web guides' - effectively classified advert-style pages allowing companies to advertise their website at a lower cost than taking out general advertising.

Online Promotion

The best methods of promoting your website will of course be online, as this is where the opportunity to attract new customers is at its greatest.

In the same way that you ensure every piece of printed matter has your online details clearly visible, make sure that everything you send electronically does too.

- Ensure that your web address appears as part of your signature in all outgoing emails.
- Also use your web address in any message you post in online forums – this is especially useful for obtaining higher rankings with search engines. This is covered in more detail later on.

Online promotion is where search engines come into play, and it is important to ensure that your site is listed in all of the major search engines.

Getting top listings in search engines is extremely difficult as there are literally over a trillion pages on the web, and rising – don't believe anyone that 'guarantees' you top ranking. Google themselves even tell

Top Search Engines

Below are the main search engines that you need to submit to:

- Google
- Altavista
- Alltheweb
- Yahoo
- MSN Search
- Lycos
- Excite
- Hotbot
- Ask Jeeves
- AOL Search

you that anyone that guarantees this is lying! This is especially true if you are in a mainstream industry as your competitors are all vying for the same space. Remember, someone has to be ranked number 1 and someone has to be ranked number 5,485. But there is a great deal that you can do to increase your chances of getting ranked within the first few pages.

For your page to be ranked higher than a competing site within a search engine, it has to be more relevant to an individual's search than the other site, and there are several stages to achieving this:

Step 1: Decide on your keywords

It cannot be stressed how important the right keywords are, so you should spend time to research the correct keywords for your business. You may be surprised to find out that what you would search for to find your site is entirely different to what others might use.

Keywords are the words or phrases that people are most likely to use to find your product or service within a search engine. They are also the words that you need to place strategically across your site in order to be ranked highly against a specific search.

Start by asking staff what they would search for to find your type of product or services on the web. Ask any prospects that found you over the web what phrases they used. This will start to give you an idea of how differently people can try to find the same information online – everyone thinks differently, so you need to try to compensate for this. Your web stats (covered later on) will also provide this information.

This is just the start – there are several online tools that can help you to select the best words and phrases based on live search data. Of course Google has one such instrument – Sandbox. This free and extremely useful little tool is hidden within their Adwords service, but you can access it directly at the following web address:

https://adwords.google.com/select/main?cmd=KeywordSandbox.

(If this is not working by the time you read this, do a Google search for 'Google Sandbox', or simply create a free Adwords account and find it within the account setup options).

Start by entering either a keyword or phrase in the box, selecting the relevant language and country and then clicking the submit button. Google will check its databases and give you a list of specific and similar matches. It won't tell you which are the most popular phrases, but there are other ways to find this information out!

Overture provides a similar service at http://inventory.overture.com – entering a keyword will show you the frequency of searches for similar words or phrases for the previous month. This system is great for checking the popularity of terms that are currently in use. Note of course that the more popular a term, the stiffer the competition you'll face. You should use this on all of your terms to gauge their popularity, and then ensure that you optimise your site for the most important ones.

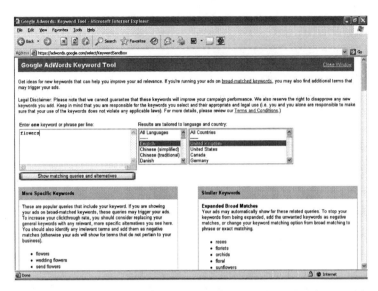

Fig 2.9.1 Google Sandbox can suggest alternative keywords based on real-world searches.

If you want to take your keyword accuracy to another level, then it is worth consid-ering Wordtracker (**www.wordtracker.com**). This is one of the most widely-used keyword assessment tools online today. Wordtracker works by compiling a database of terms that people search for. You enter keywords on their site and they'll provide you with in-depth analysis of those terms, including:

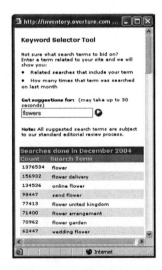

- how often people use the same words
- competing sites that use the same words
- keyword combinations that are relevant to your business
- your potential for gaining top 10 ranking in major search engines, broken down by search engine
- identify misspellings of keywords that may be worth optimising for.

All of this invaluable data does come at a

Fig 2.9.2. Overture's word search tool gives good advice on keywords currently in use.

price, although there is a free 15 keyword trial. Pricing is based on a subscription period, from one day to an annual fee.

When evaluating keywords or phrases you need to balance the popularity against the competition. Wordtracker helps you do this effectively by suggesting relevant alternatives and then showing you where they are used. In this way you can quickly identify the keywords where you are likely to face less competition.

Searching...408 row(s) returned
(These are actual queries from selected metacrawlers)

Related keywords for golf

Why do I need related keywords? Click here

1. golf
2. pga
3. lpga
4. golf courses
5. tiger woods
6. golf clubs
7. sports
8. jack nicklaus
9. titleist
10. travel

Click here to add all keywords to your basket

Count	Predicted	Keyword ❷explain
2501	14873	golf
1024	6089	golf clubs
470	2795	golf courses
438	2605	golf equipment
320	1903	used golf clubs
290	1725	golf tips
197	1172	golf games
196	1166	vw golf

Porn filter	🐎Keywords for Wordtracker : **408**
OFF ❷	◀ Delete last term ◀ Clear all

Fig 2.9.3. A search often yields a variety of possible words and phrases that you may not have considered.

As you dig deeper into the results, Wordtracker also appends a Keyword Effectiveness Index (KEI) number. This measures a keyword's competitive power and is a combination of the number of times it appears across the web against the breadth of sites that it appears on. The trick is to select words that obtain a high KEI rating across a lower number of sites. Use this in conjunction with other services such as Overture or Google Sandbox to find new keywords and rate their effectiveness.

Step 2: Add 'ALT' tags to all images
Within the HTML code of your page, every image will be placed using the <IMG> tag. Adding the ALT tag to an image (or in plain English, to add alternative text) displays a tool-tip style yellow text panel when a user hovers

the mouse over a graphic. This was primarily designed to make the site more accessible to those with screen readers, or to make the site load faster on slow connections where graphics might be disabled.

Search engines also scan ALT tags for relevance – if yours is a furniture site and you have a picture of a particular brand chair that also has the ALT tag correctly identifying the brand and model number, you will again be ranked higher. For example, for your company logo you may want to put your full company name, with the resulting HTML looking something like:

<img src="logo.jpg" alt="ABC Limited">

Keep the number of words down to a minimum and ensure that you include relevant keywords. If the image is hyperlinked to another page, add keywords relating to that page into the ALT text. Note that for full compliance to W3C standard every images should have at least a blank (ALT="") tag.

Step 3: Customise the page TITLE tag for each page

Although templates save you time when designing a site with many pages, it can mean that you forget to customise the title of each page. The <TITLE> tag of an html page is displayed in the top bar of the screen, but is also scanned and compared against the main body of your text. This is one of the most important aspects of search rankings – get the title wrong and you will probably be ranked poorly. Therefore, ensure that the title is relevant specifically to the content of that page. A title should be between 50 and 100 characters in length and, if possible should not contain all capitals or characters such as @, #, ~, +, _, $, £ etc as they can confuse some search engines. Keep it to text and numbers. For example, in the main template you may set the template to: XYZ supplies a range of furniture products across the USA, whereas on your kitchen chairs page the title might be: Metal and wooden kitchen chairs from XYZ Limited. Search engines cross-reference the page title against META tags and main text content.

Not only is it important to get keywords into your title, their position within the title is of paramount important. Note in the example above the company name was placed at the end. This is because the 'Metal and wooden chairs' part is likely to be more important as a keyword than the company name for that particular page.

Step 4: Optimising your Meta tags

This is the number one mistake that companies new to web promotion make – the omission of any Meta tags from their website. A Meta tag is a hidden piece of code that is there specifically to tell search engines about your site. Note that adding Meta tags alone is not a magic wand for your site's immediate number one placement, but they will assist some search engines in providing additional information about your pages.

Meta tags reside in the <HEAD> area of an HTML page. If you right-click over most web pages in your browser and select 'View Source' you will see that these pieces of code generally appear near the top of the page.

There are several different types of Meta tag that can be used, but we'll concentrate on the main ones for now:

Keywords
This is where you list the words that users are most likely to use within search engines to locate your site. You created these words earlier on, so it's simply a case of putting these words into the code below. You can list up to around 1000 characters, with each word separated by a comma. Many search engines will only index the first 64 characters, so put the most important words first.

<meta name="keywords" content="keyword1, keyword2, keyword3, keyword4 ">

Description
A paragraph that describes your company and/or site. This can be 200 characters in length, although some engines only display the first 20 characters, so ensure that these include the main item of interest (either company name, product name or product type). Include important keywords near the front of the description. Google does not use the Meta description in its listings; it automatically generates its own description instead.

<meta name="description" content="We sell tables, chairs and kitchen furniture. This is a short paragraph about our company and the products that we sell, with several keywords relevant to our industry such as chairs, tables, kitchens.">

The following Meta tags are optional and are unlikely to affect rankings, although are still useful to include. Some search engines do not use them.

Company
Some search engines will use this tag to categorise your site by company name

<meta name="company" content="ABC Limited">

Homepage
Where a site may span several servers and may even have several URLs, this tag helps search engines identify where the home page resides.

<meta name="homepage" content= "http://www.your_url_here.com">

Pragma

This tag forces some search engines not to cache your content, thus ensuring users get to see the most up-to-date content.

<meta http-equiv="pragma" content="no-cache">

Expires

Ensures that search engines recognise that the content of your pages does not have a specific expiry date (as some sites do). If an expiry date were set and a search is performed after that date your page would not appear.

<meta http-equiv="expires" content="0">

Distribution

Only add this tag if your site is not limited to your own region or country. It specifies that the content on your site is for global distribution.

<meta name="distribution" content="Global">

Rating

Most sites are suitable for viewing by all ages, but where you have content that should not be viewed by minors you can specify this by changing the content to 'mature', 'restricted' or '14 years'. Parents can then enable the ratings system in their web browser (Tools, Internet Options and Content in Internet Explorer) to restrict access.

<meta name="rating" content="General">

Revisit-after

The revisit-after meta tag is useful for sites where the content changes often and tells the search engine how often to revisit your site. The example below will tell the search engine to revisit your site every 7 days.

<meta name="revisit-after" content="7 days">

Robots

This Meta tag is used to tell the search engine whether you want the web page indexed or not. You only really need to use this Meta tag if you DON'T want your web page indexed. The values for this tag are:

index(default)	Index the page
noindex/index	don't index the page/Index this page
nofollow/follow	don't index any pages hyper-linked to this page/Do index any pages hyper-linked to this page
none	same as "noindex, nofollow"

<meta name="robots" content="follow, index">

Copyright
This tag identifies the copyright owner of the page.

<meta name="copyright" content="ABC Limited">

Author
Used to identify the author of the page, and will help in getting you higher rankings.

<meta name="author" content="Author name">

Once you've completed your meta tags, the top of your page should look something like this:

```
<head>
<title>ABC Limited – manufacturers of kitchen furniture including chairs, tables and cabinets</title>
<meta name="description" content="ABC manufacture kitchen furniture such as tables, chairs, cabinets, shelves and complete fitted kitchen units.">
<meta name="keywords" content="kitchen, furniture, tables, chairs, units, shelves, abc">
<meta name="rating" content="general">
<meta name="copyright" content="ABC Limited">
<meta name="revisit-after" content="7 Days">
<meta name="expires" content="never">
<meta name="distribution" content="global">
<meta name="robots" content="index, follow">
</head>
```

It is always good practice to move the Meta tags as near to the top of your HTML documents as possible. Some search engines only scan the first few kilobytes, so you want to make sure it's your Meta tags they are scanning.

Note: Do not add in competitor keywords into your Meta tags or you may find yourself at the wrong end of a lawsuit! Playboy Enterprises has successfully sued sites for using Playboy and Playmate in their Meta tags (and web addresses). It is not (yet) illegal to add in trademarked terms, however those that own the trademarks have the right to claim against you, and the stronger their brand the stronger the claim.

(If you find one of your competitors surreptitiously using your company or brand names within their Meta tags, or even hidden within the body of their pages you can report this to the search engine that you found them through. This will get them marked down or even blacklisted)

Step 5: Optimising your text

Now that you've placed your chosen keywords in the Meta tags and title of your pages, ensure that every page has keywords littered through the main body of the page. For example, if you sell kitchen furniture, make sure that in addition to 'kitchen furniture' you have words such as 'chairs, tables, sink, shelves' etc littered around the page – if a user is searching for kitchen chairs your site is more likely to be ranked highly. Use keywords within hyperlinks and for page names.

It is of paramount importance to optimise pages for specific keywords – you cannot make a single page rank highly for all of your keywords, so make sure that people find the right pages by taking the time to add in keywords thoughtfully. Many people will be arriving directly at these pages from search engines.

The more words a page has on it, the more likely it is to be indexed – search engines like content. Where possible make sure pages have over 300 words. It may be advantageous to submit specific product pages rather than your front page, which may only have a few pictures and word links to the rest of your site on it.

Note: Don't try to spoof search engines. Many web designers used to place white text on a white background – this is the oldest trick in the book and search engines will mark you down, even blacklisting you for doing it.

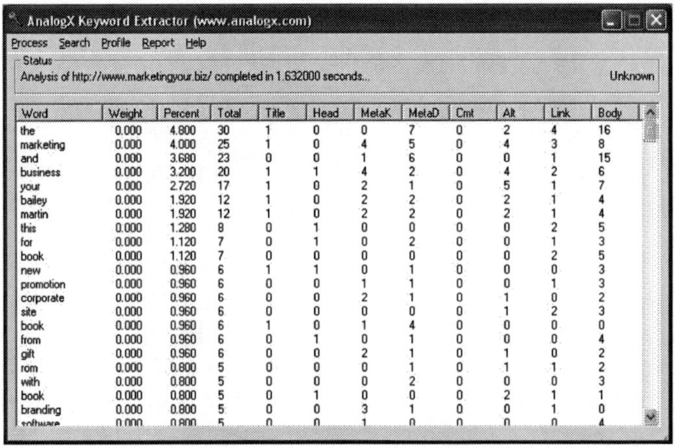

Word	Weight	Percent	Total	Title	Head	MetaK	MetaD	Cmt	Alt	Link	Body
the	0.000	4.800	30	1	0	0	7	0	2	4	16
marketing	0.000	4.000	25	1	0	4	5	0	4	3	8
and	0.000	3.680	23	0	0	1	6	0	0	1	15
business	0.000	3.200	20	1	1	4	2	0	4	2	6
your	0.000	2.720	17	1	0	2	1	0	5	1	7
bailey	0.000	1.920	12	1	0	2	2	0	2	1	4
martin	0.000	1.920	12	1	0	2	2	0	2	1	4
this	0.000	1.280	8	0	1	0	0	0	0	2	5
for	0.000	1.120	7	0	1	0	2	0	0	1	3
book	0.000	1.120	7	0	0	0	0	0	0	2	5
new	0.000	0.960	6	1	1	0	1	0	0	0	3
promotion	0.000	0.960	6	0	0	1	1	0	0	1	3
corporate	0.000	0.960	6	0	0	2	1	0	1	0	2
site	0.000	0.960	6	0	0	0	0	0	1	2	3
book	0.000	0.960	6	1	0	1	4	0	0	0	0
from	0.000	0.960	6	0	1	0	1	0	0	0	4
gift	0.000	0.960	6	0	0	2	1	0	1	0	2
rom	0.000	0.800	5	0	0	0	1	0	1	1	2
with	0.000	0.800	5	0	0	0	2	0	0	0	3
book	0.000	0.800	5	0	1	0	0	0	2	1	1
branding	0.000	0.800	5	0	0	3	1	0	0	1	0
software	0.000	0.800	5	0	0	1	0	0	0		4

Fig 2.9.5. Keyword Extractor is great for checking the 'weight' of words used in either your or your competitor's web sites.

There are several programs available that will gauge the weight of keywords in your site (and, more usefully your competitors). One such program is AnalogX's Keyword Extractor (pictured opposite) - this freeware application allows you to enter a web address and analyse the occurrence of all words on the site. It is most effective when used on competing sites to find out which words are used most frequently, achieving better rankings. It compares words against the main body of text, the Meta tags and title.

A good exercise is to pick your five top keywords and then perform the same search in a few of the main search engines. Use the Keyword Extractor on the top resulting pages and see how they have used words to good effect.

Some search engines rate pages higher if keywords appear near the top and/or bottom of the page, so it's worth adding the main words you want to be found under in the first and last paragraphs of the page. One semi-sneaky way to do this (at least for the bottom area) is to place a copyright notice followed by a tag line e.g. '© 2005 ABC Limited – suppliers of tables, chairs and kitchen furniture'. Ideally each major keyword should be relative to around 4% of the total number of words.

The format in which keywords appear can also affect ranking. Text that appears as headers (using <H1> tags, for example), is bold, italicised or in bullet points will be taken as important and ranked accordingly.

Follow this checklist whenever you optimise a page

- Make sure that the page file name has a keyword in it.
- Ensure that your top keywords or phrases appear as a header title using the <H1> tags.
- Where pages link to others, use keywords as part of the link – don't just say 'click here for more info'.
- Use keywords within bulleted text.
- Use keywords in ALT tags assigned to images.
- Use keywords in <A HREF> tags with the TITLE sub-tag.

Step 6: Add a robots.txt file to your site

Search engines use robots, or programs to automatically retrieve and reference the content from your web pages. Robots are sometimes referred to as Web Wanderers, Web Crawlers, or Spiders. Creating a robots.txt file is mainly important if there are areas of your website that you do NOT want search engines to add to their databases, thereby ensuring that users finding your site via a search engine are more likely to get to the right page first time. Perhaps, for example you have created a section for special customers or dealers that should not be accessible to the general public –

you would not want this ranked number 1 in Google!

Note: If you created a Meta tag for Robots as described in Stage 4 and are not using Gateway pages (see stage 6) then you do not need to worry about creating a robots.txt file as the meta tag overrides the necessity for a robots.txt file.

Creating a robots.txt file is easy – all you need is Windows Notepad. Normally, the file would contain text along the lines of:

User-agent: *
Disallow: /cgi-bin/

This tells all search engines not to spider any files in the /cgi-bin/ folder and ensures that only relevant pages will appear in search engines results. Repeat the second line for any other directories you do not want spidered. If you wanted to block your entire site from being scanned, adding 'Disallow: *' would prevent search engines from indexing and/or following any pages.

Once you have created your robots.txt file you need to upload it to the root directory (this is the top level folder where your index.htm homepage file also exists).

Step 7: De-clutter your code

We've discussed before the use of CSS to structure your page – this helps to reduce page file size by minimising the number of tags. Several KB can be shaved off a medium-sized page by replacing <FONT> tags with a single style applied to the total page. Not only does this make the page load fast, but, more importantly there is less for search engines to look through before they get to the good stuff – your content!

Back in chapter 2.6 we covered how the CSS code could be stripped out into a separate file that is called once and then cached by the browser. This same technique can be applied to Javascript code.

An example of the sort of code you might have is as follows:

```
<script language="JavaScript" type="text/JavaScript">
<!--
function MM_openBrWindow(theURL,winName,features) { //v2.0
window.open(theURL,winName,features);
}
//-->
</script>
```

This is only a small piece of code, but invariably today's sites can have several times the amount of code, all of which has to load and be scanned before the search robot gets to your content. As with the style sheet we can replace this by making a separate file and calling it from the main document. Here's how to do it:

1. Start by selecting all of the text between (but excluding) <!-- and //--> tags
2. Cut it from the document (CTRL & C) to the clipboard, open Notepad, paste the text and save it with a .js extension e.g. script.js
3. Now modify your script as follows:

```
<script language="Javascript" src="script.js"type="text/
javascript">
</script>
```

By moving the Javascript and CSS out of your site, and optimising your code, you can quite easily reduce a page's file size by 20%, all of which helps search engines get at the content they are interested in, as well as improving your visitor's experience of the site and reducing your bandwidth requirements.

Step 8: Add Gateway pages

Gateway pages are specific web pages that are optimised to specific products or services, and then submitted to one or several search engines. These pages consist of carefully chosen Meta tags, keywords, descriptions and main body text that are specific to each product or service you wish to promote, linking back to the main index page on your own site. As a result they will rank highly when users perform a search for the relevant keyword. A gateway page may not be required if your product pages are already achieving suitably high rankings.

Many of the web submission programs (see next stage) will generate Gateway pages for you once you provide the required text. If you decide to add in a gateway page, you can also use the robots.txt file to tell specific search spiders to index that page. If, however you are using web submission software, this will not really be necessary as you can submit each page directly so that search engines will spider that page without having to try to find it through scanning the rest of your site.

Step 9: Submitting your site

'If you build it, they will come' may have worked for Kevin Costner in the movie 'Field of Dreams', but it won't work for you unless you tell the search engines about your site – you wouldn't print 10,000 brochures then lock them in a cupboard, would you? Now that you've tweaked your site to perfection, it should be ready for submission. How you proceed from here depends largely on your budget. It can be done cheaply with limited success, but nowadays more and more search engines are charging for new submissions. Some sites have a split tier pricing policy, still allowing sites to be listed free but charging a fee for immediate entry.

If you want to start on the cheap, you can still manually submit your site to many of the major engines, including Google, which is still the most popular search engine on the web.

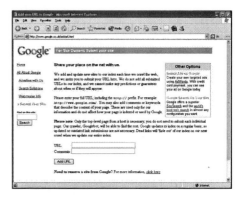

Fig 2.9.6. Submitting your site to Google is simple as well as free!

To submit your site, go to each search engine and locate the 'Add URL' or 'Add Site' link – it may not be on the front page. Use their site map if it is not immediately accessible.

There are numerous sites that will submit your URL to several of the major search engines free of charge, although the price you may pay for this could be spam, spam and more spam, as they will invariably ask for your email address. Alternatively you can invest in a software package such as Web Position Gold or Dynamic Submission (pictured) that will automatically submit your site to hundreds or even thousands of search engines automatically. A good web submission package will also include other tools, such as Meta tag creation, page keyword testing/optimisation wizards and search engine rankings. For the relatively small sum that these packages are available for, they are a worthwhile investment as they automate many of the coding procedures that would otherwise be done manually.

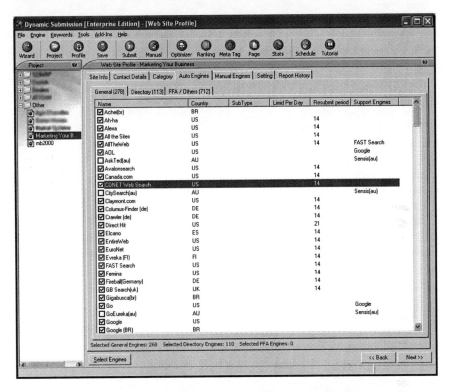

Fig 2.9.7 Dynamic Submission will submit your site to hundreds of search engines at the touch of a button.

Every search engine works in different ways – some will concentrate on single pages, where others will follow threads deep into your site, but if you follow the above guidelines your site should be acceptable to most search engines. As Google powers many search engines, this should be your main priority. Google does two types of crawl – a shallow crawl and, less frequently, a deep crawl. If you've just built a new site, it can take several weeks to appear in Google, as it won't visit it until its next scheduled deep crawl, but if you're simply updating your pages, it's quite normal to see your pages in Google within a few days. Sometimes Google will list your site without you even submitting it, as it may have found it by an external link from another site.

Note: Don't submit your site too often, as you can be blacklisted as a spammer by some search engines, although Google does not mind how often you submit. In general, submitting once a month should be adequate.

It is also worthwhile keeping an eye on search engine trends. Sites such as **searchenginewatch.com** and **webmasterworld.com** can provide valuable alerts when search engines such as Google change their methods of indexing. On November 16th 2003, Google updated it indexing methods – now known as the 'Florida' update – which had a catastrophic effect on many website, forcing many designers to rework their search engine optimisation methods. A future change could see your competitors fall from their lofty position – if you're quick enough you could re-optimise your page and take pole position!

Step 10: Get linked – get hit

Many search engines, including Google will rank your site much higher if they have sites in their databases that also link to you. Therefore, get as many other sites as possible to link to your site. This might include existing customers or general portal sites that cover your area of industry. You may have come across suitable sites while checking out competing sites that appeared when you used specific keywords.

There are some great free tools for backtracking links from your site. Aside from looking at your site statistics you can also use online tools such as Alexa (**www.alexa.com**). This site collects its data from users of the Alexa toolbar, tracking their surfing habits and placing this information in a related sites database. By entering your URL on the search field on the front page you can find out various pieces of information such as:

- similar sites that browsers visit (normally your competitors)
- general site stats (traffic ranking, speed, linking sites, number of pop-up adverts, date first online)
- subdomains within your site that users visit (useful if your site is split across several servers)
- contact information.

One very useful feature on the Traffic Details page is the ability to compare your site stats alongside another URL – great for seeing how you fare against competitors.

It is in your customers' interests to link to your site, as the reciprocal link from your site to theirs will also assist them in their efforts with search engines. This practice has a three-fold effect of generating higher rankings for you, doing your customers a favour plus delivering you additional traffic from referring sites. Make sure that you explain the benefits to them when you ask them for a link to your site. Get them to use some of your keywords within the link, e.g. 'Supplier of kitchen furniture'. By gaining more links to your sites from others within your industry you are seen as an 'authority' in

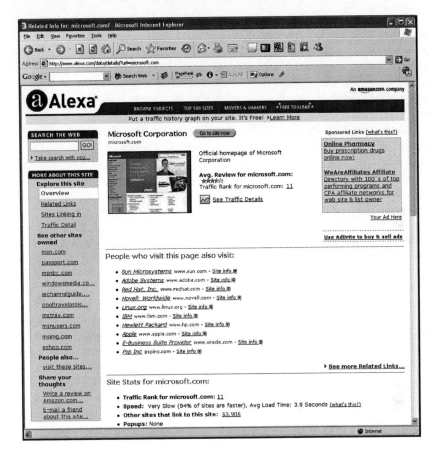

Fig 2.9.8 Alexa is a great tool for finding out information about your site, those that link to you and similar sites that your visitors also go to.

your field – the more relevant links, the greater the authority...

Another great way to do this while killing another bird with the same stone is to post messages on relevant forums. Find a forum that discusses topics relating to your industry and answer any questions that you can – be as helpful as you can. Do this regularly. Make sure that as part of your signature you include a link back to your site. This can be often set up as standard within the administration section of online forums so that you don't have to keep typing it each time. Not only do you generate more valuable links back to your site, but you also continue to build your reputation as someone who knows their industry.

One of the best kept secrets within Google is that you can trace which sites are linking to a website. Go to the Google homepage and type link:www.yourdomain.com (obviously substituting with your web address). This will provide a list of all sites that Google knows links to this domain. This is a tremendously powerful tool, especially when you insert your competitor's web address as it can identify portal sites for you to send marketing material to, or locate potential customers.

There are also free tools that will show you how many links the major search engines have coming into your site, which is also useful for gauging how you compare with competitors. A great free tool is Link Popularity Check, available for free at **www.checkyourlinkpopularity.com**. Run this regularly and enjoy seeing the fruits of your efforts as you overtake your competitors!

Step 11: Track your visitors

All good web-hosting companies will supply you with 'log files' - some even provide you with online statistic reports. These are invaluable in telling you who has visited your site, when they came, where they came from and what they saw when they got there.

One of the most important, yet frequently overlooked sections is the 'Referrer' information – this shows the website, and in some cases the actual page that visitors came from. This will mostly be either other pages on your site or search engines, but it is also a good way to pinpoint where partner site links are working well. Not only can you see the search engines that the user came from, you can also see the keywords they used to find you within the search engine in the first place. This will give you a clear indication of what is working for some pages so you can copy the philosophy over to others.

Another important part of the stats report to check regularly is the errors section. Here you can quickly identify any broken links, missing graphics or non-functioning forms. Check this on a regular basis to keep your site in tip-top condition. The errors section also has the added bonus of letting you know of any malicious attacks that may be taking place on your server (e.g. someone trying to hack you). Many hackers will try to see if they can access standard operating system files (such as CMD.EXE within Windows NT and above) to perform harmful activities like deleting the contents your hard drive, or hacking your site so that they can share files and steal your bandwidth. Any activity in the log which lists failed attempts to access files that are outside of the directory that your web pages are stored in should be reported to the system administrator or ISP. As long as you are running a computer that has a firewall and has all the latest software patches applied you should be relatively safe.

If your web host cannot supply you with automatically generated statistics reports you can analyse your log files on your computer using products such as WebTrends Log Analyser or Weblog Expert (pictured), which also has a free and very capable 'Lite' version. Once they have been configured to locate the log files on your server these programs will create comprehensive reports and charts. WebTrends will even create them in a variety of formats, including HTML, Word and Excel. Alternatively you can install server-based programs, such as Analog Log Analyser, which will perform the same function, although are a little more tricky to install, and may require certain services (PERL or CGI) to be running on your web server.

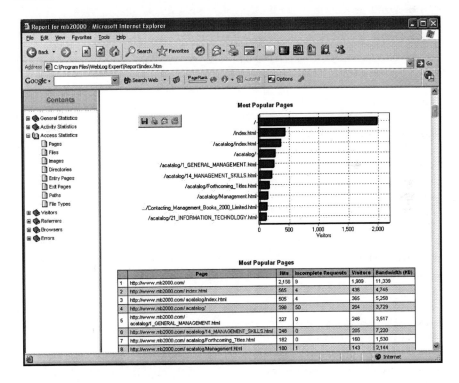

Fig 2.9.9. Logs can tell you the most popular pages on your site and how people arrived there along with the keywords they used to find you.

To summarise, these are the important points to study within your logs:

- Overall activity – is it heading in the right direction?
- Pages people visit – helps you identify parts of the site that are not attracting visitors.
- Path through site – find out where people start, and where they leave the site. Note that many users will arrive directly at individual pages from search engines.
- Search engines spidering your site – allows you to make sure that your site submissions are working.
- Keywords used to find you – are they the ones you optimised for? If not, are they more relevant and should you re-optimise or create other gateway pages.
- Site visitors – see which countries and domains are visiting regularly
- Referrer reports – find out which sites are linking to you. This often helps to locate similar sites.
- Error reports – are any pages or graphics not being found?
- Browser report – is your site optimised for the right browsers? If 10% of your visitors are using Firefox, and your site doesn't work with it, then that's 10% of business you may be losing.

If you cannot even get access to log files all is not lost – there are many free or commercial web-tracking products available. HitBox is a prime example that, with the inclusion of a small piece of code will be able to give you access to live online reports. The free products will generally require you to display a small advert with a reciprocal link to their site, but this is usually overcome by paying a small fee.

Step 12: Get an award

There are many web sites out there that specialise in reviewing web sites and offering awards for the better ones. Admittedly some of these are not worth the pixels they're lit up with, as they will offer any website an award, then try to sell them a certificate or trophy. One of the more established sites is **www.iawmd.com** (International Association of Webmasters and Designers), founded in 1997 with over 310,000 members worldwide. You can submit your website for

Fig 2.9.10. An award can add credibility to your site.

256

review free of charge to be reviewed for their 'Golden Web Award' by entering a few details on their website. Within a few weeks you will receive an email confirming whether your site is deemed worthy. Of course, if you win they will try to sell you a certificate, but you also get to place a small award icon on your website giving your site credibility in the eyes of your visitors. It is also a talking point when discussing the site with customers and could even be the subject of a press release for your trade press - 'Top XXXXXXX site wins web award'.

Step 13 – Add affiliated content

If your site is suitable, you may want to consider signing up to be an affiliate of sites such as Amazon.com. This free service allows you to add suitable products from their online catalogue onto your site – if users click on the link and subsequently purchase you will receive a small percentage of the sale value. Admittedly, unless you are receiving a lot of traffic you are probably not going to make much money from this, but the side benefit is that search engines will harvest all of the keywords from the products you list. Many companies find that by promoting similar products in this way, they can bring extra traffic to their site that includes people that may have been searching from a different perspective. Make sure that you add in text as well as pictures, otherwise you will not get the full benefits of such an affiliation.

Another option is to add a free news feed to your site. Depending on your industry, there may be an online media publication (such as **www.worldpress.org**) that can offer you the ability to integrate their news headlines into your site. This is normally delivered through javascript plugins or RSS feed, pulled from their server. These dynamically update as their site changes without you having to make any additional modifications to your site. This gives users (and search engines) new, fresh content, although the downside is that when users click on a story they will generally be directed to another site. This is a reasonable trade-off if this is done via a pop-up window, but disregard any news services that don't offer this capability – you don't want to drive visitors away from your site without an easy route back.

Summary

❑ Remember, a website is not like other media that is finished as soon as it is printed – it is never finished and can grow at an alarming rate as news, case studies, further product information and other relevant details are continually pumped into it.

❑ E-commerce experts Actinic suggest that the more targeted your pages are the more likely you are to convert browsers to buyers. Bruce Townsend, Marketing Manager suggests; *"Try to get at least one first page position on the top three search sites. Choose a very specific phrase that's relevant to your products, e.g. 'discount running shoes'. Put it in the title and description of your home page, and repeat it three or four times in the page text and within text links to relevant pages of your site. Then submit to the search engines. Free submissions take a few weeks to process, so use their paid inclusion option if there is one, or try some pay per click advertising on the same sites. Also, arrange reciprocal links with as many related but non-competing sites as you can."*

❑ Perform searches regularly on the keywords you have chosen to ensure that you are going up in the rankings, and analyse competitors' sites and keywords regularly – especially if they are above you.

❑ If you ensure that the content is relevant and useful, that all of your other literature backs up and promotes your web address and that you continually tweak your site in response to statistical analysis you will have a healthy, popular site that helps in winning and maintaining business.

2.10

How to: Create Audio/visual Multimedia Content

On the CD

- Video Software
- Audio Software
- Multimedia Authoring Software
- Video Screensaver
- Web links

A good multimedia presentation, either as part of a demonstration CD-ROM, DVD, video or for use at a trade show can heighten an observer's opinion of your company. With standard PCs now many times more powerful than the technology that put man on the moon or the computing power that rendered the original Star Wars movies, the availability of the hardware required that could create a professional presentation has widened greatly. Obviously the product you sell will dictate the necessity for multimedia, but simply knowing what tools you have available to create such material widens your options.

For this exercise we will again use our fictitious company Eyeglaze to cover some examples of how several multimedia applications may be created. This chapter does not go into such detail as previous chapters as the scope is so wide, but it should give you a good indication of the most suitable method for your application.

Example 1: The training guide
The requirement here may be to demonstrate to users how to install and set up software supplied with the Eyeglaze products. For this we need to record what is happening on-screen as we follow the installation and configuration procedure, then put this into a format that the user can access.

Step 1: Recording
For this stage we will use Techsmiths Camtasia Recorder, which was used

to record all of the video demos on the accompanying CD-ROM. It allows you to capture either a specific portion of the screen, a window or the entire screen area. You can also add audio simultaneously if you have a microphone configured. In reality unless you are a newsreader you may find it's better to narrate roughly, then record a separate, cleaned up narration and overdub it over the movie later on – we'll cover this next.

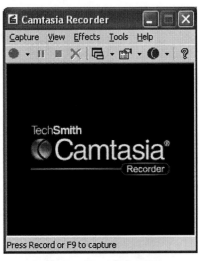

Recording is simply a case of presetting your preferences (e.g. screen area, audio etc) and hitting the record button, and then using the computer as normal. When finished you either press F10 to stop recording or click Stop.

Fig 2.10.1. The Camtasia recorder window.

The recording will be saved as a movie file, ready for editing. You may wish to record several separate files that each focus on a particular area or function – these can be spliced together later.

Step 2: Editing

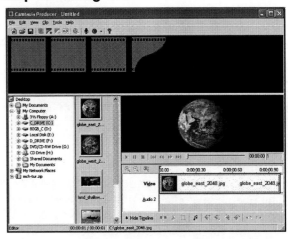

Fig 2.10.2 Camtasia's editor allows a simple time-line approach to compile your still and video screen capture clips.

For the uninitiated, this can be a little tricky at first, but the technique is similar to the old way of splicing film clips together, but without the knife and tape! With Camtasia Producer (pictured) you can pull in your video clips, cut out the pieces you don't want, then drag the edited clip to a timeline at the top of the screen. Use the mouse to drag and select areas that you wish to delete (which will be highlighted in blue) then click the Cut Section icon underneath. Repeat this process with any additional clips.

You may also wish to insert a title screen at the start of your movie. This can simply be one or several JPGs or similar file created in a graphics package such as Adobe Photoshop – remember to save it as the same dimensions as your movie. Just drag it from the thumbnail view of images and drop it into position in the timeline at the top of the screen.

Special effects and pauses can also be easily included into any of the separate elements within your timeline. For example, you might want your existing title screen to stay visible for 3 seconds, then to slide to the left with the proceeding movie scrolling in from the right. By right-clicking over the thumbnail in the timeline you can configure both of these options.

Step 3: Adding Audio

The Camtasia suite is also supplied with an audio editing tool, allowing you to record and edit sound for overdubbing over an existing file. Alternatively you could use an editing suite such as Goldwave or Adobe Audition.

Recording a new file is simple – open your video file within the audio editor and just click on Record to begin recording from your micro-phone. You may want to do a test-run first to make sure the microphone is at the correct recording level – this can be adjusted if necessary. Trim the audio to the right length, editing out any mistakes – as you record you will be able to see where you are within the video file so that the

Fig 2.10.3 Camtasia's audio editor allows for simple editing - anything more and you'll need a dedicated audio editing program.

narration matches what's happening on-screen.

Both Adobe Audition and Goldwave have noise and hiss reduction tools. No matter how good your microphone is, it's worth running these tools over the final edited file before insertion to make it sound that little bit cleaner.

Step 4: Compiling your final file

Once you have edited your movie clip(s) and added any narration there are two final processes you need to complete. The first is the compilation of your timeline into a single movie. This is achieved by clicking Produce Movie under the File menu. You'll be prompted to select a file format, along with several other settings – for the most part you can leave these as they are but you should take time to familiarise yourself with the options available. If file size is an important factor (either because users will be downloading it, or you have several large files to fit onto a CD), play around with some of the different audio codecs – choosing a codec with greater compression can significantly reduce the final file size, within minimal loss of quality. MP3 codecs are the best, normally above 128kbps. Do a test run with several settings to find a file size/quality trade-off that you are happy with.

You should now have a single 'AVI' format file, but not everyone will be normally able to view it, especially if you have used the Techsmiths Codec (a special compression algorithm that reduces the file size without much loss in quality). Fortunately, Camtasia has the ability to create an 'executable' file, containing your movie, a movie player and the required codec. The Pack and Show option under the File menu will create this in one easy step – make sure you tick the 'Include TSSC codec' box! Once created, you'll end up with a single file that most users will be able to view on any PC.

If you use Macromedia Flash on your website, you can also import Camtasia files directly into Flash using a free plug-in. This allows you to wrap a rich user interface around your content in a compressed format that can stream off the internet.

Example 2: The trade show movie

Perhaps Eyeglaze have decided to exhibit at a forthcoming trade show, with a plasma screen as an integral part of their stand design? They'll want something eye-catching to run on it. Previously, creating media content such as a movie was confined to the realms of production companies, and while they still offer a better service than many users can provide for themselves, you can create professional quality movies using a standard PC. Granted, you will need a fast PC and specialist software but the investment is well worth it if you intend to produce content regularly.

Step 1: Structure your content

Before you can start filming, you need to draw out a storyboard for your movie. Let's say that this movie is to demonstrate a new product for our fictitious company Eyeglaze – we may want to illustrate the product's ease of upgrade with a video clip of a user removing their old graphics card from their computer and adding in a new one, followed by a clip of setting the card's software up, and finishing with demonstrations of improvements. For a show this may or may not have narration, depending on whether it is just to catch people's attention, or if it is the centrepiece of your presentation.

Draw out a storyboard of the clips you will need. In addition to standard video clips you could also insert Camtasia screen-captured clips (see the previous example). Decide where you may also want background music.

Step 2: Record your content

When filming video it pays to have the right equipment, driven by someone who knows how to get the best out of it – the finished article is only as good as the source material. Today's camcorders are better than ever but are still no match for a professional video camera. This is also true when recording audio – a standard camcorder normally houses a built-in microphone, whereas professionals usually take sound through different sources, such as lapel microphones and overhead booms delivering a much cleaner and true stereo sound. Therefore, even if your budget is tight, buy or hire the best equipment to record the source material as you can afford.

For filler material you may want to consider purchasing royalty free video clips from sites such as **rocketclips.com** or **digitaljuice.com**. These are generally available on CD-ROM/DVD or Mini-DV tape. You can also purchase royalty-free music from companies such as Sound Dogs (**www.sounddogs.com**). A quick search for 'royalty-free video clips' should provide you with a good list of content suppliers. Royalty-free means that once you pay to purchase the sound or video clip you will not have to pay the artist for the number of times you use it.

Your aim is to end up with one or a series of tapes or files that can then be imported into your PC. The most common tape format is currently DV, or Mini-DV. Importing DV format tape ensures there is no loss of quality as the content is digital. This is also true after editing and output.

To import DV tapes, your PC will need to be equipped with a 'Firewire' interface, also known as IEEE1394 – this connects to the Firewire port on your DV camcorder. You'll also need the associated software to import the files, which should have been supplied with your Firewire hardware. Video editing packages such as Adobe Premiere also have this capability. Where a professional film company has been used it would be easier to request DV-AVI formatted files on DVD-ROM. Don't request a true DVD Video disc as you will then have to convert it back to AVI format, which is a time-consuming process and may also result in loss of quality if not performed correctly. Note also that DVD-ROM discs (which are formatted differently to DVD Video discs) currently have a single file size limit of 2GB – equating to approximately 9 minutes of film – so they may have to split movies up if they are supplied in the highest quality DV-AVI format.

Step 3: Edit your content

Again, investing in the right tools for the job will not only accelerate the production process but also widen your options for adding design flair. For this stage you will need a good video-editing suite that provides easy manipulation of film clips, precision editing and an array of audio/visual special effects. Adobe's suite of video applications does just that. Adobe Premiere is the tool best suited to the editing phase. While the price tag initially appears expensive, it will cost much less than getting a video edited professionally. Its timeline approach falls directly in line with the thought process you will have used back in stage 1 to map out how your video will play.

Fig 2.10.4. Adobe Premiere is the standard for professional video editing, with an easy-to-use timeline.

Video editing is not as daunting as it sounds – as mentioned in the previous example, it's the same as the age-old method of slicing and splicing original cine-film but in a digital medium – old-style film editors never had on-screen precision and several levels of 'Undo'! Within Adobe Premiere (pictured) you have a 'bin' of all of your files, which can include video, audio and stills of various graphic formats. These are placed on a timeline, with the option of applying sound or video effects. A generous selection of effects are supplied with Adobe Premiere, which are just dragged and dropped onto the timeline where required. You can easily create cross fades and titles with literally a few clicks of a mouse – Premiere is as simple or as comprehensive as you need it to be, and there are many third party filters available that can overlay truly spectacular effects.

Depending on how you envisage the finished movie will look like, you may be able to produce a satisfactory final cut directly from Adobe Premiere. If you're happy with the results at this stage you can skip directly to stage 5.

Step 4: Adding the final polish to video

Where a more slick and professional finish is required you may also want to work with products such as Adobe After Effects. Drawing files from other applications such as Adobe Photoshop and Premiere, it provides 2D and 3D compositing, animation and video effects. A 'Pro' version is also available, which includes features such as motion tracking/stabilisation tools that can be used to reduce/eliminate camera shake during filming, together with additional visual effects. Admittedly, this is not an application that you are likely to be able to install and run with straight away, but the learning curve is well worth the effort if you have a requirement for video processing. The software is also provided with a fairly respectable training DVD to get you started.

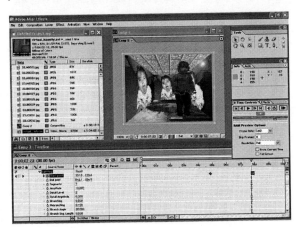

Fig 2.10.5 Adobe After Effects is best described as PhotoShop for video!

Adobe After Effects has too many features to list here, but an example may be that you may want to add a moving background behind a person being interviewed. You would do this by filming the person against a solid background (ideally a blue or green 'chroma-key' screen), then use After Effects' 'keying' technology to make the background transparent, and then applying another movie to appear behind the person talking.

Text manipulation is also another powerful feature. Many of the title or opening sequences for TV shows are created with programs such as After Effects, so you could easily produce a video animation of your company's logo and/or slogan to pre-empt your movie, then add in textual animations over the top of your main content.

If you don't have the time or resources to take your composition this far you could use Adobe Photoshop to design static title graphics that can be imported into Premiere. Alternatively Premiere does have reasonable titling capabilities built in.

After Effects is also great for producing animated logos. If, for example your original company or product log is stored as a layered image within Adobe PhotoShop you can animate each layer individually within After Effects!

Step 5: Outputting your media

Now that you have got your completed movie rendered, you have a variety of output options available. Both Adobe Premiere and After Effects allow you to output a completed project in several formats, so your movie could be used on your website, a CD-ROM, DVD or VHS.

Web site format: Unfortunately there are several different standards of video format that appear on the web, and not everyone will immediately have the software installed to be able to view all of them. Two of the safer formats to output web content in are Windows Media (WMV) and Quicktime movies (MOV). They also have the advantage of 'streaming' - as soon as enough of the movie has loaded it will start to play while the rest continues to load in the background. You can also embed movies into Flash files, which is ideal if you already have other Flash content or want to include a movie as part of an interactive website. Macromedia has made major strides forward with video integration into Flash, offering a video toolbox to work in conjunction with many popular video applications to generate its FLV format videos, which can easily be embedded into web pages through a freely distributed plugin for Dreamweaver. Your main constraint for this format is file size – if your main target audience is still using 56kbps modems then your file needs to be encoded to reflect that, and the resulting quality will be low – this is unavoidable.

CD-ROM format: Again, there are a myriad of formats available, from producing a VCD (Video CD) that can play in many DVD players to encoding the movie as an MPG, higher resolution WMV, MOV or AVI files. If the CD is to be used in a standard PC then MPG or WMV will be suitable as these will most likely play on most computers without additional video decompression codecs being required. A movie could also be subsequently be imported or embedded into another application, such as Macromedia Flash, so ensure you choose a codec format compatible with your target application's import capabilities.

Fig 2.10.6 Adobe Encore DVD builds professional DVDs, complete with subtitles, menus etc.

DVD Movie: Now becoming more

popular in business, DVD authoring is no longer only within the realms of large multimedia companies. For a relatively small outlay you can purchase programs such as Adobe Encore DVD that will give you the capability to produce an extremely comprehensive and professional DVD, including menus, multi-angles, subtitles and alternative audio channels – essentially everything you would expect to see on a commercial DVD.

VHS: For users that handled the original import of video footage from a video camera, the simplest way to export the content to VHS is to output the finished video back to the camera via the Firewire port, then connect the video camera to a video recorder and record to VHS tape. Bear in mind that if your VHS tape is destined for other continents there may be alternative tape formats. The USA uses the NTSC format, whereas PAL is popular elsewhere – granted some PAL videos have NTSC compatibility but do you really want to take the chance that your customers will have this? If you don't have the ability to output to your video camera, produce a DVD video or a data DVD with the final video cut and pass this to a video production company for VHS duplication. Note that some DV cameras have the DV input disabled as standard by the manufacturers to kerb piracy, but many third-party companies can override this with a software page (similar to removing the region coding from a DVD player) - this will probably invalidate any warranty though.

Example 3: Presentation CD-ROM

Although this may be less media-rich than the above two examples, a presentation or demonstration CD still needs to deliver graphical appeal as well as ease of use. Let's say that Eyeglaze now want to create a CD for use with both prospects and customers that contains material such as:

- fact sheets and product literature in PDF format
- the latest software drivers
- video demonstrations, perhaps produced with either Camtasia and/or Adobe Premiere
- demo/trial software
- technical support documents, in Word, PDF or HTML format.

All of the material to be included on the disc may already exist but there needs be a mechanism that pulls them all together and presents them in an intuitive fashion to the user – you need a menu system! There are dozens of applications available that give users the ability to create a menu-driven interface, but because of their complexity and the fact that resulting output may differ greatly, this example cannot be broken down into stages. Instead we'll look at some of the options available and the factors you need to consider.

A place for everything and everything in its place

Before we discuss the front-end menu we should consider that many people would bypass it and want to browse the CD contents. Creating a sensible directory structure will in itself provide an immediate navigation structure. It does not have to be complex – folder names such as DOCS, MOVIES, DEMOS, SUPPORT and SOFTWARE will suffice. Look at the structure on the CD-ROM that accompanies this book as an example.

The quick route: HTML

One of the easiest ways to build a quick menu system is to write a web page! A static web page does not need to be delivered over the Internet for a PC to be able to view it. Designing the CD navigation is exactly the same as for a website, so use the website tutorial in this book.

Note that Windows XP Service Pack 2 disabled certain scripts from running if the page is viewed statically rather than being served by web server – this often means that you'll get that annoying information bar telling you that Internet Explorer has blocked a potentially harmful script. It also means that whatever code it has blocked will not function – this could be your main menu navigation system!

Fig 2.10.7. This is what your users might see if you use HTML to build a menu, so be careful of the code you use!

Alternative options

The alternative options available will depend on your skill (if you intend to write a system yourself) or your budget. Many language applications can fashion an application that will do the task required, including Visual Basic, C++ and Borland Delphi, but these are not as graphical and are likely to be prohibitively expensive if you have to outsource.

A simpler and much more media rich solution would be to turn to another web-centric solution such as Macromedia Flash, or its big brother, Director.

Flash has the power to create an executable version of a flash movie, which itself can be used to create excellent user interfaces – just look at any good Flash-based website! Camtasia also includes a menu making facility – it's fine for a single page menu with a few options, but don't expect to create anything more complex than this.

If you're really stuck for resources, you can even create a presentation with Microsoft PowerPoint, and then use the in-built Pack and Go facility to create an executable presentation that can link to external files. Macromedia Director has a higher price tag and learning curve but is specifically designed for CD, DVD and kiosk applications.

Finishing touches

Assuming that you now have your content segregated neatly into appropriately named directories, and have created a suitable navigation interface, your CD is almost ready to go, but there are still a couple of tricks we can do to make the user's experience a little slicker. Firstly, we want the CD to play automatically after insertion. Windows 95 and above automatically looks for a file marked 'autorun.inf' on the CD – this simple text file contains instructions such as what file to run on insertion and what icon to display for the disc in Windows Explorer. Creating an autorun.inf file is simple – open Notepad and add the following lines:

```
[autorun]
OPEN=file.exe
ICON=file.ico
```

Rename file.exe to be the file you want to run on insertion – this example would expect the file to be in the same directory as autorun.inf, but you can add in a path to a file in a subfolder; just don't put a drive letter, as this probably will not be the same for every system!

Note also that if you have used an HTML-based menu system, you will have to use another small program that opens the appropriate page, and then point the autorun file at this program. The reason for this is that you cannot 'run' a web page directly from an autorun file. The CD that accompanies this book uses this technique.

Icon files are quite easy to create, or alternatively even easier to source online. There are many sites that have free icons, or free programs to create them. These programs normally take a standard graphic and convert it to the desired size, which is 39 x 39 pixels.

Duplication of effort

Where only a small number of discs are being produced, it is not cost-effective to get them printed professionally, but there are two options – printing on labels or directly onto the CD surface. Label printing can give a very good quality finish on matt, gloss or clear materials. Alternatively, certain inkjet printers can now print directly onto specially coated CDs. You must calculate the time factor for printing and handling for both methods as this will quickly mount up if you are producing hundreds of CDs.

If you only want to make small numbers of CDs or DVDs at any one time, why not consider a duplicating unit. For the price of a low or mid-range PC you can get dedicated multi-disc unit that can burn dozens or even hundreds of discs per hour. It also frees up your PC, as burning discs requires a lot of PC resources. VHS duplicators are also available, but are likely to be more expensive as VHS is a dying media.

Fig 2.10.8 CD & DVD duplicators can allow you to produce small quantities of discs in-house cheaply and quickly.

Summary

❑ With the cost of CDs, DVDs and VHS cassettes now down to virtually throwaway prices, it is cheaper (not to mention more environmentally friendly) to provide prospects with electronic information rather than their printed equivalent. An assortment of very different applications can be used to create an informative and enjoyable user experience. If you are prepared for the financial investment and a learning curve, products such as Adobe Premiere and After Effects present superb opportunities for producing high-quality video content. Macromedia Flash should also be considered where content is being delivered over the Internet and perhaps also on CD-ROM.

❑ Where CD/DVD/VHS content regularly changes consider purchasing your own duplicating equipment as the initial outlay will quickly be recouped in the time you save by not burning discs singularly.

2.11

How to: Structure and Store Customer Information

On the CD

- CRM Software
- Office Software
- Web links

The most important part of your entire marketing programme is your customer and prospect information – without this you have no one to send information to or call on. Therefore the structure that you put into place to record this information and the way you make it available to sales staff is important. We are essentially talking about CRM (Customer Relationship Management) databases here, and there are two routes you can go down – off-the-shelf or homegrown.

CRM unfortunately is an often neglected part of the business sales cycle. Recent CRM research undertaken by Sage found that although take-up of CRM products by UK SMEs (Small to Medium Enterprises) was small – about 8% - over half expressed a wish to be able to manage their customer bases more effectively.

Off-the-shelf

There are many standalone contact management packages available, such as Goldmine or Act! These have the benefit of being very easy to install and configure, allowing you to get on with the business of selling. All of the standard reports you are likely to want to run will be there, with the ability for you to write customised reports. David Pinches, Marketing Director for Sage CRM Solutions, suggests that Act! really can improve marketing technique; *"Act! gives you a complete profile of customers that allows you to conduct targeted campaigns using direct mail, email, telesales etc. Companies using ACT! can also buy in databases and import the lists into their system to do direct marketing or email campaigns. They can then log responses against specific campaigns and see a percentage return."*

Off-the-shelf systems give you an immediately accessible template with which to start with, although customisation and integration with other systems may require a degree of technical skill and may have limitations, depending on the product you choose. Act! and Goldmine are designed to be installed on a local area network, so access over the Internet is restrictive unless you have a VPN (Virtual Private Network). Act! comes in two flavours – the Professional and Workgroups editions. The professional version is suitable for small businesses, while the workgroups edition is for larger companies looking for in-depth business analysis, customisation and integration with other business software.

Fig 2.11.1. Act! is one of the leading CRM systems, best suited to localised databases.

There are alternatives that are web-based, such as Sugar Suite CRM – an Open Source product running through PHP scripts on a MySQL database. Sugar Suite comes in two versions – open source freeware and commercial licensing, with the latter including additional features. It comes with the features you would expect from any competent CRM, including contact and company database, calendar, task lists, lead, bug (problem) and opportunity tracking, email marketing and a 'dashboard' that displays live chart of prospective sales. At the time of writing the freeware version does not have reporting capabilities, although you can easily export any element to CSV for external analysis. Marketing and support modules also compliment Sugar Suite, both of which are available on the same business module, offering an idea way to test the complete suite for suitability.

Tara Smith Spalding, Director of Marketing for SugarCRM believes that housing your database on a web server is better than a local in-house database; *"Today, employees are mobile and are connected to the web at all times. Having a web-based enterprise software system allows companies to manage their data in real-time, and not have delays or redundancies with synchronising. Also, the Sugar Suite is built in a manner so that each user interface is customisable, and can be managed by the administrator. Independent offline systems don't have that kind of control. Lastly, the data security model and data management is centrally managed versus separately managed."*

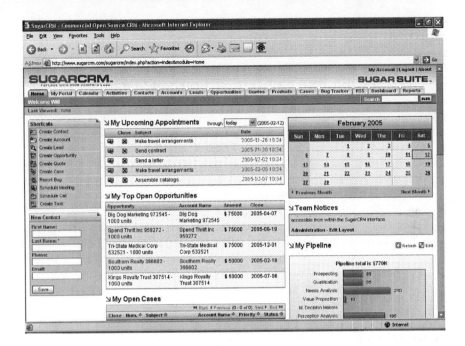

Fig 2.11.2 Sugar Suite CRM offers a complete online CRM for free.

Getting Sugar Suite up and running is reasonably easy, and in fact follows the same procedure as covered in chapter 2.8. As mentioned earlier, you'll need a web server running PHP and MySQL. Download the source files from sugarcrm.com, upload them to your website, edit the included config.php file and run the setup script online. A short wizard takes you through a series of screens to verify your server is configured correctly, and then you're away.

One refreshing methodology that the company employs is the passing down of features between releases – a roadmap on their website (**www.sugarcrm.com**) shows timescales for features that will pass over from the commercial release over to the open source version.

Homegrown

If you want to have total control over the way you can interrogate your data, and you have the time, skill or funds to develop it then you can write your own database. You may also want to access it over the web, which will require a scripting language such as PHP, ASP or Cold Fusion, and effectively twice the development – once to write the database table structure, and then again to write the web interface. Tara Smith Spalding of SugarCRM advises; *"It is always easier, less expensive and faster to customize a robust application versus building one from scratch. Sugar Suite is an inclusive CRM system that an IT professional who understands PHP can customize so that the application can easily adapt to any company's needs. The technology, interface, architecture, algorithms, and database structure has been built by CRM experts and enhanced by the open source community to be one of the most advanced CRM applications."* In other words, you may be better off taking something that meets 90% of your need and tweaking it for that extra 10% rather than building an application from the ground up.

The market leader for small business database solutions is Microsoft Access, although most other database products such as EasyDatabase (included with Easy Office) may also suffice. For web-based systems either mySQL or SQL Server are standard, with mySQL favoured, probably due to its price tag – free. These applications will allow you design the way you structure your data tables in a way that fully supports your business, rather than reconfiguring your business to match one of the off-the-shelf systems mentioned above.

Most homegrown systems will be written for small businesses running from a single location, and discussing how to write a web-based system is outside of the realms of this book. This section, therefore, will concentrate on what you would need to store basic information in a locally stored/accessed database.

> **Try before you buy!**
>
> If you are not sure whether you want to do it yourself or buy a pre-configured system, why not try out one of the Contact Management programs - most have a 30 day downloadable trial on their website which will allow you to see whether you can customise it to your needs. Alternatively, test demos of online products such as Sugar Suite. If it does the job then there is no point spending what will be (I guarantee you!) days or weeks in front of a screen designing tables, forms and reports.

Writing an elementary database in MS Access is relatively straightforward. Once you know what data you want to store (see the following section) simply create a blank table, go into design view and enter your field names, followed by data type. Don't forget to create an AUTONUMBER primary key field that will contain your unique identifier (think of it as an 'account number' that is unique to each record; never getting reused, even if a record is deleted). Once you have your table designed, you can now go into the form view and create the page that you will use to input your data. Of course, this would cover only the most basic of systems – a well-structured system will have various data filters (such as drop-down menus with pre-populated options) with 'one to many' relationships, covered in more detail further on.

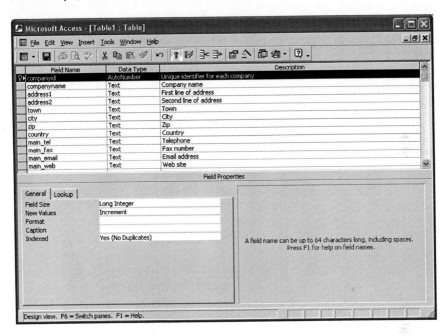

Fig 2.11.3 A basic table within Microsoft Access. The highlighted line is set as a Primary Key, and is therefore unique for each record.

You will, however require a relatively high level of technical expertise to develop a custom database application with suitable security and error trapping, so you should only consider this if off-the-shelf packages just don't fit the gap. For example, do you need to set user permissions so that all staff log in, and certain staff cannot view or amend certain fields/record types? Do you need to check that certain fields have been completed and in a specific format prior to saving? In MS Access, all of this would require the use of a scripting language called Visual Basic, which has a steep learning curve for those not familiar with programming.

What information should I store?
Regardless of which type of system you go for, you must have a clear idea of how you need to structure your data, although most of the work will be

done for you with a pre-designed CRM system. You still need to check to ensure that it meets your entire needs, although adding new fields is never too complex with off-the-shelf systems. Act! comes complete with a form designer, while SugarCRM allows similar functionality through it's web-based administration section.

When applications such as Microsoft Access first made an appearance, many budding programmers wrote simple databases that held little more than name, rank and number plus a comments field that held every piece of information about the company/individual. They then realised that they sometimes needed to separate records by information in that comments field, e.g. customers that required products configured a certain way, or perhaps the last time they were called – in other words, pigeon-holing data correctly. If this information is held in separate fields, it is possible to manipulate the data much easer. For example:

- If you have a 'salesman' field with a drop-down menu listing all of your sales staff, once you have allocated a salesperson to each record you can run reports of records by salesman.
- If you then separate records by type, e.g. prospect, customer, dead lead etc, you can write a report to display all the prospects for a particular salesperson.
- If you have some tick boxes which show the record's main area of interest you can then write a report that shows all prospects for a particular salesperson that are interested in a particular product range.

With only three fields we already have the makings of a very specific marketing campaign!

You need to examine your customer base and how each customer differs from each other to decide this, so it is impossible to provide a finite list of fields to create for your business within this book. If you opt for an off-the-shelf CRM package, then you can skip this section as it will undoubtedly have all of the main bases covered. If you're building your own database here are most of the common fields that you should have.

- company name
- invoice address (broken down to street, city, county, zip, country)
- delivery details
- additional delivery addresses (broken down as Invoice address)
- telephone
- fax
- email
- website

- contacts
  - name
  - job title
  - direct number
  - mobile number
  - email address
- call log
  - date of call
  - name of person who called
  - details of call
  - outcome of call (this could be a pull-down menu with set options, such as 'complete', 'to call back', 'not available' etc)
  - notes
- due follow-up date
- sales person (drop-down list of all sales staff)
- record type (drop-down list showing customer, prospect, dead lead etc).

Note: Where items in the list above are sub-bulleted, this will indicate a 'one-to-many' relationship. This means that, for example with contacts and call logs, you will probably have several contacts and many call logs for one company. In the screenshot taken from Act! (pictured) you can see that the bottom part of the screen would allow for many sub-records/logs to be appended to a single company record.

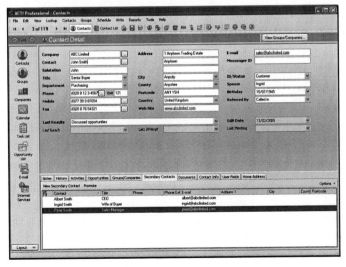

Fig 2.11.4 Act! takes care of 'one-to-many' relationships with a tabbed view at the bottom half of the screen and a tabular list of sub-records.

The importance of breaking down your data into manageable, searchable chunks cannot be stressed highly enough, especially the custom fields relating to your products or company's method of doing business. Where you have a finite, structured list for a specific field, create a separate table with a field for your item and an 'autonumber' field. Now list the contents of that table as a drop-down menu from your main table. For example, if you wanted a field for 'source of enquiry' you could create a table calls Source that lists all of the options (which you can easily add to later), and then use the 'Lookup Wizard' in Access to link this to your main table. This will store the unique identifying number of the enquiry source table in the main table. As you add new enquiry sources they will automatically be reflected in the dropdown field in the main table.

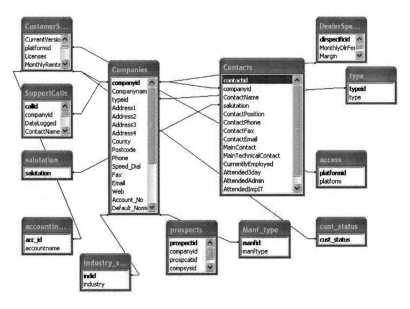

Fig 2.11.5. This database shows many tables linked to two main tables. The smaller sub-tables all populate drop-down menus.

How do I export data from the system for mailshots?

This depends very much on what you intend to do with the information, but generally you will either be exporting into a separate file (for importing into another application) or exporting data into a reporting module within your software (which may also include mailing label 'reports').

Off-the-shelf products such as Act! have simple to use yet powerful reporting functions that allow for easy extraction of very specific record types into any desired format, so in reality you will almost never need to export data out of it. By running a wizard you can create a 'report' of mailing labels or letters based on a 'look up', which might be all prospects that have expressed an interest in a particular product range. MS Access has good reporting, mail-merge and label creation facilities, but they require a little more skill (not much more, but a little more nonetheless!) Merging between MS Access and MS Word is covered in Chapter 2.3. For bulk emailing you are better off exporting your contacts to a CSV file and importing to a dedicated package such as Infacta Groupmail, covered earlier in the book.

The importance of accuracy

It is all very well having a database that allows for quick and detailed information entry and retrieval, but if the users of the system do not understand the relevance of data integrity, or indeed what each and every field means then you will quickly end up with an unorganised heap of irrelevant data. For example, if users start entering information into a Notes field rather than ticking appropriate fields or using pull-down menus, then running reports based on those fields will result in missed records.

Whether using an off-the-shelf package or an in-house system built from a database product such as Microsoft Access, ensure that you set 'error-traps' on fields you want to specify as mandatory, or fields that must have a certain type of entry or format such as phone numbers. You can never completely eliminate these types of errors, but you can dramatically reduce them with a little forethought. You may even want to design some queries that look for errors, e.g. email addresses without @ or companies without contacts attributed to them. Before going live, get some of your users to enter some sample data so you can see how they interpret the information they receive or ask for. Ideally the system should be designed around the way your company works, not the other way around. Give training to all system users, and back this up with training documents or online help that they can refer to. If you are designing your own application, add 'tooltips' to each field with a concise description of its use and data format.

Data protection issues

Depending on which country you are based in, you may have to adhere to legislation relating to the storage and use of personal data. UK laws for example, state that businesses must register details of the data controller within their business with the Information Commissioner (governor of the Data Protection Act) and must comply with eight basic principles of good practice. Data must be:

- fairly and lawfully processed
- processed for limited purposes

- adequate, relevant and not excessive
- accurate
- not kept longer than necessary
- processed in accordance with the data subject's rights
- secure
- not transferred to countries without adequate protection.

Over the last few years, you may have seen the tick-boxes underneath the small print of anything you fill in (be it for a new bank account, magazine competition etc) asking if you wish to opt out of receiving 'carefully selected offers' - this is normally to ensure that the company is in compliance with data protection laws. They are ensuring that there is no legal recourse when they sell your details onto other companies for marketing purposes. The laws are not so stringent if you intend to use the details only for in-house purposes, but must be adhered to nonetheless. In the UK, there is a £35 (around $60) fee to register your company on the Data Protection register (more info at **http://www.dpr.gov.uk**). If you are not already registered, do it immediately as there are heavy penalties for non-registration or abuse of this law.

Summary

❑ The choice of CRM you make will depend on the technical ability within your company. For an immediate customisable solution for staff in a single location, buy Act! If you need a highly customised solution (and have the skill, time or deep pockets), then build your own system. For those with staff working remotely, products such as Sugar Suite may offer a more flexible solution, especially as the basic product is free and highly customisable due to its open source architecture.

❑ Once you have a well-structured database in place the opportunities are limitless. With junk mail – both electronic and paper based – being high on people's hate lists these days it is important to make your direct marketing efforts as targeted as possible. If a user is likely to have an interest in the product you are informing them of they are less likely to regard your company (and therefore future mailings) as junk. Also, your campaigns are likely to have a higher success rate and cost you less. This is of even greater importance with email marketing, as a simple click of the 'Add to Junk Mail' filter can forever banish you from your prospect's in-box. Ensure that all users of the database understand the importance of accurately entering data into the system and make sure that there is adequate training and help documentation.

Conclusion

If you create more leads, close more sales or reduce your marketing costs because of implementing just one of the ideas covered in this book, then you have already justified your expenditure, probably many times over. Hopefully you now have a much better insight into the many methods of low-cost promotion and may even be more creative because of a newfound ability to identify the successful campaigns of others and modify them to meet your own needs. Although marketing is about the promotion of your company and products, without a solid foundation of material the job is made much more difficult.

The second edition of this book pays greater attention to online promotion as it continues to grow in importance for the success of many businesses. A good web presence can come very cheap if you have the design and technical skills to build it yourself. If you don't possess these talents, hopefully this book will at least give you a firmer foundation of knowledge for tackling such projects, either by yourself or through a web design agency. Search engine placement can make a major difference to the level of enquiries you receive, so pay particular attention to this area. If you are in a niche market, you stand a greater chance of getting to the top of the pile.

Marketing covers such a broad area and every business needs to be marketed differently, but it does need to be marketed. Many companies make the mistake of only allocating more time, resources and budget when times are hard. The fact is that times are probably hard because of a lack of effective marketing in the first place. Well-marketed businesses are successful because of a continual drip-feeding of material to relevant groups – prospects, customers, media, partners etc. With that in mind here is a final top ten guide of the most important marketing tips:

1. **Get your own house in order first.** Ensure that you have a good database structure that allows you to easily access and extract information so that, for example, you can print out a mail shot or perform an email-shot in minutes. A quick response to an emerging situation can really make a difference to the bottom line.

2. **Have a single source for marketing material.** Whatever form of media you distribute, be it electronic, CD-ROM or printed material, make sure that everyone knows where it is and keep everything together. Make sure that sales reps or dealers have stocks and are using up-to-date material.

3. **Do it now!** If an editor asks for a picture to be emailed, or a prospect wants additional information mailed make sure you respond promptly. This is why it's all the more important to have a well structured and immediately accessible repository of material. If you've just received an enquiry from your website why not call the prospect straight away – even while they may still be on your site! A prompt response creates a lasting impression.

4. **Make the website the first place for new information, not the last.** Customers will not visit your website if they know that it's going to look the same as the last time they came. If you make it a useful resource they will visit it before calling you. Whenever you produce a new brochure, case study or press release, ensure that it goes online first. Press releases (and associated images) should appear on the site before distribution to the press. Revisit the site regularly and get feedback from customers and prospects about what they like and dislike about it.

5. **Make electronic versions of all brochures and forms.** PDF creating programs such as Cute PDF Writer are freely available and will continue to save you money in postage and printing costs. Any piece of paper that is sent to a prospect can be turned into an electronic document, and can then either be emailed or posted on your website allowing prospects to serve themselves.

6. **Build good relationships with the media.** Treat your relationship with editors as a win-win – you want to give them a story that will be of use to them. Negotiate exclusive deals for specific editorial, such as case studies to guarantee good exposure. Be approachable and offer yourself as a voice in the industry.

7. **Check, check and recheck.** Before you send anything out of your company (or even internal emails/memos), it takes no time to run your both your spell checker and your eyes over it. You'll be amazed how many minor mistakes it'll pick up, but these all make a difference. Get others to check your work as well, as it is very difficult to proof read your own material. I didn't proof read this book myself!

8. **Be a wheeler-dealer.** Look for co-op marketing and contra-deal opportunities. Can you offer someone a product or service in return for some free or joint publicity? Also, maybe one of your customers can provide you with a required product or service in exchange for an upgrade, new product etc. giving you an opportunity to perhaps use them as an upgrade case study.

9. **Network with similar companies.** If there are companies that market non-conflicting products to the same customer base then build relationships with them. Maybe produce a joint newsletter, host a joint event or share costs at a trade show. Where such relationships exist ensure that this crossover is also reflected on your websites, which could result in high search engine rankings and traffic.

10. **Enjoy yourself!** This repeats the statement that I made in the introduction, but it is probably one of the most important aspects of marketing and communication in general, especially if your role requires a degree of face-to-face contact. If you take pleasure in your work this will come across and affect others – enthusiasm is actually very infectious. Also, ask yourself this: Do you prefer to be around positive, happy people or those with a negative approach to life? If you've successfully practiced all of the above it is genuinely possible for you to positively change the working environment of those around you, by making their jobs easier – through more sales enquiries, less paperwork, better information retrieval, self-serving customers, good company reputation etc.

Now that you've read the theory and seen how this can be brought into practice, don't forget to keep the continual drip-feeding going. In the following Appendices you'll find additional information and online resources. The accompanying CD-ROM is also backed up by a website that lists the latest discoveries to help you market your company quickly, cheaply and effectively.

I hope you've found this book as interesting to read as it was to write. Despite being in a marketing role for over fifteen years, I constantly pick up new ideas, tips and tricks not only from colleagues and customers but also by simply observing how other companies are promoting themselves. In fact I re-wrote the entire search engine submission chapter just before finishing this book, as I'd encountered several new useful techniques.

If you have successes as a result of this book, visit my website at **www.marketingyour.biz** and share it with everyone. We are all still learning and I am always encouraged and excited by seeing others stretch their boundaries. See Appendix 6 for further information on the site and its content.

While I don't advocate complete plagiarism, it is common practice to take elements of an idea you like and tailor it to meet your own needs. So, now that you are armed with your newfound knowledge I wish you luck as you go forth and market!

Appendix 1 – Marketing Manager's Calendar

It is useful to compile a list of tasks that you should regularly perform to keep your company's profile in the public eye.

Every week

- Check your website log statistics, especially the error log to make sure there are no dead links. Immediately fix problems and recheck.

- If you have a search facility on your site, check the search keywords people are using. Modify or add content accordingly, paying particular attention to the title of the pages on your site.

Every month

- Send out at least one press release

- Ensure at the very least that new content appears on your home page

- Check your site's rankings in all the major search engines using your chosen keywords. Also use online tools such as Google Sandbox and Overture to ensure you are using the most relevant keywords. Check your site's performance in Alexa against your competitors. Collate and compare all of this data to identify your site's strengths and weaknesses

- Visit your competitors' web sites to see what's new. Run a keyword checker over them to see which words they are using, and check where they appear in the search engines

- Organise at least one product review for the press (if relevant)

- Organise at least one case study

Every quarter

- Send out at least one newsletter to your customers and/or prospects. Also make it available electronically on your website

- Extensively review the content on your website, refreshing where necessary

Every year

- Call every magazine in your database to verify that your contacts are still correct

- Organise at least one major press event, such as a product launch

- Organise a user day to keep loyal customers informed and to gain useful feedback

- If your company offers service contracts, perhaps make a special offer for companies or users that have allowed this to lapse

- Ensure you have the latest editorial calendars from all relevant magazines, making note of issues with articles that you may be able to submit editorial for

- Perform a major review of your web design and content – does it still match the current company image? Is all of the old content still relevant to be included (such as press releases on deals which may have fallen through – do you still want people to read about them?)

Appendix 2 – Case Studies

Here is a small selection of case studies relating to how different companies have maximised their exposure at minimal expense.

1. The small retail outlet

Two 'computer techies' set up a company from home, building and repairing PCs. After a couple of years, they had grown out of working from home (and their garages), deciding to make the move to a retail-based business while still maintaining and growing their consultancy and support trade. Much of their business was from existing customers due to strong customer service focus.

Marketing Strategy

The initial issue to tackle was that of perception. Previously all of their business was either conducted at the customer's site or over the phone, so working from home did not matter. They were now trying to attract customers to their premises, so priority needed to be placed on decorating the shop to give customers visual assurance of their stability and professionalism. The shop front window was transformed into a series of interchangeable adverts (simply by printing large format adverts onto paper, laminating them and hanging them vertically with thread). Their suppliers were able to provide empty product packaging and posters – some larger companies can supply more elaborate display material. As a talking point, a display cabinet was built in an unused but easily visible part of the store that contained several old (early 80s) computers with a timeline showing how the computers had evolved. This gave the perception to new visitors that the company had been trading long enough to sell such computers!

An open day was planned and the local weekly papers contacted. This resulted in news articles appearing before the event – drawing visitors – and press with accompanying photos after the event.

A website was constructed (using Actinic Catalog) not only covering items that they stocked but also products that could be delivered quickly giving the perception that they carried a large amount of stock. The site mainly focused on parts rather than complete systems to promote the growth of higher turnover products. The site was submitted to search engines with keywords optimised for the products carried and the geographical region.

Results

The local press coverage worked extremely effectively, with many visitors to the shop carrying the newspapers with them. Customer referrals increased, as did their number of web sales. Many customers would visit the showroom and subsequently make a purchase online later. The website also yielded a higher than expected number of sales outside of the geographical region due to successful search engine rankings. An indirect benefit of the web turnover was greater purchasing power. The parts business also required less work than system building and repair, so although more staff were required (and hired) the additional overhead was substantially less than the profit achieved.

Customers' perception of the company, both online and in the shop was that of a small, but robust business with a long-standing history, wide product range and friendly staff. More store staff of a higher knowledge level were afforded by the increase in web sales, which required minimal resources to sustain.

2. The recycling company

The company was started in the early 1990s, originally set up to sell waste compaction machines and balers for recycling. In 1994, they developed a complete one-stop shop waste management package hoping to take advantage of the substantial business opportunities relating to environmental issues generated by the UK's production of millions of tonnes of commercial waste.

A small team of sales consultants were used to sell directly to their target market of supermarkets, hospitals, hotels, food manufacturers, logistic & distribution companies and more. The majority of sales were secured via a sequence of on-site visits, an often time-consuming and expensive exercise, taking into account travelling time etc. Many organisations were not aware of the ever-changing legislation relating to waste disposal and also the equipment and products were often highly visible on a customer's site. The MD was also concerned about global warming and wanted to raise awareness at a corporate level.

Marketing Strategy

The aim here was to increase awareness of the company within its industry, reduce internal overheads, reduce the sales cycle period and increase customer awareness of their legal obligations.

Regular press releases to relevant trade magazines in each sector with case studies of target customers ensured that the company received exposure and drew prospective clients' attention to some of the legal issues they faced.

Products were branded with the company logo and phone number (and later on the website) and a USP was identified – to supply the equipment in the purchasers corporate colours, or to match their building, or to have a slogan of their choice sign written on the waste containers.

A rental plan was designed that reflected the savings the customer would make by recycling, but that also required no initial large financial outlay.

An Intranet was set up to allow remote staff to easily access the company database. Plans were also drawn up to build an Extranet for key customers. A demo CD was created containing videos of all products in use.

A separate website was set up (using phpNuke) to allow the MD the ability to add news and items relating to global warming. It was focused on positive actions as well as negative so as not to appear 'all doom and gloom'. The MD was also put forward as a candidate on radio debates on the subject.

Results

The CD-ROM not only succeeded in reducing the time to close an order, but also reduced literature printing and postage costs. Customers were able to sign up to the rental agreement with minimal risk and a range of guarantees substantially increasing sales. The flow of information, both internally and to larger, more demanding customers was increased. Overall customer perception was improved because of the demonstrated quality of service.

By providing customers with self-service access to information they reduced overheads and increased customer retention simultaneously. The company itself ran smoother and leaner because of an infrastructure geared towards ensuring online information was accurate. A good brand was established with a reputation for affordability and flexibility. The MD has become more of a voice in the industry and is now called upon for quotes from the media when related situations arise. Their overall success led them to become the 14th fastest growing company in the UK in 2003, according to UK accounting and business advisory company Vantis.

3. The notebook PC distributor

This company imported notebook computers from Taiwan and resold them to a network of resellers, which either had retail outlets or dealt with local businesses or government bodies.

Marketing Strategy

A brand name was created and the notebooks were customised to give them a unique brand image. Resellers were giving marketing funds (a percentage of the advert cost) to advertise the products exclusively. Notebooks were sent for single and group product reviews in monthly technology magazines. Adverts were placed in trade journals to entice new resellers, and the Sales and Marketing Manager also performed an interview for a trade magazine. (This was in the early 1990s and therefore web sites and Internet access were not commonplace).

A notebook PC was supplied for a competition in a magazine. This coincided with a review in the same issue. The Sales and Marketing Manager also did a video interview that appeared on the cover disc of an end user related magazine.

A relationship was set up with a similar importer to jointly import from the same supplier, cutting shipping costs and increasing buying power. A subsidiary company was also set up to facilitate direct telesales.

Results

The products themselves were good and as a result received positive reviews in the press. This not only created a great deal of end-user interest, but also gave resellers confidence to take on the product range. The co-op marketing ensured that the products were covered in virtually every major computer magazine, giving the perception of a widely available brand. Resellers had a good range of marketing material supplied to them, which was in addition to the increasing number of product reviews available.

The agreement with the magazine that ran the competition was that they supplied the names and addresses of all entrants, which was several thousand names. These were provided to the direct sales subsidiary company to pursue both over the phone and by direct mailing.

The company went from an initial staff of two to a £2m ($3.3m) company within two years. A strong brand was established with a geographically well-spread dealer network operating effectively, backed up by constant press and advertising coverage.

4. The small software/hardware manufacturer

Initially specialising in bespoke hardware and software, this company needed to increase revenue in other areas as the market they were serving was in decline, both due to current market conditions and technological advances. The company's products handled the flow of programming information to factory shopfloor machinery. One main problem (especially with larger prospects) was that of the perception of company size and stability, as the company had only four staff and was disorganised. As a result many of their customers, who were loyal only because there was a limited choice of alternative vendors, had a poor opinion of the company and its level of support.

Marketing Strategy

An office-based General Manager was employed to handle day-to-day running of the business, as the other staff members were often called out of the office.

The company diversified into increasing sales of PCs, components and software to its existing client base. PCs were already manufactured to accompany hardware and software products; therefore internal mechanisms were already in place to handle this.

Laser-printed newsletters were produced in-house and mailed out regularly to customers. Technical articles were written for specific trade magazines to demonstrate the company's technical skills. A price list of systems and components (most of which were ordered as required) was also sent out regularly.

An opportunity arose to partner with another company to provide prizes for a competition featured on a national TV programme.

Results

The business ran much smoother as customer enquiries were answered within acceptable timescales, stock arrived when required and staff were kept informed of day-to-day requirements. Maintenance contract renewals which were previously in decline were now regularly renewed, adding a steadier base to the company's cash flow.

By raising the profile through direct mail, product range expansion and press coverage this drastically reduced new customer's fear of dealing with a small organisation. The TV coverage added to this further, while also allowing future newsletters and price lists to include the coveted 'As seen on TV'.

Within six months sales were split 50/50 between bespoke products and PCs, reducing the company's reliance on their diminishing market, while also opening up a B2C sales channel. Computer component sales increased turnover with minimal resource requirements, plus the company image was improved by the perception of a much larger product range.

5. The electronics catalogue company

A relatively large organisation with approximately 800 staff, this company sold a wide range of electronic components via a large 'telephone directory-sized' catalogue, produced annually. Each division of the catalogue was split into sales divisions – this study focuses on the Computer Products section.

Marketing Strategy

The main problem for this department was that the product range and pricing changed much more frequently than the catalogue's production cycle. As a result their main vehicle for product promotion was normally several months out of date.

A fax-shot mechanism was set up to send out weekly single-page updates with push products and special offers. Deals were set up with suppliers to run special 'blitz days', with push products being subsidised by the vendors. Adverts were placed in computer trade magazines, again subsidised by vendors to move the perception of the company away from being a supplier of components such as resistors and cables.

A CD-ROM was developed to accompany the catalogue. (At the time group politics prevented a specific website from being created to handle online sales).

Results

Part-paid adverts and fax-shots helped to quickly increase sales of new products and reduce inventory of slow-moving stock. The CD-ROM, which could be updated more frequently, gave a more up-to-date reflection of the current product range, while also being cheaper to produce and distribute.

The sales team was more motivated because of the excitement generated by the blitz days, as these generally also included prizes for the top sellers.

Using the company's strong catalogue brand helped secure excellent co-op funding agreements with suppliers, thus allowing for increased advertising to targeted magazines to build a wider customer base.

6. The vertical market software company

Selling through a worldwide network of resellers this company relied on them to market the products in their own region, supplying brief product literature and offering little in the way of support to allow them to enhance their own marketing material. Although the product itself was very strong there was no press or advertising to back it up, with the exception of annual trade fairs that dealers funded and attended. The company's website was designed in-house but consisted of a few pages containing basic text and images, with a domain name suffix that was difficult to guess.

Marketing Strategy

New brochures and a new website were designed. All major country suffixes of the domain were purchased and pointed at the new site, which was also optimised and submitted to search engines. Additional domains with specific keywords were also purchased. The site was geared towards lead-generation, with all pages having direct link to the brochure request form. A 'marketing CD' was created and distributed to all dealers, allowing them to quickly create quality literature that was customisable and translatable.

Regular case studies and press releases were distributed to the press worldwide (both direct and through dealers). Several video case studies were also produced, and made available on the web, demo CD and in DVD-ROM format for running as looped demos at exhibitions. At annual trade shows a unique theme was created to differentiate the company from its competitors – one year featured a tank ('crush your competition') and a helicopter ('Fly XXXXX'), while another featured a Laurel and Hardy lookalike duo (see case study 7 for more details).

A demo CD was created using Macromedia Flash for customers, containing product videos, case studies in PDF format and a short movie featuring the Laurel and Hardy duo used at a trade show. The disc was designed to be customisable and translatable, so dealers could also add their own content as required. Videa case studies were also added.

A download section was created on the website to give a slick self-service mechanism for both dealers and end users. It was built in such a way as to allow dealers the ability to plug it into their own site seamlessly, thus giving a value added service to their clients. Other 'plug-ins' were also written that allowed dealers to take content from the main site and display it as their own. One example of this was the creation of several video case studies, which dealers could 'stream' from their websites, with content being drawn dynamically from the manufacturer's server. The company's in-house Marketing Manager also offered free web design and promotion services for dealers who did not have the skills to develop their own site.

Results

Emphasis was placed on helping resellers to help themselves by removing the bottleneck of marketing where they did not possess the skills or time. Existing resellers grew their market share because of better customer perception and market awareness. A constant press presence backed this up, and the company grew a reputation for innovative displays at exhibitions.

Web site traffic and sales leads grew, with search engines playing a major part in this success. Sales lead also leapt up after increasing the visibility of the online brochure request form. The web plug-ins also proved successful, allowing the company to maintain control over content while giving dealers easy access to good quality material for their own sites.

New dealers were easier to recruit and get up and running because of the wide availability of marketing tools available to them. Web sites were constructed for dealers as required, with customised PDF documents containing the dealer's contact information being generated as required.

The demo CD proved extremely effective, with dealers making their own as needed, ensuring that the latest information was always included.

By providing the dealers with tools to create their own material, a level of professionalism was maintained regardless of the individual dealer's design skills. The company recruited more dealers and gained continual media coverage, which led to more sales with a quicker closure cycle. Their brand perception was improved, which was of additional importance when the company branched into a new business sector.

7. The comedy double-act

A Laurel and Hardy double-act had achieved considerable success at minor events, but the two actors were only able to generate enough work for a part-time income. Although they were well known by the relevant entertainment agencies they were not receiving many new offers of work, despite critical acclaim wherever they appeared.

Marketing Strategy

A chance meeting with the software company featured in case study 6 allowed a contra deal to be set up. Already contracted by the company to appear at a trade show, the duo agreed a free day's filming in exchange for the company's Marketing Manager to design them a website, and free use of any of the material created.

It was decided that a short comedy film would be created that would be included on the company's demo disc. A script was written relating the duo's antics to the software products, and the company contacted one of its customers for permission to use their premises for filming in exchange for a free software package. The local newspaper was also contacted, with a piece appearing in the following issue.

A website was created that contained a variety of pictures of the duo in action at previous events, many of which included several major celebrities, and even Royalty. A full history of the lookalike duo and the original Laurel and Hardy was added, together with details and links to all of their films on Amazon.com – this also generated revenue through Amazon's affiliate program, albeit in small amounts. The site was optimised for keywords relating to tribute acts, body doubles and look-alikes, then submitted to search engines. Similar sites such as comedy portals and fan sites were also contacted, requesting links to the new site. A .com domain name was purchased and pointed to the site, as the existing domain was long and difficult to remember. Desktop wallpapers and high-resolution images were also available for download.

A DVD and VHS cassette were created using both previous footage and content taken from the day's filming.

Results

Web traffic increased dramatically, as did the number and quality of enquiries. Many leads arrived as a result of users following links on other relevant sites, or by using specific keyword searches. Customers liked the idea of being able to download high-resolution pictures that they could then incorporate into their own marketing initiatives for the events they were promoting. Adding free giveaways such as the desktop wallpapers drew additional traffic and gave more substance to the site.

The DVD and VHS cassette greatly enhanced customer perception of the duo as a reputable class act by demonstrating the types of events they attend and the breadth of their talents. By crossing over from theatre and public events to entertainment at business events a new market was opened up to the duo, with several companies contacting them directly after their first event.

The perception of the duo as a serious double-act was raised exponentially, as many of their peers operate on a low-cost part-time basis and have little more than promo photos or business cards to promote themselves.

From a cost perspective, much of this was achieved by a trade off of services – a day of their time filming got them a high quality website that generated good leads and excellent content for their DVD.

8. The holiday resort hotel

A family-run hotel near Venice, Italy was looking to increase the number of direct bookings they received. Previously they relied heavily on tour operators, who made tough demands for very low profit margins. The hoteliers also wanted to extend the seasonal opening period of the hotel to cater more for business bookings, which would also make use of the recently refurbished conference facilities. Guests that had previously visited the hotel frequently booked directly the following year, but there was little in the way of pre-prepared information to assist them.

Marketing Strategy

It was clear that guests visiting the hotel needed more information about organising future visits. It was suggested that a leaflet be designed that guests could take away detailing the following year's prices (with a 'direct booking' discount), together with information on booking direct flights to various local airports.

A website was constructed that listed the hotel's facilities, including a gallery of dozens of photos showing locations in and around the hotel. Additional information such as hotel history, flight information, live and updated weather information, local attractions and links to various sites of interest was also posted on the site. It was also written in four European languages to cater for the majority of visitors.

Results

By the following year direct bookings were substantially up, allowing the hoteliers to reduce their reliance on tour operators and making the business much more profitable. Even customers that came via tour companies used the website to plan their holiday, and frequently praised the content of the site. Two years after the initial website was launched a 'micro-site' was created to publicise a villa that the hoteliers had also built. This was let almost entirely through web-based bookings.

As the dependency on the tour operators had been reduced this also gave the hotel owners greater bargaining power when negotiating rates. They were able to cost-effectively and immediate promote their new property online with great success.

9. The Book Publisher

Management Books 2000 (the publisher of this book!) had a website that, as with so many small businesses, had been written in-house. It was constructed using an old version Actinic Catalog and separate HTML pages. The author subsequently left the company, leaving staff with limited HTML experience to maintain the site. As a result pages outside of Actinic bore no resemblance and there were many graphics that did not appear on the site. The publisher felt that the site did not offer his authors the level of marketing support that he would like, but he did not have the technical skills in-house to bring it to the desired level of quality.

Marketing Strategy

An upgrade was suggested to the latest version of Actinic, which allows 'brochure pages' to be created. This removed the need for HTML pages to be created outside of the easy-to-use catalogue interface of Actinic. It was recommended that a newsletter be sent to all existing authors, advising of the site – this was not only to demonstrate the publisher's commitment to them, but also to request links from the author's own site (where relevant) to mb2000.com, which should assist the site with search engine rankings. Additional training was given to the publisher to optimise the site for search engines from with Actinic.

The Results

After the new site went live there was a marked increase in sales, although traffic did not immediately rise. This was because the conversion rate of 'browsers to buyers' was much higher. The feedback from existing authors was encouraging, and new authors confirmed that they felt they were dealing with a larger, professional company. The newsletter inspired several authors to contact the publisher to discuss new projects. Web traffic continued to rise, not only due to the search engine optimisation, but also through to a rise in links back from authors websites back to mb2000.com.

Case studies summary

In all of these examples, the companies concerned were able to raise their profile through cost-effective methods such as PR or low-cost contact methods to their customers and/or prospect. While advertising played a part with some of them, it was only ever a part of the overall marketing strategy.

Online presence has also played a major part in the success of most of the above. Again this is a relatively low-cost method of reaching new prospects and should be at or near the top of any marketing strategy.

Appendix 3 – CD-ROM Contents

The accompanying CD-ROM contains a wide range of applications covering the majority of tasks that a Marketing Manager is likely to want to perform. Note that the CD-ROM has been added after book production and is in continual development, therefore please view the index on the CD-ROM for a complete and accurate list of programs as some applications may have been added/modified/removed from the list below.

Please also check the license agreement with each application as 'freeware' may only apply to non-commercial use of the product.

Analog Log Analyser
Source: www.analog.cx/
Dubbed the most popular log analyser in the world, this product is excellent if you want a quick method of generating statistical analysis of the visitors to your website. Requires a reasonable degree of understanding of web server configuration to set up. *Freeware*.

Ace HTML 5
Source: http://freeware.acehtml.com/
AceHTML 5 is a powerful HTML editor designed both for novices and professional webmasters. Includes an extensive array of features such as the HTML syntax code checker, ensuring the validity of the user's HTML code, the code explorer, providing rapid document navigation, and over 175 built-in DHTML and JavaScript samples helping you add interactivity to your website. *Freeware*.

Act!
Source: www.act.com
Used by over 4 million people worldwide, Act! offers a complete and integrated contact management solution, providing a full diary and task list that are linked to each contact record. *Trial version*.

Actinic Catalog
Source: www.actinic.com
Actinic Catalog delivers an easy method of getting your company's products online. It offers the ability to import/export information, link into online payment services (including PayPal) and place up to 10,000 products online. Actinic Catalog is suitable for direct selling whereas Actinic Business

allows for the creation of individual customers, each having access to their own special pricing. *30-day trial version.*

Active Media Magnet
Source: www.myrasoft.com
Media Magnet allows targeted submission of press releases. With four easy steps you can create and send out to over 20,000 media contacts a press release. You can submit and re-submit your release as often as you like. You can also create your own list from your contacts. This is definitely helpful for newsletter generators. *30-day trial version.*

Adobe PhotoShop
Source: www.adobe.com
The standard for imaging editing on both PC and Apple Macintosh computers. Includes a variety of filters to create stunning special effects. *Trial version.*

Audacity
Source: http://audacity.sourceforge.net
Excellent freeware open source audio editor. Built in effects include amplify, echo, fade in/out, reverse, bass boost and noise removal. Also supports export to Ogg Vorbis, WAV and MP3 formats. *Open source freeware.*

AVG Antivirus
Source: www.grisoft.com
AVG Free edition is an antivirus solution suitable for home and non-commercial use. This version is completely unrestricted and acts as a good demonstration of Grisoft's full professional and network version. *Freeware.*

Camtasia Studio
Source: www.technsmith.com
Screen capture software that allows you to make a recording of your screen as you narrate. Ideal for producing demonstrations or tutorials that can be emailed or added to a CD-ROM. *Trial version.*

Cute PDF Printer
Source: www.acrosoftware.com/
An extremely useful program that sets itself up as a virtual printer. You can then 'print to PDF', creating Adobe Acrobat documents that can then be emailed or used on your website. *Freeware.*

DHTML Menu Builder
Source: http://software.xfx.net
DHTML Builder allows you to build 'drop-down' menus easily and without much knowledge of HTML. Each menu can have sub-menus, together with graphics and special effects. The version on this disc allows you to create and embed menus, however no hyperlinks will work. *Trial version.*

Dynamic Submission
Source: www.dynamicsubmission.com
One of the leading website submission tools. In addition to submitting your site to over 1000 search engines, it will also help you to optimise your pages by pointing out where you can increase the strength of keywords, meta tags and titles. Meta tag and gateway page generators are also included. *Trial version.*

GIF Animator
Source: www.microsoft.com
Basic but useful program from Microsoft that allows you to quickly create animated GIF files for use on websites. You start by creating a set of images in your favourite image editing program, then import them into GIF Animator. You can then set the duration of each 'slide', and the export quality. *Freeware.*

ICQ Lite
Source: www.icq.com
An excellent instant messaging software that allows you to see when colleagues are online, wherever they are in the world. Can drastically reduce call cost and improve productivity. Full version (also free) includes many additional features. *Freeware.*

Infacta Groupmail
Source: www.infacta.com
Bulk email solution that allows you to easily control large email lists while sending professionally formatted messages that are personalised to recipients. A variety of free plug-ins are available for the Plus and Pro versions. *Freeware.*

Inno Setup
Source: www.jrsoftware.org
A setup creation file, this program is ideal if you want to distribute software or files in a single package, with the user installing them in a pre-determined method, order and location. Creates a single EXE file with the ability to

compress included files, compare file info, create shortcuts, registry entries and an uninstall routine. *Freeware.*

Irfan View 3.75
Source: www.irfanview.com
This is a popular freeware image viewer and converter. The list of file types supported is one of its greatest attributes, including: AIF, ANI/CUR, ASF, AU/SND, AVI, BMP/DIB, CAM (Casio JPG), CLP, Dicom/ACR, DJVU, EMF/WMF, EPS, FlashPix (FPX), FSH, G3, GIF, ICO/ICL/EXE/DLL, IFF/LBM, IMG (GEM), JPG2000, JPG/JPEG, KDC, LDF, LWF, MED, MID/RMI, MOV, MP3, MPG/MPEG, NLM/NOL/NGG, PBM/PGM/PPM, PCX/DCX, PhotoCD, PNG, PSD, PSP, RAS/SUN, RealAudio (RA), RLE, SFF, SFW, SGI/RGB, SWF (Flash/Shockwave), TGA, TIF/TIFF, WAV, WBMP, XBM, XPM. *Freeware.*

JPEG Optimiser
Source: www.xat.com
JPEG Optimizer squeezes JPG images by applying special algorithms. This is ideal for compressing graphics to appear on web pages so that they take less time to download. You can choose how much quality you are happy to lose, then save the new image – this can sometimes be half the size of the original file, or even less. Note: Many high-end graphics packages such as Photoshop also have similar functions. *Trial version.*

Keyword Extractor
Source: www.analogx.com/
Have you ever wondered why some web sites end up higher on search engine results than others? Now there's a new tool to add to your search engine analysis – AnalogX Keyword Extractor! AnalogX Keyword Extractor (KeyEx) extracts all of the keywords from a webpage, then sorts and indexes them based on their usage and position. Once indexed, you can adjust search-engine specific weighting factors and keyword criteria to get the best possible view of how a search engine sees your site. KeyEx can load up both local files as well as files off other web sites, can work through a proxy, and can have separate configurations for as many search engines as required. *Freeware.*

Listmaster Pro
Source: www.analogx.com/
If you run an email mailing list (or have been considering starting one), then AnalogX ListMaster Pro will be a useful tool. AnalogX ListMaster Pro allows you to quickly and easily manage a mailing list – from a couple hundred

people, to lists spanning hundreds of thousands – all from a simple to use interface. It helps you identify which email addresses are valid or invalid, and lets you sort them by a number of criteria. It will also let you see how many people are subscribing from different countries (based on their domain extension). Best of all, it's ULTRA fast, it can load and sort a list of over 100,000 addresses in under 10 seconds! It can remove duplicate entries from that same list in less than 2 seconds, and it's completely multi-threaded for maximum performance when performing any time consuming task. *Freeware.*

Macromedia Contribute
Source: www.macromedia.com
Macromedia Contribute is the easiest way for individuals and teams to update, create, and publish web content to any HTML website. Administrative controls let non-technical users make content changes while Contribute maintains site standards for style, layout, and code. *Trial version.*

Macromedia Dreamweaver MX
Source: www.macromedia.com
The industry standard product when it comes to HTML editing. Dreamweaver is also expandable through a variety of free extensions available online. *Trial version.*

Macromedia Flash MX
Source: www.macromedia.com
Macromedia Flash MX is the solution for developing highly visual interactive content and applications that can be used either on the web or a CD-ROM. Flash can also pull content directly from a Macromedia Cold Fusion server to deliver live content in a rich media environment. *Trial version.*

Open Office
Source: www.openoffice.org
Completely free office suite (originally called Star Office) consisting of word processor, DTP, presentation, spreadsheet and database tools. *Open source freeware.*

PDFmoto
Source: www.pdfmoto.com
Extremely useful utility that can be configured to monitor a local or network folder and automatically convert any document (such as Word, Excel etc) placed there into a PDF, then publish it automatically to one or several web sites with links and navigation structure. It also detects documents that have

been added, deleted or amended, reflecting these changes on the site automatically. *Free version limited to 50 products, with commercial versions available.*

Typographicus
Source: www.visual-design.com/ENG_Welcome.htm
Typographicus is a powerful semiprofessional DTP-Application – creating professional labels and business cards, beautiful letter papers and practical serial letters is as easy as making multi-page brochures, foto calendars of high quality and extensive magazines. *Trial version.*

VentaFax and Voice
Source: www.ventafax.com/
VentaFax is a powerful fax/voice messaging software for Windows 9x/ME/NT4.x/2000 and XP boasting features and reliability available only in high-end products, but cheaper and less greedy on system resources. Effectively this will turn your PC into a fax machine and an answer phone. *Trial version.*

Video Screensaver
Source: www.microsoft.com
A small application that allows you to specify a series of videos as a Windows XP screensaver. This is ideal, for example to have configured on PCs at trade shows or seminars so that when they are not in use they are still actively promoting your company. Requires Windows Media Player 9 or above. *Freeware.*

VNC
Source: www.uk.research.att.com/vnc/
VNC is a remote display system which allows you to view a computing "desktop" environment not only on the machine where it is running, but also from anywhere on the Internet, and from a wide variety of machines. There are PC, Unix and even smartphone versions available. It is ideal if you need to access your PC or server when away from the office. *Freeware.*

VPOP
Source: www.download.com
VPOP3 is a powerful e-mail server and gateway that can be used to connect your network or standalone PC to the worldwide Internet e-mail system. VPOP3 is specifically designed to provide internal and Internet e-mail capabilities for a LAN or single machine with many different ISP accounts. It supports many features, such as automatic responders, mailing lists, aliases, scheduling, and download rules. *Trial version.*

Weblog Expert Lite
Source: www.alentum.com
This program differs from AnalogX Log Analyser as you can use it to analyse logs stored on your computer. You can normally download the logs files from your webserver, or some ISPs allow you to automatically receive them via email. This simple program will analyse the files and present you with a reasonably thorough report in HTML format. There is also a Pro version available, providing in-depth analysis for those that require it. *Freeware.*

Whois Ultra
Source: www.analogx.com/
AnalogX WhoIs is a graphical application that goes out on the net and looks up domain registration information. WhoIs also lets you enter previously registered domains and supplies the administration/owner contact information, in case you want to contact the people directly. You can also automatically launch your web browser and have it go to the page you just did a request on. You can enter in keywords and have it scan for different domain name combinations – then generate HTML reports from the results. WhoIs ULTRA supports ALL top level domains (e.g. .co.uk, .org etc), and you can quickly and easily add your own to the list! *Freeware.*

Winzip
Source: www.winzip.com
Industry standard software for compressing files. Can also create self-extracting files, so a single 'EXE' file can be sent which will decompress all files to a desired location – ideal for emailing files that need to be installed. *Shareware.*

WordWeb
Source: http://wordweb.info/free/
You can easily use this application to transform your everyday writing into something more eye-catching and impressive. The user interface of WordWeb is extremely easy to understand. Simply type in your word and press the search button and one frame displays the definition, the other shows synonyms, antonyms, type of, types, part of, similar and attributes. This program comes highly recommended and is well suited for anyone, from students to professionals. Pro version also available. *Freeware.*

WS_FTP LE
Source: www.ipswitch.com
WS_FTP LE is the limited edition version of WS_FTP Pro, allowing only

multiple file transfers and the auto re-get or resuming feature. *WS_FTP LE is shareware, available for free to educational users, government employees (U.S. local, state, federal and military) or to non-business home users only.*

Zoom Search
Source: www.wrensoft.com
Zoom search allows you to add a search capability to your site. The free version is good enough for the majority of small (<50 page) sites and can generate output in PHP, CGI or Javascript, so it's good for CD-ROMs as well! *Freeware.*

Zone Alarm Firewall
Source: www.zonelabs.com
Excellent firewall to reduce the risk of your computer being hacked – this is especially important if your computer has a permanent connection to the Internet. *Freeware.*

Appendix 4 – Online Resources

Here are a selection of useful web sites for software, information and assistance.

Audit Bureau of Circulation (UK)
Provides free access to the circulation, distribution and attendance data for ABC certified magazines, newspapers, exhibitions and directories within the UK and Republic of Ireland.
www.abc.org.uk

Audit Bureau of Circulation (USA)
As with the UK site above, this site provides an excellent resource for finding information on circulation or attendance of a particular audited publication or event.
www.accessabc.com

Actinic
An award-winning e-commerce software package that allows users with little or no web design skills to create and manage an online store.
www.actinic.com

Adobe Studio Tips & Tutorials
Official site from Adobe, developers of industry leading graphics, video and web development software.
www.studio.adobe.com

Adwordsmarket
Alternative to Google's Sandbox and Overtures keyword information tools.
www.adwordsmarket.com

Alexa
This site provides information about site traffic and links from other sites. Useful for finding information on sites that link to you and their influence on search engines.
www.alexa.com

AlldayPA
A 24 hour call handling and message taking service that can give a business a professional telephone service. It can be used as a receptionist service,

switchboard, overflow call handling, order taking or holiday cover. Low setup fee and charge per call/per minute.
www.alldaypa.com

Amazon.com
Ideal affiliate partner with a comprehensive range of tools to help plug their product content into your site.
www.amazon.com

Analog-x
Site that offers a variety of tools, including Keyword Live, which allows you to analyse how often a keyword is used on a website – great for checking to see why your competitors rank higher than you in search engines!
www.analogx.com

Anonymizer
Software product that offers 'anonymous surfing' by hiding the trail that most computers inadvertently leave as they browse web sites. A cut-down free version is available online.
www.anonymizer.com

Archive.org
Not exactly useful, but quite fun. This site has archives of virtually every site ever built. Try looking back at your company's old website!
www.archive.org/

Arelis
Stands for Axandra's Reciprocal Links Solution. This program finds sites that link to sites similar to yours (or your competitors) and allows you to email them to suggest a link to yours, thus raising your site's importance in the eyes of search engines.
www.axandra.com/

Association of Exhibition Organisers (AEO)
UK-specific site that offers information, advice and statistics on trade shows.
www.aeo.org.uk

Boxedart.com
Online resource for web templates, buttons, interfaces and photos. Pay an annual fee for unlimited access.
www.boxedart.com

Blogger
A site that allows users the ability to create a web log, commonly referred to as a 'blog'. Owned by Google.
www.blogger.com

Bobby
A free online service that allows you to test your site for accessibility, offering advice on any problems it finds. It is very interesting to see how your site will appear when used with alternative screen readers such as those for partially sighted users.
http://bobby.watchfire.com

Bravenet
Excellent site for free web tools for web designers, from scripts (guest books, forums etc) to free clipart. Many services will be co-branded.
www.bravenet.com

Buylistonline
Online purchasing of US B2B or B2C mailing lists that can be broken down through various criteria.
www.buylistonline.com

Cable TV Advertising Bureau
Site representing most ad-supporting cable TV networks and most ad-insertable network systems.
www.cabletvadbureau.com/

Charge
US-based online credit card company offering credit card transaction services for websites.
www.charge.com

Commission Junction
Online affiliation company allowing you to either buy ad space on other sites or feature ads/products on your site to earn revenue.
www.cj.com

Companies House
Online resource for the registration and provision of information relating to all businesses in the UK. An excellent resource if you need to find financial information on a company. Reports can be downloaded for a nominal fee.
www.companieshouse.gov.uk

Cunning Stunts Communications
An adventurous ambient marketing agency based in the UK that has pulled several major publicity coups in its time. The website may well be able to provide you with inspiration through a number of listed case studies.
www.cunningwork.com

Data HQ
UK-specific mailing list company providing a complete direct marketing service.
www.datahq.co.uk

Data Protection Act
The official UK government website relating to the Data Protection Act and how it affects your business.
www.dataprotection.gov.uk

Dialog Central
Places a small graphic on your web page which, when rolled over, allows users to rate the effectiveness of the page. You are then supplied with all of the stats so that you can tweak content according to user comments. Best of all, it's free!
www.dialogcentral.com

Download.com
Excellent resource for free, demo or shareware software.
www.download.com

Erol electronic retailing software
Another low-cost e-commerce product, allowing you to quickly add an online store to your website.
www.erolonline.co.uk

Exhibitor Online
The online home to Exhibitor magazine – the magazine to read when preparing for an exhibition. The site includes directories, buyers guides, tips and tricks etc.
www.exhibitornet.com

Fastpay
FastPay is a Natwest-owned company that offers users a quick, easy and secure way to send and receive money by email or mobile phone. Sign up is free, and you can start using FastPay immediately. A good alternative to

PayPal if you want to take credit cards online but cannot get a major transaction company to accept you, or if you only take minimal number of credit card payments. For UK residents only.
www.fastpay.co.uk

Gallup Organization
The Gallup Organization provides 'measurement tools' to help companies increase customer engagement. Their site boasts an excellent database of polls, delivering excellent statistical information
www.gallup.com

GotoMyPC & GotoMeeting
Two services offered by the same parent company that allow remote access or sharing of a computer's resources. GotoMyPC allows you to access a PC over the Internet. GotoMeeting allows several people to view an single PC, with the option to pass 'presentation' (or screen display) from one PC to another.
www.gotomypc.com and www.gotomeeting.com

Guerrilla Marketing
Site that focuses on getting the maximum exposure for your brand at a fraction of the cost of traditional marketing techniques.
www.gmarketing.com

HitBox
Providers of online website statistics, including Hitbox personal, a free service.
www.hitboxcentral.com

InetStore
E-commerce software product using either Microsoft Access or SQL.
www.inetstore.com

Infacta
Home to Groupmail – excellent bulk email software, including a free edition.
www.infacta.com

ivisit
Free video conference software that allows several users to see and hear each other simultaneously.
www.ivisit.com

Link popularity check

Invaluable free program that allows you to check how many links the search engines count coming into your site. (In general, the more links you have, the higher your site will rank.) Also great for running comparisons against your competitors.
www.checkyourlinkpopularity.com/

Live Person

LivePerson's live chat, email management and knowledge base services enable online businesses to increase online revenue, productivity and responsiveness to customer needs while decreasing the overall cost of customer support. A freeware version (Humanclick) is available on Bravenet's site.
www.liveperson.com

Magazine Publishers of America

An association for consumer magazines in the US with fact sheets, calendars and other resources related to printed media.
www.magazine.org/

Marketing Power

Official website of the American Marketing Association, which also offers a free newsletter containing customised information. An excellent resource for marketing ideas and guidance.
www.marketingpower.com

Maxrefer.com

A web-based referral system allowing you to let visitors recommend your site to others, inform them of special announcements and invite them to sign up for newsletters. An ideal tool for viral marketing on the web.
www.maxrefer.com

Mplans

A website offering resources and advice on building a marketing plan. Several sample plans are available for download.
www.mplans.com

Nationmaster

A website that carries general statistics and comparisons of nations. Their slogan says it all - 'Everything about everywhere'. Includes general information, such as richest, highest crime etc but also includes more niche stats such as Internet usage, budget expenditures etc.
www.nationmaster.com

.net magazine online
Online home to one of the UK's biggest selling Internet magazines. Has an excellent forum where you can get free advice, both from editors and industry professionals.
www.netmag.co.uk

Nimlok
Leading manufacturer of exhibition solutions worldwide.
www.nimlok.co.uk and www.nimlok.com

Nochex
Another online payment system that offers services similar to PayPal and Fastpay. UK residents only.
www.nochex.com

NUA
Online internet surveys, separated by categories such as advertising, e-commerce, entertainment and travel.
www.nua.ie/surveys/

Open Office
Another free alternative to Microsoft Office, which also works on Apple Mac and Linux systems.
www.openoffice.org

OsCommerce
Open source freeware e-commerce suite. Requires PHP, MySQL and medium to advanced skills to set up.
www.oscommerce.com

Overture
A company offering 'pay-per-performance' advertising, listing your site on several major search engines as sponsored links. Also has a handy keyword research tool.
www.overture.com

PayPal
Online payments and shopping cart facility – an easy method of adding basic e-commerce facilities to a small website.
www.paypal.com

Picasa
Graphic viewer and basic editing tool, now owned by search engine goliath Google. Freeware.
www.picasa.com

Picosearch
Excellent free service to add a search facility to your site. Fully customisable, also providing useful stats on the keywords people have searched for.
www.picosearch.com

Pixel2life
Site packed with tutorials on a diverse range of software packages, including, 3D Studio, Photoshop, Illustrator, Flash and Visual Basic.
www.pixel2life.com

Plaxo
A useful tool for keeping email and other contact information up-to-date. Free online/offline service that integrates with Outlook Express.
www.plaxo.com

Promotional Products Association International
International trade association dedicated to the promotional products industry.
www.ppai.org

PRWEB
Free newswire service, allowing you to post press releases that are syndicated across many sites. Making a donation gets you greater exposure.
www.prweb.com

Radio Advertising Bureau (UK)
Large database of stats and information relating to UK radio advertising and the type of audiences it attracts. The case study section may be of particular interest, detailing campaigns specific to a wide variety of industries and market sectors.
www.rab.co.uk

RL Rouse
21 step guide to getting top rankings in Google and Yahoo.
http://www.rlrouse.com

Robots Text page

Information on how to create a robots.txt file for your website.
www.robotstxt.org/

Search Engine Watch

Site focusing on news on the latest search engine developments.
www.searchenginewatch.com

Site Confidence

Company offering site testing to monitor a website's technical performance from the outside as users would experience it. This is useful for busy sites where browsers on a slow connection might be experiencing long delays. Technical staff can be immediately notified when site performance is affected in any way.
www.siteconfidence.com

Site Meter

Site Meter is a free, fast, and easy way to add a web counter to your web page. Not only does it display the number of visitors to your website, it also keeps statistics on the number of visits each hour and each day.
www.sitemeter.com

Sitepoint

Site offering excellent series of tutorials covering all aspects of web design, from buying a domain name to designing to promoting.
www.sitepoint.com

Skype

Free internet telephony product that also allows (at a cost) calls to be made to standard telephones.
www.skype.com

Sound Dogs

A site specialising in the sale of royalty-free music and sound clips, which are ideal for use in multimedia applications.
www.sounddogs.com

Sourceforge

The world's largest open source software development website. A great resource for open source (and usually free) software products, from office applications/suites to web portals and content management systems.
www.sourceforge.net

Stocked Photos
Online image bank which, instead of charging per-image has a fixed annual fee. Sister site to boxedart.com
www.stockedphotos.com

Sugar Suite CRM Software
Superb freeware and commercial CRM package. Requires a web server running PHP and MySQL, plus basic understanding of these technologies. It is trouble-free once up and running. Also has marketing and technical support modules integrated with the CRM engine, giving a total communication solution.
www.sugarcrm.com

Television Bureau of Advertising
Non-profit organisation for the US TV industry with a variety of online tools and resources helping advertisers make the most out of local television.
www.tvb.org

Templatesheaven.com
Alternative to Boxedart.com that sells at a price per template. Worth considering if Boxedart.com does not meet your needs.
www.templatesheaven.com

Teneric
Very useful business and marketing plan site. It also plays host to an excellent forum where you can ask business and marketing-related questions.
www.teneric.co.uk

Traffic Swarm
Free web traffic generation service. Add a banner on your site and earn credits to receive adverts on other sites. Alternatively you can buy credits to have your ad shown on related sites.
www.trafficswarm.com

Tucows
Excellent resource for free, demo or shareware software.
www.tucows.com

Typo 3

Freeware alternative to Macromedia Contribute, allowing website content managers the ability to easily modify authorised text and graphics on a web page without damaging the core template. Requires PHP and MySQL to be running on the web server, as well as a fair degree of technical knowledge to configure.

www.typo3.com

Webex

Industry-leading service delivering online meetings, web conferencing and video conferencing services.

www.webex.com

Web Master World

Site offering in-depth search engine optimisation advice, along with building and marketing tips.

www.webmasterworld.com

Webmonkey

A website dedicated to offering tutorials and advice for building better web sites.

www.webmonkey.com

Webtrends

Authors of Log Analyser software for creating reports detailing statistics of visitors to your website.

www.webtrends.com

World Press

Site offering free news feed – an ideal way to add dynamic content to your site so that visitors always see something new.

www.worldpress.org

XAT

Home to the excellent JPEG Optimizer shareware program – ideal for squashing image file sizes down to make them load faster on your web pages.

www.xat.com

Zen Cart

This is an open-source shopping cart system written in PHP that interfaces with a MySQL database on a web server. A good alternative to many of the off-the-shelf systems available. Once configured it is easy to add/modify products and customise the site's look and feel
www.zen-cart.com

Zoom Search Engine

A free package for web developers to add an industrial strength custom search engine to a site within minute. Features include Google-like context descriptions, wildcard and exact phrase searching, spider and offline indexing, statistics and more...
www.wrensoft.com/zoom/

Appendix 5 – Recommended Reading

Building your Business with Google for Dummies – Brad Hill
ISBN: 0764571435
This book focuses on using Google's business functions as a revenue model. Any business looking to gain a higher profile on the world's favourite search engine should be reading this book.

NLP at Work: The Difference that Makes a Difference in Business – Sue Knight
ISBN: 1857883020
Neuro Linguistic Programming explains how you make sense of your world and how to be what you want to be. In this edition, the author explores recent developments in NLP and shows how NLP has become even more significant in our increasingly unpredictable business and personal lives.

How to Handle Media Interviews – Andrew Boyd
ISBN: 1852521244
A complete guide to being interviewed – whether on the tv, radio, or by the press. Practical tips are given by media masters from both sides of the divide; from the angry men of UK TV and politics, Jeremy Paxman and Tony Benn, to the Today Programme, the CBI, PR professionals and senior corporate spokesmen. They reveal their secrets of success and point out the traps for the unwary.

Public Relations for Your Business – Frank Jefkins
ISBN: 1852523476
A practical, down-to-earth guide to public relations – how it works, what it can do for your company, and how to do it. Written by a well-known PR guru and recently updated, this book is a classic introduction to the world of Public Relations.

Corporate Entertaining as a Marketing Tool – Andrew Crofts
ISBN: 185252362X
Corporate entertainment accounts for an ever-growing proportion of marketing spend, and offers a unique opportunity to target specific groups of people – whether customers or employees – to develop productive long-term relationships. But the pitfalls are many, and it is all too easy to spend the money without getting the desired result. This guide shows readers how to do it right.

The Frog Snogger's Guide – Susan Lancaster & Sean Orford
ISBN: 1852523484
A guide to getting on with toads … We all have to get on with people we don't instinctively like – bosses, colleagues, customers, mothers-in-law, sons-in-law ... the list is endless. However slimy and unappealing they may be, we have to find a way to get through to them. *The Frog Snogger's Guide* is a guide to overcoming initial aversion and forming a constructive bond or rapport with the many frogs and toads we need to get on with to progress our own ambitions or aspirations.

Appendix 6 – The Marketing Your Business Website

To compliment this book, a website has been created that will provide up-to-date information on the latest marketing tips, software and news.

In addition to information to prospective buyers of this book the site will contain comments and quotes from companies around the world relating to successful marketing campaigns they have performed. You are also invited to submit your own advice and comments to share with others.

The site has been set up to be an extension of this book, and will continue to develop. The author welcomes your suggestions and feedback as to how it can be improved to be a better resource for you.

Martin Bailey is available for consultancy work; covering projects such as web design/redesign, search engine optimisation and submission, PR or general marketing support services. Contact him directly through this website.

Visit www.marketingyour.biz to:

- find the latest information about the author
- get news and events relating to the book's publicity
- find links to the latest useful marketing software
- read news and reviews about useful hardware and software
- pick up tips and tricks to help your own marketing campaigns
- contact the author for consultancy services
- find about co-branding options for the book.

Glossary of Terms

B2B   Business to Business. The nature of trading between your business and another business.

B2C   Business to Consumer. The nature of trading between your business and consumers, which requires different methods to B2B.

Bleed   Term used when designing artwork for printing. It signifies the area of material outside of the cut area that is still printed on to ensure that any errors in cutting are not highlighted by the print edge being shown.

Blog   A blog is basically a journal that is available on the web. The activity of updating a blog is "blogging" and someone who keeps a blog is a "blogger." Blogs are typically updated daily using software that allows people with little or no technical background to update and maintain the blog. Postings on a blog are almost always arranged in cronological order with the most recent additions featured most prominantly.

Broadband High speed, permanent Internet connection.

Case Study A document that details information about one of your customers, detailing why they chose you and the benefits/savings they have achieved due to your products/services. Can also be used as a press release. Ideal to send to new prospects that may be in a similar position to the existing customer, allowing them to more readily see your product or service advantages.

CMYK   Represents the four colours used in the four colour lithographical printing process – Cyan, Magenta, Yellow and Black.

Codec   A plugin responsible for encoding and decoding a file format. Normally used with video and audio files to provide various levels of file compression. MP3 and MPG are examples of compression codecs.

CRM   Customer Relationship Management. Term used to describe the management of information on customers and prospects (e.g. contact and sales lead management software such as ACT, Goldmine or

SugarSuite CRM).

CSS   Cascading Style Sheets. Used within web pages to maintain a common look and feel across all pages. Once a CSS document is created all font sizes, styles and colours are defined in one place, allowing all pages to be updated from one source.

CSV   Comma Separated Values. Standard format for importing or exporting data. Each field is separated by a comma.

DPI   Dots per inch – description of size of graphic files. The number of dots per inch signifies the quality of the picture. Standard resolution for adverts is 300dpi.

Extranet   An intranet that is opened up to customers. An example of this might be a courier company that allows customers to track parcels online.

FTP   File Transfer Protocol. The name used for the software that transfers files between your computer and a web server.

GIF   Graphic file format mainly used for images on web sites. Is limited to 256 colours or less – decreasing the number of colours reduces the file size, so can result in a very graphical page that can load very quickly.

Guerilla Marketing   Term given to 'off-the-wall marketing and promotion 'stunts'.

IM   Instant Messaging. Used to describe applications such as MSN Messenger and ICQ; programs that allow you to see when others are online and communicate with them through text, audio or video.

Intranet   An internal 'Internet' designed to be used within the confines of your organisation. Ideal for improving internal communication and making a single source for company information and materials.

ISP   Internet Service Provider. A company that provides you with access to the internet, either through dial-up or ADSL/Cable modem (broadband).

JPG   (pronounced Jay-Peg and also known as JPEG). Graphic file format mainly used for pictures on web sites due to its high compression ratios, which result in small file sizes.

LAN   Local Area Network.

Open Source Software that is not only free, but the source code is also openly available for modification. The Linux operating system, OpenOffice suite and SugarSuite CRM systems are good examples of this.

Newsgroup An electronic discussion group allowing you to post messages that others can see and reply to, building a 'thread' of messages linked by a common subject. Newsgroups are generally free to subscribe to.

PDF   Portable Document Format – standard format for electronic document distribution. Developed by Adobe. A free PDF viewer is available from www.adobe.com

Press release A document that is sent out to relevant media, such as radio stations, magazines etc detailing information on an event within your company, such as new product releases.

SEO   Search Engine Optimisation. Many web submission companies now call themselves 'SEO Experts'. Also referred to as SEM (Search Engine Marketing).

SIC code   Industry recognised codes with each SIC code being unique to a specific industry, product or process.

SPAM   The nickname for unsolicited junk emails, which stands for Stupid Pointless Annoying Message. The term was originally derived from a Monty Python sketch!

SSL   Secure Socket Layers. Any secure site (that starts with a URL of https://) is using SSL to encrypt its contents. This gives visitors to online stores confidence that their credit card details cannot be stolen.

TIF   Graphical file format normally used when producing artwork. Standard requested format is CMYK TIF at 300dpi.

Trim   A term used in artwork production. The trim size is normally the finished size of the item (e.g. brochure, business card etc).

USB   Universal Serial Bus. A type of computer interface used to connect devices such as printers, scanners and digital cameras to a PC.

USP   Unique Selling Point

URL   Term used for a web address. Stands for Unique Resource Location.

VPN   Virtual Private Network. A term used to describe connecting to a network (such as your office) securely over the Internet.

W3C   World Wide Web Consortium. This is the organisation behind many of the web standards, such as HTML and CSS. Their web address is www.w3.org.

WAN   Wide Area Network. This differs from a LAN as it is normally spread across several geographical locations.

WYSIWYG   What You See Is What You Get. Term used to describe applications that display on-screen what will be output to a different media e.g. printer.

Zip   A compressed file format, ideal for reducing the size of one or many files (such as graphics).

Index